Handling Change

A HISTORY OF THE IRISH BANK OFFICIALS' ASSOCIATION

Handling Change

A HISTORY OF THE IRISH BANK OFFICIALS' ASSOCIATION

PAUL ROUSE
& MARK DUNCAN

The Collins Press

First published in 2012 by
The Collins Press
West Link Park
Doughcloyne
Wilton
Cork

British Library Cataloguing in Publication data
Rouse, Paul
    Handling change : a history of the Irish Bank Officials'
    Association.
    1. Irish Bank Officials' Association—History. 2. Banks
    and banking—Ireland—History—20th century.
    I. Title II. Duncan, Mark.
    331.8'81133212'09417-dc23

ISBN-13: 978-1-84889-141-8

Design and typesetting by Patricia Hope, Dublin
Typeset in Sabon
Printed in Sweden by ScandBook AB

Contents

Acknowledgements

It has been a pleasure to write this book. The offer to get involved in this project came from Séamas Shiels, the communications manager at IBOA The Finance Union. Throughout the process, Séamas has been a model of support: assured, calm and reasonable. Invaluable assistance was offered by Rosemary Platt, whose knowledge of the archives of the Union is remarkable and whose willingness to assist was vital to the completion of this book. Margaret Browne, a long-time stalwart of the Association, was equally supportive of the project altogether from her personal support, her knowledge of the Union and its people ranging back across the decades was a vital resource.

Further thanks are due to the current General Secretary, Larry Broderick, and his predecessors, Ciaran Ryan and Job Stott, as well as the current President, Jessie Doherty, and the Union's Honorary Secretary, Tommy Kennedy. Former Union officers and activists Brendan O'Donoghue, Pat O'Connor Hegarty and Des Sheridan also contributed many thoughtful observations and clarifications. Jane Higgins ensured that our team received the necessary administrative and logistical support during our time in IBOA House. Almost all of those mentioned above also undertook to read various drafts of the manuscript together with Marian Geoghegan and Joan

MacSwiney. Finally we wish to thank the many IBOA members, retired members and their families who contributed memorabilia and reminiscences, which greatly enhanced our work.

The Research Assistant on this book was Maren Muckler. Maren's diligence, attention to detail, integrity, work ethic and organisational skills ensured that this book was finished on time, despite a pressing deadline. More than that, it is a simple fact that without Maren this book would never have been written: our debt to her is huge. Assisting Maren in the latter stages of her work was Sinéad Egan, who also did an excellent job. Further research – particularly on trade unions in Ireland – was carried out by Dr Irial Glynn, a talented young historian who produced fascinating material which was used in the early chapters of the book.

Colleagues in UCD, Boston College-Ireland and in InQuest Research Group were of great assistance, especially Prof. Diarmaid Ferriter, Prof. Mike Cronin and Seán Kearns. Great thanks are due to the staff of the National Archives of Ireland – particularly Catríona Crowe and Aideen Ireland – who once again have provided great assistance, despite the pressures of their working environment. The photographs that fill these pages were sourced from multiple repositories. As well as the IBOA archive, which yielded a wealth of material, we are grateful for the advice and assistance provided by the staff of the National Library of Ireland, the RTÉ Stills Library, the Kennelly Archive, Getty Images, Lensmen, Robert Redmond Photography and Davison and Associates.

On a personal note, great thanks are offered to the assorted members of the Duncan, Egan, Rouse and Pozzey families. Writing a book is a selfish endeavour, which affects the lives of more than just the authors. So thanks in particular to Nuala, Sophie, Cáit, Éilis, Joe and Olivia for putting up with us and our ways.

Mark Duncan and Paul Rouse
2012

Foreword

For over ninety years, IBOA The Finance Union and its forerunner, the Irish Bank Officials' Association, has sought to defend – and where possible, advance – the interests of staff in the Irish financial services sector. The history of the Union is marked by stunning achievements and some disheartening setbacks as the IBOA and its members have grappled with the changing circumstances within financial institutions and within Irish society as a whole.

Of course, the Union itself has also been constantly evolving in response to these developments: as expectations and preconceptions appropriate to one era eventually gave way to new ideas and redefined objectives in light of previous experience. So this is a history of an organisation on a journey – adapting both its external strategies and its own internal structures to changing economic and social conditions.

Paul Rouse and Mark Duncan chart the IBOA's gradual transition from a staff association to a trade union; from a body with quite narrow and unashamedly middle-class pretensions to one which is now far more socially diverse; and from an organisation that began largely as an old boys' club to one in which women make up three out of every four members and under 35s are in the majority.

This book also illustrates very clearly that the IBOA is far from being a grey and faceless edifice. Its pages are full of colourful characters – some loud and flamboyant, others rather more modest and unassuming – but all contributing to a vivid narrative of men and women striving for fulfilment both in work and at play.

Paul Rouse and Mark Duncan also identify many events from times past which resonate with more recent developments – not just the bread-and-butter concerns of pay and working conditions – but also the bigger questions about the direction of banking policy and practice.

Measured against the standards of today, it could be argued that some of the positions adopted by the Union were deficient in certain respects. But, of course, hindsight is twenty-twenty vision. We can all be wise after the event – as the current banking crisis clearly illustrates. It is much more difficult to make the right calls in the middle of a fluid, rapidly changing situation.

Nevertheless, one consistent concern for IBOA members over the last two decades has been the issue of banking culture – which has not only had negative consequences for their own working conditions but has also contributed significantly to a business environment in which reckless decision-making was allowed to flourish to the detriment of the institutions and the economy as a whole.

The near collapse of many key financial institutions is an unprecedented crisis in Irish banking of staggering proportions: but it also offers an unparalleled opportunity to change the culture of banking – if the relevant authorities can rise above short-term expediency to make the necessary strategic shift.

Our history indicates that the IBOA has risen to major challenges in the past. Our future will be determined by the extent to which we are able to rise to this, our most profound challenge, in the months and years ahead.

Larry Broderick
General Secretary

Margaret Browne
President, 2009–2011
Chair of the Union History Project

Introduction

This book is a history of the Irish Bank Officials' Association (IBOA). It records the history of that Association from its inception in March 1918 up until the autumn of 2011, by which time it was apparent that Irish banking was in the throes of monumental change. It is a history of a representative association which became a trade union – to the point of formally changing its name in April 2009 to IBOA The Finance Union – in a country which moved from relative poverty to illusory wealth before sliding back once more into the gloom of recession and economic misery. This history locates the story of the IBOA within the broader context of Irish history. It is an organisation which was founded before partition and retained an all-island unity despite that partition and despite the subsequent violence which stained twentieth-century Irish life. The shifting political allegiances of Irish bankers are manifest in these pages.

Also manifest are matters of class and of gender. The IBOA was profoundly and proudly middle class in its ethos for much of its history. Indeed, it was a badge of honour for the Association to draw a distinction between its members and those of the 'ordinary working classes', as its leaders described them. This distinction was even used as the principle reason for the earliest pay claims of the Association. The logic was clear: in order to fulfil the social obligations expected of their class, bank officials required higher

3

rates of pay. This ethos prevailed for much of the twentieth century. So, too, did the notion of discrimination against women. In the years immediately before the foundation of the IBOA, women were called to work in banks for the first time in Ireland due to the outbreak of the Great War. Steadily, through the decades, their numbers increased until they became a majority. The rise of women in Irish banks was attended by gross male chauvinism. This was a reflection of sentiment in wider Irish society, but also a reflection of the particularly chauvinistic notions which prevailed in Irish banking and was evident not just in bank management but also within the ranks of the IBOA.

Although the broader forces of Irish history shaped the story of the development of the IBOA, this is also the story of life in a particular type of institution. Much of what happened to the men and women who worked in Irish banks also happened to those who worked in other places. But there is also much that happened in the lives of Irish bank officials that was peculiar unto themselves. This book is an attempt to capture a lot of the fun which Irish bank officials were fortunate to experience through their place of work. There can be no disguising the fact that work in the bank could be filled with drudgery and it certainly bored many who spent their days pining to be elsewhere. Nonetheless, the social life that was wrapped around work – sporting clubs, social events, day trips and much more – was an essential part of the life of bank officials for generations.

In general, the IBOA has done much for its members; of that there can be no doubt. Inevitably, of course, there are members who have lamented – and will continue to lament – that not more has been done, or that certain mistakes have been made. Inevitably, too, there will be people who have entirely different memories of events than the ones recorded in these pages. There will also be people who will be disappointed at the failure to mention or give due regard to a whole range of activities undertaken or events organised by the IBOA. This is inevitable. No book can possibly compete with the experience of a lived history. That is not to walk away from any of the views expressed in this book, merely to recognise that there will be those who will dissent from some (or, maybe, more than some) of those views.

Equally, the IBOA has been at the centre of a number of

significant public controversies, often associated with strikes. The Union – and its members – has been the subject of trenchant criticism. Some of this criticism has been merited; other parts of it have been misguided. It is a tribute to the integrity of the IBOA that the Union has not sought to influence the text, or made any attempt to distil criticism or amplify compliments. Further, this is a history written at a clear watershed in the history of the Union. Amidst the collapse in the Irish economy, thousands of jobs have been lost from Irish banks and it is clear that more will follow. More than that, the reputation of Ireland's banks lies in ruin. Against this backdrop, the IBOA remains a vital presence for its members; indeed, its presence might be considered more vital now than at any point in its history. The next chapter in the history of the Union will undoubtedly prove to be a compelling one; in the meantime, what follows in these pages is its story so far.

The Mansion House on Dublin's Dawson Street. It was here, on Monday 17 March 1918, that 350 bank officials from across Ireland gathered for a meeting at which the IBOA was founded. *(NLI, Eason Collection)*

1

Foundations

On 17 March 1918, 350 bank officials from across Ireland gathered for a meeting in the Mansion House in Dublin. The Mansion House had been given to bank officials for the evening by Laurence O'Neill, a Dublin corn merchant who was Lord Mayor of the city. Presiding at the meeting was Charles Hutchings Denroche, another Dubliner, who was a solicitor and was also a former official of the Provincial Bank of Ireland. Denroche had been asked to act as chairman because it was considered unfair by the organisers to ask a serving bank official to assume too prominent a position in an enterprise that was sure to be opposed by their employers.[1]

As the meeting gathered momentum, a motion was put to the floor that 'an Association be formed and that the Association be called "The Irish Bank Officials' Association".'[2] The motion was passed unanimously. Soon afterwards, a constitution for the new Association was adopted, an executive committee was elected and votes of thanks were passed to those who had made the meeting possible. By the time the bank officials departed from the Mansion House, the meeting could be considered to have been entirely a success: Irish bank officials now had their own representative body, the IBOA.[3]

I

The road to the Mansion House

The manner in which the emergence of the IBOA was influenced by wider social, cultural, economic and political factors is fundamental to understanding its history. After all, the backdrop in March 1918 was international war and national revolution. Exactly a month after the IBOA was formed, Laurence O'Neill again opened the doors of the Mansion House, this time to a meeting of Irish nationalists who supported a pledge which had been drafted by Éamon de Valera in opposition to the British government's moves to conscript Irishmen into the British army.[4] Within a short few years of the establishment of the IBOA, the Irish Free State was established and the island was partitioned. This political upheaval had inevitable consequences for the activities of the Association.

While the IBOA was influenced by the political environment in which it was founded, of still greater importance were social and economic impulses. The men who had planned the meeting in Dublin had themselves already organised local committees in the cities of Dublin, Limerick, Cork, Galway, Belfast and Derry through the previous winter. They had been moved to act by the manner in which Irish banks treated their officials and by the apparent decline in their economic fortunes as the Great War drew to its climax. As we will see, the pay and conditions of bank officials were greatly at odds with their imagined place in Irish society. This, more than anything else, led bank officials to establish the IBOA.

In many respects, they were unlikely activists. Bank officials were perceived – and perceived themselves – to be of a different order from those workers who usually formed themselves into trade unions. Indeed, the IBOA was at pains to avoid presenting itself as a trade union as it made its first uncertain steps.[5] And yet the emergence in the nineteenth century of representative unions for Irish workers had an obvious impact on the establishment of the IBOA. In time, the IBOA would acknowledge that heritage by formally integrating with the trade union movement, but even at the outset in 1918 the influence was obvious.

To understand the genesis of the IBOA, it is important to understand the long history of workers' associations in Ireland. From the time of the Normans, some Irish workers had organised themselves in guilds. These guilds 'brought journeymen and masters together for the good of their common calling' in order to 'regulate working practices and apprenticeships' by helping to set wages and prices.[6] They also had the ability to help members in need. The rise in religious animosity between Catholics and Protestants in the sixteenth and seventeenth centuries saw guilds divided upon religious lines. By then, the guilds had become the preserve of masters, leaving journeymen to fend for themselves in so-called 'combinations' that fought for working and wage rights in Dublin from the 1670s onwards.[7] From 1729, government introduced a series of mainly ineffective acts attempting to limit the power of combinations and guilds. In 1780, approximately 20,000 artisans protested against moves to allow masters employ as many apprentices in Ireland as they wished; this was a move which also proved futile.[8]

The industrial revolution saw the emergence of trade unions. In response to the development of trade unionism, the British government passed the Combination Act in 1799 which prohibited trade unions and collective bargaining by workers. This was repealed by parliament in 1824. A new Combination Act was introduced in 1825, which permitted the existence of unions but placed controls on their activity. This was undertaken in response to the strikes that followed the repeal of the original 1799 Combination Act. It is claimed that Dublin acquired a reputation for being the strongest centre of trade unionism in the United Kingdom during the 1820s, with construction unions the most active and representative; Cork, Limerick and Belfast also recorded union activity.[9] 'Ribbonism', a form of verbal and physical abuse of men who had not served their apprenticeships, known as 'colts', and of the employers who hired them sometimes took place in cities such as Dublin.[10] Nevertheless, violence did not play a key role in union protest in cities, especially when compared to the often bloody acts sometimes carried out by secret agrarian organisations, such as the Whiteboys, across rural

Ireland in the second half of the eighteenth century and first half of the nineteenth century. Significantly, these rural protest movements did influence Irish emigrants involved in trade unions abroad during the nineteenth century, particularly the activities related to the Molly Maguires in Pennsylvania.[11]

Cross-channel cooperation between Irish and British groups remained difficult in the first half of the nineteenth century because communication was slow and costly.[12] Opposition from Daniel O'Connell, the Catholic Church and employers meant that mobilising Irish people to support the Chartist movement, which emerged in Britain in the late 1830s and 1840s with Irishman Fergus O'Connor to the fore, was even more difficult.[13] The Young Irelanders' support for Chartism met with more success following the death of O'Connell, but their doomed 1848 rebellion meant 'working-class politics lost its revolutionary edge'.[14] Groups, such as the Amalgamated Society of Engineers, formed in the decades thereafter often 'restricted member-ship to properly qualified, apprentice-trained craftsmen' and, as a consequence, 'ignored the great mass of unskilled labourers'.[15]

In the early 1860s, Dublin craft unions combined to form a new trades council, the United Trades Association (UTA), to lobby employers on behalf of workers. Various societies quickly affiliated and the UTA encouraged towns and cities around Ireland to form similar associations, a proposal taken up in Cork, Limerick and Waterford and one met with favour by workers in Galway, Ennis and Enniskillen.[16] The eventual goal was for all trades councils to come together to form a confederated Irish association, but the establish-ment of the British Trades Union Congress in 1868 meant that most union members turned to London for leadership.[17] Dismayed at the seeming lack of interest from the British Congress in Irish union affairs, certain Irish unions, which had grown in number since the Trade Union Act conferred legal status on trade unions in 1871,[18] decided to form their own Irish Trades Union Congress (TUC) in 1894.[19]

By this time, trade unions were no longer confined solely to the skilled trades.[20] 'New unionism', which saw skilled and unskilled workers coming together, began to take hold from 1889 onwards.[21] Of the unskilled workers, dockers, coal porters and gas workers made up the most important part of this 'new unionism' since they had the ability to affect a wide range of economic activities if they went on strike.[22] Encouragement for these unions came both from Britain and further afield, as socialism and syndicalism developed across Europe and America. International figures such as Eleanor Marx (Karl Marx's daughter), and her husband, Edward Aveling, for example, addressed a large demonstration in the Phoenix Park in May 1891 alongside the prominent Cork trade unionist Michael Canty.[23]

The Local Government Act of 1898 heralded another source of change by giving working-class people real power through suffrage – a factor reflected in the 1899 election of eight candidates in Dublin associated with the trade union movement.[24] Trade unions further benefited from the Trades Disputes Act (1906) and the Trade Union Act (1913). The first helped define trade disputes, authorised peaceful picketing and absolved the trade unions from being sued by employers as a result of trade disputes; the second enabled unions to raise political funds and to engage in political activities.[25]

The rise of James Larkin and James Connolly brought a new dimension to Irish trade unionism. Larkin came to Belfast from Liverpool in 1907 to take up an appointment as Irish organiser of the British-led National Union of Dock Labourers (NUDL). That year, he successfully organised dockers of all religious backgrounds in Belfast before graduating to various other Irish cities and then eventually settling in Dublin.[26] After falling out with the NUDL, Larkin founded the ITGWU in 1909 in Dublin. Connolly's writings from America – to where he had emigrated at the beginning of the twentieth century – also gave the ITGWU political direction.[27] By June 1911, Edinburgh-born Connolly, who returned to Ireland from America in July 1910, became the ITGWU's organiser in Belfast. The union gathered huge momentum and at the beginning of 1912, the ITGWU had over 18,000 members.[28]

In August 1913 employers combined with William Martin Murphy in the infamous lockout of employees unwilling to sign a document pledging to disown the ITGWU. What Andrew Boyd has referred to as the 'bitterest struggle between capital and labour in the whole history of Ireland' only ended several months later in January 1914 with defeat for the union,[29] although the employers

James Larkin addresses a crowd in Dublin in the early 1920s. Larkin was central to the rise of Irish trade unionism, founding the influential Irish Transport and General Workers' Union (ITGWU) in 1909. By 1911, the union claimed a membership of 18,000 workers. *(Getty Images)*

also failed in their primary objective of destroying the ITGWU. Some of the later strikes that took place in that decade related to nationalist politics, with the Irish TUC calling for a one-day general strike to protest against the British government's plan to impose conscription on Ireland in April 1918 and in April 1920 calling for a general strike in support of republican political prisoners who had gone on hunger strike.[30] The Limerick Soviet was declared in April 1919 when the United Trades and Labour Council initiated a general strike in the city in protest at the declaration by the local British army commander, Brigadier Griffin, that Limerick was a Special Military Area. Nonetheless, not all industrial action related to nationalist politics, with builders and railworkers notably prominent in attaining better conditions for themselves during the latter years of the First World War under the syndicalist movement. Agricultural workers also began to attach themselves to the labour movement, thereby facilitating the rise of unionism in rural Ireland, especially during the ITGWU's 'land campaign' in 1919, which saw two county-wide strikes taking place in Meath and Kildare and the seizure of thirteen Limerick creameries in the 'Knocklong Soviet'.[31]

At this time, clerical unions also began to expand and display, according to O'Connor, 'a strong and unusual affinity with the Labour movement'.[32] Bank officials, however, did not. That Irish bank employees did not move to organise themselves until 1918 was due to a complex set of reasons related to class, commerce and culture. In 1920, Serjeant Henry Hanna, a barrister representing the bank officials, laid bare the image which bank officials constructed of themselves. He claimed that 'bank officials form a class by themselves,' that they were

> drawn from a good class of society, they are men of education, they must be men of high character . . . By reason of the class from which they are drawn, the standards that have been set out for what have been called

The IBOA was born into a decade of political and industrial unrest. For the labour movement, the iconic moment came with the lock-out of Dublin workers in a dispute over the right of workers to join trade unions in 1913. This photograph shows members of the Dublin Metropolitan Police baton-charging passers-by, as well as union members attending a union rally in Sackville (now O'Connell) Street in August of that year. *(RTÉ: The Cashman Collection)*

The impressive Ulster Bank building in Belfast, *c.* 1910. Founded prior to the partition of the island, the IBOA would continue to represent bank officials on either side of the border that divided Northern Ireland from the Irish Free State. *(NLI, Lawrence Collection)*

14

the working classes . . . do not apply. The majority of these officials whom I represent are the sons of – some of them – the middle classes, some of them are the sons of officers in His Majesty's Army, some of them are what may be called the sons of local gentry in connection with provincial towns, and many of them are sons of the professional classes. They are nearly all gentlemen who have had before they entered the bank a good, high-class secondary education, some of them as a matter of fact have degrees out of the universities . . . The fact of that will impress upon you that the people I represent are men of considerable ability, considerably above the ordinary working classes, and that they approach more nearly to the professional classes than any part or portion of the community who are not actually in the professional line.'[33]

The problem for bank officials lay precisely in that ground between working-class and professional-class life. Bank officials were supposed to lead lives which aped the lives of those who had money. According to Hanna, they were required to be in the same clubs as 'the best class in the community', to join the same public organisations, to mix socially with that class, to send their children to appropriate schools and even to marry under the supervision of the bank.[34] And yet it was apparent to all that the working conditions of the employees of Irish banks simply did not allow them to lead such a life. That all of this was the case was due, in part, to the manner in which banking in Ireland had developed over the centuries.

II

BANKS AND THEIR EMPLOYEES

The first Irish banks emerged at the end of the seventeenth century and in the early part of the eighteenth century. The growth of trade in eighteenth-century Ireland brought the further development of banking facilities in cities and towns, with Dublin emerging as the most important banking centre on the island. In 1783, the Bank of Ireland was established as a national bank by royal charter, almost a century after the establishment of the Bank of England and the Bank of Scotland. The Bank of Ireland operated as government banker, though it did not immediately establish a network of branches around the country. This function was left to the private banks, whose fortunes rose and fell in line with the sharp fluctuations so characteristic of the Irish economy, with the profits of boom years offering little protection from failure in times of recession. After 1815 and the end of the Napoleonic wars, for example, post-war deflation and agricultural depression was the signal for the collapse of several banks. Ultimately, Irish banking at that time 'relied too much on land as security, lacked a dynamic commercial influence and was overstretched following the exceptionally large increases in currency during the war years'.[35]

During the 1820s and the 1830s a range of private banks were established – amongst these were the Northern Bank (1824), the Provincial Bank (1825), the National Bank (1835) and the Royal Bank (1836) – and their dominance of the banking system extended well into the twentieth century. The second half of the nineteenth century saw the establishment of a range of savings banks and, then, of building societies, all of which contributed to the development of the sector. As well as offering deposit accounts and a range of credit facilities from loans to overdrafts, the growth in banking allowed for the wider use of money in the Irish economy. Coins had first been issued in Ireland under the authority of the Hiberno-Norse king Sitric III in Dublin during the 990s and, through the centuries that followed, the circulation of coins existed side by side with barter. In the nineteenth century, the amount of currency notes in circulation increased significantly.[36] Banking became more diversified, offered more services and became more central to the Irish economy. This was reflected in the increase in the number of bank branches. As the nineteenth century progressed, more and more branches were established across the countryside to the point where by 1913 there were more than 850 bank branches in operation.

Northern Bank, Mohill, County Leitrim, *c.* 1915. Banks already sat at the heart of the commercial life of Irish villages, towns and cities by the early twentieth century. *(NLI, Eason Collection)*

Despite a couple of spectacular bank failures, by the early years of the twentieth century Irish banks had a widespread reputation for caution and conservatism.[37] This caution extended to the pay which was granted to its officials. The first honorary secretary of the IBOA, J. F. Eager, was later to explain that although the cost and standard of living has been 'rising for many years before the war, little, if any, improvement was made in the scale of salaries, and officials . . . were barely able to exist on the salaries paid prior to August, 1914. The position then was becoming acute. The very rapid increase in the cost of living occasioned by the war was inadequately met by the directors of the banks, and all bank officials in Ireland are quite unable to live in any comfort or to rear and educate their families.' What further irritated Eager was the belief that the 'financial position of the banks when war broke out was

due to this conserving of profits, not at the expense of the shareholders but rather by the withholding of a living wage from their
employees'.[38] It was against this backdrop that Irish bank officials
were emboldened to act.

III

AN ASSOCIATION FOR BANK WORKERS

The deterioration in their living standards prompted 40 bank clerks
in Limerick to convene a meeting in that city for 27 September
1917. It was a step whose boldness was defined by the innate
caution of the environment in which bank officials worked. The
meeting was held in the Glentworth Hotel in Limerick city with a Mr
Dickinson in the chair. The chairman defined the purpose of the
meeting in a short speech which outlined their ambition as 'the
formation of a union of Irish bank officials'.[39] A series of speakers
rose in support of the motion, their remarks were greeted with great
enthusiasm and the idea of the establishment of a union was
unanimously endorsed. All 40 men present then signed a pledge to
support the formation of a union.[40]

As a mark of their desire to translate their pledge into practice, it
was then agreed to circulate to all the banks and bank branches in
Cork, Dublin and Belfast a proposal that a representative meeting be
organised in Dublin for the purposes of establishing a national
union.[41] That meeting should take place on 'St. Stephen's day or some
suitable day'. Finally, the Limerick bank clerks agreed that a subscription of 2/6 be collected from all present to defray the costs that would
inevitably emerge from their endeavours and also agreed that the
proceedings of their meeting and all resolutions passed 'should be kept
strictly confidential'.[42] When the Limerick bank officials met again on
30 November 1917 they had some progress to reflect on. Reaction
from Cork had been positive and the Cork and Limerick clerks had
agreed on a joint circular in an attempt to promote support in Belfast
and Dublin. The meeting also agreed that all Limerick clerks should

engage in 'a bit of propaganda work' by writing to any bank officials in Dublin and Belfast.[43] In the context of the times – and particularly in the context of the environment in which the Limerick clerks worked – their actions were most courageous.

The reaction in Dublin to developments in Limerick was hugely positive. Several attempts had been made to organise bank clerks previously, but all had been stillborn. This renewed effort, too, almost collapsed even as it was undertaken. Some Dublin bank clerks came together and organised a meeting for a city centre hall. A rather theatrical account of what transpired was subsequently written by J. F. Eager, an official from the Hibernian Bank who was later to gain great prominence in the IBOA, serving as president in the 1920s. Eager painted a dramatic portrait of the night, recalling: 'It was openly conceded that it bordered on madness to imagine that it was likely that any organisation of bank officials could be formed, and it was hard to find any who really regarded the matter seriously.'[44]

The extent to which bank officials were cowed – or were perceived to be cowed – by their employers can be seen from Eager's (undoubtedly exaggerated) recollection that 'on the night of the meeting every doorway in the vicinity of the hall concealed in its darkness a number of bank officials all peering to see who might pass in'.[45] Eventually, the reticent were coaxed into the room. This, in turn, led to further shocks to the system for those who were uncertain. The paraphernalia from a previous political meeting had yet to be removed from the room and, with police raids a feature of life in the city since the 1916 Rising, the prospect of being associated with such a raid worried several present.[46]

There was worse to follow for the anxious. The meeting was chaired by a friend of one of the bank officials who had organised the meeting. This man spoke to the meeting of the value of organisation and attempted to allay any concerns held by those present. The meeting appeared to be progressing positively until it emerged that the chairman was actually the secretary of one of the largest clerical unions in Britain who was in Ireland on a short visit. This alarmed 'many present who considered it beneath the dignity of bank officials to form a union' in the style of those organised by ordinary working people. Later, when the chairman announced that he had to leave the meeting early in order to attend a meeting at Liberty Hall, the headquarters of the Irish Transport and General Workers' Union, it became too much for some who simply abandoned the meeting.[47]

Those who were left, however, were determined to pursue the establishment of a representative association. They formed a Provisional Committee with two representatives from each of nine banks: Bank of Ireland, Belfast Banking Co., Hibernian Bank, Munster and Leinster Bank, National Bank, Northern Bank, Provincial Bank, Royal Bank, and Ulster Bank. That committee set to work immediately. Circulars were sent to banks in Belfast, Derry and Galway urging the formation of local committees. These were duly formed and took their place alongside the existing committees in Cork and Limerick. The Dublin committee took the lead in drawing up a provisional constitution for the proposed association. This was sent to the other committees for discussion and a meeting of representatives of all the committees was arranged for Dublin on St Stephen's Day, 1917.[48]

At that meeting, efforts by the six committees to establish a national association took further shape. It was agreed to work together to organise the country generally. A complete directory of every bank official in Ireland was compiled and, armed with this information, a personal invitation to join the proposed association was issued to officials in every bank in Ireland. Their efforts brought a resounding response. By the time the inaugural general meeting of the Irish Bank Officials' Association was held in the Mansion House on 18 March 1918, there were 1,441 bank officials already registered as members on the books of the association.[49] Around 350 had travelled to Dublin to formalise the establishment of the 'The Irish Bank Officials' Association'.[50] The adoption of a constitution and the election of an executive committee completed the formalities. The question was: now that bank officials had their own representative association, what precisely would that Association do?

What immediately became apparent was what they would not do. At the first meeting of the newly elected executive of the IBOA on 20 March 1918, the issue of registering as a trade union was considered. The matter was put to C. H. Denroche, the solicitor whose work in chairing the inaugural meeting had led to him being essentially co-opted onto the executive of the IBOA. Denroche responded that it was his opinion that 'it was undesirable and that nothing could be gained by doing so'. As Gordon McMullan has pointed out, this opinion was entirely in keeping with the line taken by its English counterpart, The Bank Officers' Guild, which had described itself in February 1918 as 'not a militant trade union, but a Guild, conciliatory in its methods'.[51]

Charles Hutchings Denroche, the first Organising Secretary of the IBOA. *(IBOA Archive)*

The IBOA's initial approach to dealing with the banks was moderate as it set out to represent the interests of its members. A copy of the IBOA's constitution was forwarded to each of the banks on 24 May 1918. The executive of the IBOA had asked C. H. Denroche to act as intermediary and in his letter to the banks enclosing the constitution, Denroche had written:

> The officers of your bank who belong to this Association believe themselves to have certain grievances relating to their employment, which they are confident would be redressed by your directors if they were known to and realised by them . . . I have no doubt your directors realise the importance of having a happy and contented staff and would be desirous of doing anything reasonable to attain that object.[52]

A month later, letters were sent to each bank in which the members' grievances over pay and conditions were detailed. These letters had been compiled after the executive committee had solicited statements setting out the problems experienced by bank officials across the country. The grievances ranged from pensions and holidays to pay and promotion. The replies from the banks were at best non-committal, and at worst dismissive, while several were merely formal acknowledgements of the receipt of letters.[53]

In an attempt to find a focal point for the development of the new Association, it was decided to draw up a proposed scale of minimum salaries. That scale saw a proposal that salaries would commence at £80 in the first year, rising to reach £140 by the seventh year, £400 by the twentieth year and £500 by the thirtieth year. All salaries were to be paid free of income tax and after 40 years' service, bank officials were to be entitled to retire on a pension of not less than two-thirds of their salary. Officials who reached management positions would also receive further increases in pay.[54] The proposed pay scale was then sent to the banks and to the Ministry of Labour in London. The IBOA did not seriously believe that the banks would agree to the proposed salary scale. Instead, they hoped that the banks would agree to arbitration on the matter.[55]

In an attempt to defuse the situation, various banks offered minimal increases in pay and bonuses to their staff. It was deemed much too little by the IBOA. In August 1918, the IBOA wrote to the Ministry of Labour in London with a request that it seek to establish an arbitration board. The Ministry wrote to the banks asking that they agree to arbitration. Several banks responded with letters of acknowledgement; one claimed to be unaware of any grievances amongst its staff; and another simply declined the proposal.[56] These letters were forwarded to the IBOA from London, along with a letter from F. H. Greenhalgh, an official at the Ministry, noting the refusal of the banks to engage with arbitration and stating that the Ministry was therefore unable to pursue the matter.[57]

Although it had failed in its designs to secure an arbitration board, the IBOA had progressed in other ways. By March 1919, it had enlisted a membership of more than 2,300 members and could claim the allegiance of 80 per cent of Irish bank officials; by the summer of 1919 it was claiming 95 per cent of all officials as members.[58] More than 500 members attended the first AGM of the Association in City Hall in Dublin on St Patrick's Day, 1919. There were signs of increased militancy. A motion was unanimously passed which pledged the meeting to 'support the Executive Committee in any action it may take in order to achieve the objects of the Association'.[59] Against that, when the question of registering the IBOA as a trade union was again raised, it was effectively quashed with C. H. Denroche – again acting as chairman – telling the meeting that 'he did not think that there were any real advantages to be gained' from such a move.[60]

Nonetheless, it was apparent to delegates at the AGM that a more militant approach was on the way. There was open discussion of the possibilities of establishing a fund in the event of a strike being called and, although this idea was not adopted, the very fact of its suggestion evidenced a more militant approach. This approach soon manifested itself. Bank officials across the country approached local public representatives asking for support. County Councils, Corporations, Boards of Guardians and Urban and Rural District Councils passed resolutions in support of the demands of bank officials.[61] Copies of such resolutions were published in the press and forwarded to the banks.

Bringing a new dimension to their endeavour, the Executive Committee deputed C. H. Denroche to represent it at meetings of shareholders in various banks. They had secured this right by buying a single share or some stock in all of the banks. This led, in turn, to some testy exchanges. At a meeting of the shareholders of National Bank, Denroche informed the meeting that the conditions being endured by its staff had left them on the verge of strike. The chairman of the bank, Sir John Purcell, was reported to have replied 'they would not be interfered with in the administration of the bank by Mr. Denroche or by any outsider, nor would they be dictated to by a parcel of boys.'[62]

The growing militancy of the IBOA was further reflected in a new-found willingness to use the newspapers to publicise their case. Letters sent by the IBOA to the British government in pursuit of their ambitions were forwarded to *The Irish Times* in April 1919.[63] Denroche wrote to the press reporting that he had been 'contemptuously' treated by the banks; this willingness to use the press promoted a sense of the justice of the cause amongst the general public and, in time, increased the pressures on banks. Understanding the power of the press, the Executive Committee also launched its own magazine which helped to unify the membership and promote the development of the IBOA. In one of its first editions, the magazine had demanded of bank officials that they commit to the cause. In big, bold type, it declared: 'Everyone who is not for us is against us . . . You must organise . . . This is urgent.'[64]

Before September 1919, C. H. Denroche had acted in a voluntary capacity as adviser to the IBOA, but in that month he accepted the revised role of Organising Secretary. Immediately upon assuming the role, Denroche wrote to the banks asking that they should recognise the IBOA. He said that the request was yet another appeal for recognition and made clear – albeit in diplomatic language – that failure to grant such recognition must inevitably result in strike.[65] In response, the various Irish banks sent only notes of acknowledgement, with the exception of Hibernian Bank which looked for clarification of the welfare issues which the IBOA wished to address. When that list was provided, it included rates of pay, working hours, overtime, pensions, holidays and marriage restrictions. The response of the Hibernian Bank was stark. It said that it could not agree to recognition as this would 'be prejudicial to the efficient control of the bank's business, might in some respects prove embarrassing to the bank's customers, and would practically amount to an abdication by the Board of their proper functions in respect of the internal management of the bank'.[66]

During the autumn of 1919, Denroche travelled to towns across Ireland, meeting bank officials and assessing the mood of IBOA members. The mood was for strike. At a meeting in Cavan, a huge crowd turned out to hear Denroche say that he believed that bank directors simply did not believe that bank officials were capable of strike, that it was 'all gigantic bluff'.[67]

A ballot on industrial action saw 2,437 IBOA members vote in favour of staging a strike; just 91 voted against. The results were considered at a meeting of the Executive Committee at the Gresham Hotel in Dublin on 23 November which was also attended by special delegates from across the country.[68] The upshot of the meeting saw notice served on nine Irish banks which read that after 'eighteen months of fruitless appeals', the IBOA was declaring that 'on the 31st day of December next, all bank officials who are members of this Association . . . will cease work in every bank'.[69] The response of the banks was swift. Already they had established a Joint Committee in response to the establishment of the IBOA and now they sought to undercut support for the approaching strike. Banks demanded of their employees a written personal statement that they would not support the strike. The Belfast Bank Co., for example, circularised their employees with a form which they were asked to sign and return. The form read: 'Dear Sirs, I do not intend to absent myself from work as from 31st December, as directed by the Irish Bank Officials' Association. Yours faithfully, _____.' In an appended letter, the bank noted: 'In cases where the form is not returned we will naturally assume that the official who declines to extend to us the courtesy of a reply is leaving our service.'[70]

The response of the IBOA was definite. The Executive Committee stated that unless the declaration was withdrawn, there would be an immediate strike of all bank officials across the country. As general public dismay at the prospect of a bank strike rose, the IBOA increased the pressure on the banks by ordering a strike of its members from 3 December 1919. Public bodies, chambers of commerce and the press called on the banks to agree to arbitration. Finally, on 2 December 1919, the government intervened with the secretary of the Ministry of Labour, Gordon Campbell, negotiating an agreement by which the strike was called off, after the banks had agreed to a conference with the IBOA.[71]

That conference duly took place on 4 December 1919 at the Ministry of Labour's Dublin offices. It opened at 2 p.m. and lasted seven hours. The upshot was victory on all the key points for the IBOA. In return for agreeing not to strike, the IBOA was recognised to have the right to represent its members in discussions on salaries, bonuses, working hours, overtime, pensions, holidays, widows' and orphans' funds, marriage facilities and lunching facilities. Crucially, it was agreed by the banks to enter into arbitration on matters relating to salaries, bonuses, working hours, overtime, pensions and holidays.[72] Gordon McMullan has written: 'The significance of this breakthrough . . . cannot be over-estimated. This decision to threaten strike action and the ensuing developments represent probably the most important single decision in the history of the Irish Bank Officials' Association.'[73] Its consequence was that the IBOA had succeeded in its first ambition to secure recognition and to bring the banks to arbitration. The question now was what would that arbitration bring?

The first IBOA Executive Committee: Top row (l–r): H. E. Henry, C. I. Murray, J. Purcell, C. Byrne, G. F. Kerin, J. S. Fitzsimmons. Middle row (l–r): M. O'Connell, F. M. Mease, E. H. Flint, J. T. Scarlett, D. Aylward, R. A. Calvin. Front row (l–r): W. G. Bradley, P. J. Kelly, J. F. Eagar, C. H. Denroche (Organising Secretary), H. L. Dowd, Geo. Marlow. *(IBOA Archive)*

2

The 1920s

The first years of the 1920s brought momentous change to the lives of Irish bank officials. The last days of the previous decade had seen the IBOA secure official recognition from the banks which employed its members and had seen agreement that those same banks would enter into arbitration with the Association in respect of pay and conditions. That arbitration took place in March 1920 and ultimately transformed the working lives of officials by providing a standard of living which had previously been unattainable. What also transformed the lives of bank officials was the dramatic political upheaval under way in Ireland which provided the backdrop to arbitration. The year 1920 was a violent one, characterised by murder, hunger strike and execution. An increasingly aggressive IRA campaign was followed by the deployment of the Black and Tans by the British government. Eventually, this Anglo-Irish War drifted into stalemate and a political solution of sorts. This solution involved the partition of Ireland, initially through the Government of Ireland Act of 1920 and then through the Anglo-Irish Treaty of 1921. Where initially the IBOA had looked to Westminster to adjudicate on matters of dispute, from 1922 it dealt with two governments: that of the Irish Free State in Dublin and that of Northern Ireland in Belfast. This presented obvious challenges for an Association which had, itself, only been founded

Dáil Éireann in session in the year of the Anglo-Irish Treaty, 1921. The political developments of 1913–22 left Ireland divided. Where initially the IBOA had looked to Westminster for political guidance, from 1922 it dealt with two governments: that of the Irish Free State in Dublin and that of Northern Ireland in Belfast. *(Getty Images)*

in 1918. Inevitably, the IBOA was affected by the wider changes in Irish society; that it was not itself sundered by those changes was its own success.

I

ARBITRATION

At 11 a.m. on 1 March 1920 representatives of eight Irish banks and of the IBOA began formal proceedings of what was immediately termed 'this very important arbitration'.[1] The venue was in keeping with the importance of the occasion: the Old House of Lords at the Bank of Ireland in College Green had been part of the Irish Houses of Parliament before the Act of Union, 1801. The building had then been sold by the British government to the Bank of Ireland in 1803 and the House of Lords had since served as the boardroom for the bank. On both sides of the room hung enormous tapestries, and on one end sat the dais upon which the throne of the Lord Lieutenant of Ireland had rested in splendour.

If the surroundings spoke of the importance of the occasion, so too did the key personnel. The Umpire of the arbitration was the Lord Chancellor of Ireland, Sir James Campbell (later Lord Glenavy). He was a former unionist MP who had also served as Attorney-General for Ireland, before assuming the role of Lord Chancellor, the most important judicial position on the island. Later, the Lord Chancellor served as the first chairman of the senate of the Irish Free State. His performance in the role, it has been written, was characterised by 'dismissive haughtiness towards his fellow senators, and by adjourning the house to suit his own convenience'.[2] The arbitrator chosen to represent eight Irish banks was Stewart Blacker Quin and their counsel was S. L. Brown. The Royal Bank had declined to enter arbitration, preferring to leave the process to continue to its end and then decide whether or not to accept its terms. In the event of that bank not being content, a further separate arbitration would be entered into. Representing the IBOA as arbitrator was S. W. Maddock, while its counsel was Henry Hanna, a future high court judge.[3]

The arbitration opened with the words of the Lord Chancellor: 'Now it is fully 11 o'clock and we had better get to work.' And work they did.[4] Over the following three days, eighteen witnesses were called, ranging from bank officials to bank managers and directors. In the course of their evidence a vivid picture was painted of the lives of bank officials and of the implications of class and culture in towns and cities all across Ireland. Two central themes immediately emerged. The first was that the decline in the living standards of bank officials since the outbreak of the Great War, in particular, was real and distressing. This was essentially acknowledged by all parties at the arbitration. The second was that the economic difficulties of bank officials were compounded by the notions of social and occupational superiority which attended their work. Again, this was something which was accepted by all who sat in the Old House of Lords in March 1920.[5]

It would, of course, be a mistake to consider that every bank manager was a dyed-in-the-wool conservative, whose life was defined by service to his employer and whose piety and rectitude overwhelmed every other aspect of his character. Equally, it would be folly to imagine that bank officials then – and in the decades that followed – sought only to live up to the image of them which was constructed for the benefit of the arbitration. There is sufficient evidence of socialising – notably drinking – to confirm that any suggestion of absolute propriety is simply untrue. By the same token, it is also clear that there was compassion displayed by many managers towards staff and that managers were more flexible in their dealings with customers than is usually portrayed. Naturally, the thousands of men and women who passed their lives as bank officials did not conform to any one type. Irish banks held their share of eccentrics and individualists.[6]

Allowing for that, there is no denying that the image which the banks wished to present extended to their staff and was rooted in an acute sense of their place in Irish society. This sense of social status emerged repeatedly across the three days of the arbitration. It was woven into the entirety of an official's career and was a determinant even in the prospect of getting employment in the first place. In his evidence to the arbitration, C. H. Denroche, secretary of the IBOA, explained that bank officials were drawn from the sons of the landed gentry, of professionals, of substantial businessmen and, in 'some of the banks', the sons of large farmers. Their selection was 'by nomination . . . If anyone in a country town thought that he would like to get his son into the bank he went to the bank manager, and the bank manager saw him . . . If he thought he was a suitable man from every point of view, he would send his name forward to the directors, and the directors considered all the circumstances of the case. If they thought the boy suitable, they would have him up for examination at Head Office.'[7] This process was confirmed by Henry Johns, the managing director of the Belfast Bank. Where Denroche and Johns disagreed was on the competitive nature of examination undertaken by the candidate. Johns regarded the competition as 'very considerable', with just 50 per cent succeeding in gaining a position. Denroche, on the other hand, believed that there was barely enough demand to meet supply: 'I do not think you could ever look at the examination as a competitive examination.'[8]

Staff taken into the banks were sometimes as young as fifteen, with the average age at start of employment given at seventeen. Before they might be considered full-time employees of the bank, they were placed on a period of probation which lasted for three years. Andrew Jameson, a director of the Bank of Ireland, was asked what an official was tested for during this probationary period. He replied: 'His conduct, how he lives, and whether he shows general efficiency.'[9] Initially, while on probation, the new clerks were charged with copying letters, keeping postages, and assisting in the exchanges of cheques and notes between their bank and the others in a town. The new clerks would then begin to do basic bookkeeping and, in this function, to look after both the accounts of the bank and of the customer.

Following probation, the clerk might then move to work as a teller in a bank – not always immediately – but, certainly, in time. The teller was, in 1920, responsible for looking after the cash received and paid out by a bank on any given day, a sum which at the time could range between £60,000 and £100,000. To discharge this duty properly, the teller was required to be aware of the condition of a customer's account and of the amount of credit the bank was prepared to extend to individual customers. On top of that, a teller was charged with the responsibility of being able to judge whether to accept or refuse cheques, sometimes for large sums. In time, a clerk might be promoted to the role of sub-agent, with responsibility for all those working under him and the decisions they made, as well as being able to give advice to customers and to the bank manager.[10]

Almost always, it was only with promotion that bank officials saw their pay increased. And the evidence presented by the IBOA suggested that it was not always ability that saw a man promoted; rather it was 'largely by reason of favouritism'. In this it was argued that 'the man who made himself the greatest favourite' was the one who got promoted, ahead of men who showed a 'certain independence of character' and who did not have it in themselves to approach the directors in pursuit of advancement.[11] The charge of promoting those who most successfully endeared themselves to directors was rejected out of hand by Sir Thomas Esmonde, a director of the National Bank, who said: 'I do not know how these charges got abroad about favouritism. It is one of the things we have been always fighting against – the very idea of it.'[12]

What was clear, however, for any man who coveted promotion, choosing a wife was no mere matter of love and commitment. A *de facto* system had existed whereby a bank official wishing to marry effectively sought the permission of his employers to do so. For example, letters survive in relation to an employee of the Hibernian Bank in the north-east of Ireland where it is made explicit that the employee will furnish particulars in relation to his marriage 'sufficient to satisfy the Directors' of the bank. The satisfaction sought, in this instance, related to the financial stability of the marriage.[13] On the first day of arbitration, Henry Hanna told the assembly that 'in some of the banks in pre-war days, an official could not marry without the consent of the directors', and unless he earned £150 per year, the amount deemed the minimum to support a man and his wife. Hanna described this practice as 'a humiliation' and a 'curtailment of a man's liberty'.[14]

When C. H. Denroche gave evidence to the court, he laid bare the dilemma which faced a bank official who wished to marry. They did not make enough money, he said, to marry women of their own class, but 'if men in the bank married outside their own class it would be a serious thing for them. The Directors would look askance at them.'[15] The result, according to Henry Dowd, a senior teller in the Bank of Ireland and the first President of the IBOA, was that the marriage prospects of bank officials were greatly diminished: 'A small percentage of the men get promotion, but naturally so late in life that he is really absolutely unable to marry . . . It is astonishing how few have been able to marry. Many have waited 10 and 15 years before they can support a family.'[16]

May, 1924.   IRISH BANKING MAGAZINE.   177

THE PRESIDENT OF THE IRISH BANK OFFICIALS' ASSOCIATION.

Henry Dowd, the first President of the IBOA, as portrayed by the *Irish Banking Magazine* in May 1924. In testimony to an arbitration on pay in 1920, Dowd spoke of how the low pay of bank officials had contributed to the frustration of their marital prospects. 'It is astonishing how few have been able to marry,' he remarked. 'Many have waited ten and fifteen years before they can support a family.' *(IBOA Archive)*

Evidence presented to the arbitration suggested that those bank officials who did manage to get married depended upon income outside of their bank salary to survive. A. G. Palmer, an official of the National Bank at College Green, who had been working at the bank for twenty-six years and had risen to the position of ledger keeper, was married with two children. He was a non-smoking, teetotal vegetarian and yet gave evidence that he struggled to make ends meet. He said that his family had moved to a smaller house, had sold several pieces of their furniture and had used up a private income of £300 to make ends meet in recent years. Asked by Henry Hanna whether he was able to keep a servant, he replied 'no', that everything was done by his wife. Palmer agreed that his wife's health had suffered 'owing to the constant drudgery', while they had not been to 'any place of entertainment at all' over the previous four years.[17] In great overstatement, counsel for the IBOA was later to say: 'A sadder story was never told in court . . . He goes home at night and what does he see? His wife with no servant to help her, the wife of a clergyman's son, turned into a domestic servant, drudging and patching the whole night through, and scraping and watching to see that no crumbs fall from that table.'[18]

Further evidence was provided as to the educational demands of the families of bank officials. Henry Hanna told the arbitration court: 'The bank officials had to encounter a great many difficulties about the education of their children, about the manner in which they could educate them properly, and in many parts of the country and in some of the towns in which the officials lived it would be considered derogatory for the bank manager to send his children to the local National School.' Usually – and this could apply to officials other than the bank manager – children were sent to boarding school.[19]

Again, the financial pressure under which bank officials operated was presented in the evidence of female witnesses, whom Henry Hanna designated as 'lady clerks' as he made the simple point that 'they should be given a sum that they may be able to live in decency.'[20] In 1920, their number amounted to 100 permanent 'lady clerks' in the Bank of Ireland and three in the other banks combined. There were at least 300 further temporary 'lady clerks' across the banks. Hanna told the court that the salaries paid to lady clerks were 'scandalously inadequate', particularly because they were given to a young lady of education, who probably has gone through a good high-class secondary school, who comes of respectable people of the upper middle class, and who goes into the bank for the purpose of being able to support herself. 'After all, the ladies who go into banks are of a good class. The Bank Directors know they are of a good class, possibly some of the parents of these young ladies are of as good a rank as the Directors themselves.'[21]

One witness, Helen Alexander, a permanent clerk at the Bank of Ireland, said simply of her level of pay: 'You cannot live on it, it is an impossibility.' She further told the court that her salary was insufficient, 'especially as they are doing the work of men'. Then in her sixth year of working for the bank, she lived at home with her family, saying she simply did not earn enough to live in lodgings. Other 'lady clerks' had their income supplemented by their families.[22] Many of these women had been taken on by the banks in the years immediately after the war, while others had been taken on in a temporary basis during the war itself. Many women were designated as 'temporary' even though it was apparent that they had established themselves as permanent employees. According to C. H. Denroche, banks had taken on women as clerks on a temporary basis to fill a gap during the Great War and 'they found them useful and retained their services'.

Denroche acknowledged to the arbitration that the IBOA had its own difficulties in respect of accepting female members and had decided to accept membership only from those who were permanent. How these women were represented at arbitration presented further difficulty for the IBOA. Denroche told the court that there was no sentiment within the IBOA against the continued employment of women in the banks, but that the Association, 'which is mainly composed of men, think that the ladies won't be satisfied if we don't say: "Equal pay for equal service." On the other hand, if we say that, the Directors may dismiss them.' Before the arbitration, the IBOA held meetings of its female members in Dublin, Belfast, Cork and Waterford to canvass opinion. Some demanded equal pay; others took a more moderate view. In the end, the IBOA sought a lesser scale of pay for women than for men, 'leaning to the side of moderation', with a low salary affording a basic standard of living which would go up in small increments.[23] Earlier on the second day of arbitration, the Lord Chancellor appeared to be supporting that idea, saying that the salaries of 'lady clerks' should be fixed on the same scale as that of men, 'subject to taking off, say, 20 per cent . . .'[24]

The question remained: what would the scale of pay for men be? This was the crux of the arbitration. Before the arbitration, the IBOA had presented its proposal for a scale of pay, and the banks had done likewise. There was a considerable difference between the two. Evidence presented by a series of witnesses called by the IBOA clearly outlined the financial struggle for bank officials. This struggle had worsened considerably since the outbreak of the Great War, even though it was argued that bank officials were considerably underpaid even before that war.[25] The cost of living increase between 1914 and 1919 was estimated at 120 per cent, while by 1920 it was claimed that this figure had risen beyond 130 per cent.[26] The IBOA sought to present the revised pay scale it was seeking as moderate in proportion to the increase in the cost of living. C. H. Denroche said that they took into consideration 'that everybody must expect to be worse off now than he was before the war, and that everybody must pay some portion of the increase.'[27]

What was agreed was that the banks were eminently capable of meeting the increases in salaries requested by the IBOA. They made no serious attempt to deny that this was the case. Rather, they argued that the scale proposed would tend against efficiency in the bank, that it would make the pursuit of promotion less important and, by that, officials would 'not work as they did to secure these posts'.[28] In response to this statement, Jameson was asked: 'Can you imagine anything less likely to promote efficiency than men having to live for years on what I may call a starvation wage?' His simple reply was: 'No.'

But how much was enough? In arguing for the increase it proposed, the IBOA repeatedly asserted that the position of the bank clerk in Irish society required a different standard of living from others. This assertion was accepted by the banks. Henry Hanna referred to other awards given at arbitration: 'The lowest wage here, under the award for railway workers, is as to a third class worker at a Class II. station, 56s. a week. He does not require to buy the same kind of clothes; he may be getting a uniform from the railway company; he does not require to live in the same class of house; and perhaps has not been brought up on the same kind of food – you have to take these things into consideration, and look round and see what other people are getting?'

C. H. Denroche argued that the cost-of-living increases since the outbreak of the Great War had disproportionately affected bank clerks, by comparison with workers. In accepting that the cost-of-living increase was 125 per cent in comparison with the pre-war cost of living, Denroche claimed that that figure was itself a compromise, saying '125 or 120 per cent, only deals with the increase of the cost of living for a workman's *ménage*. There are things which may be necessary to one class that are not necessary to another. These figures merely deal with items that come into a workingman's *ménage*. If you go above that you find that there are things 250 and 300 per cent above pre-war figures. What may be necessary for a bank official may not be necessary for a coal porter.'[29]

As the arbitration was drawing to a close, it became apparent that bank officials were going to get a substantial award in their favour. Counsel for the banks accepted this as he said that 'the banks are most anxious to approach this matter in a spirit of absolute fair play, with a view to seeing that the clerks and officials get absolutely everything they are entitled to'.[30] As if to underline this, the banks volunteered to pay the entire costs of the arbitration. C. H. Denroche replied that the IBOA 'appreciates very much the spirit in which the directors have met them, and while the Association is prepared to pay their own entire costs, they recognise the action of the directors as most gracious, and they thoroughly appreciate it'. All of which prompted the Lord Chancellor to note, on behalf of the arbitrators: 'I think we are able to say that we have been greatly struck with the spirit of fair play and conciliation shown on both sides.'[31] All that remained was to await the decision.

When the arbitration court made its findings known, it was a clear victory for the arguments of the IBOA. A standardised pay scale would now apply across all the banks. The starting salary for men and women alike would be £100, which would rise in annual increments for the men of £10 until it reached £140 and would then increase by £15 annually to reach £230, before finally increasing by £20 annually to reach £450. The increase for female staff would be £10 annually to £150, and £5 annually thereafter to reach £190. These minimum scales would be augmented by a bonus of 20 per cent of salary for as long as the cost of living remained between 115 and 135 per cent of pre-war values. All salaries would be paid by the bank free of income tax. One disappointment was the failure to secure adequate pay and protection for temporary 'lady clerks'.[32]

Further decisions in respect of working conditions were also announced. The banks agreed, for example, that 'where practicable, every official shall have half an hour free from duty to enable him or her to lunch', and where this was not possible 'arrangements

The bank officials' workplace: this photograph shows the interior of a National Bank building in the south-east of the country *c.* 1920. *(NLI, Poole Collection)*

should be made whereby a light luncheon may be partaken of while on duty.' Holidays were to amount to between 15 and 21 working days, depending on length of service, with managers and agents entitled to a calendar month. A weekly half-holiday was agreed to, with banks committed to allowing their staff leave on such days at 2 p.m. Further, a comprehensive agreement was reached on the payment of pensions. In all matters, the proposals of the IBOA were largely satisfied; it was not an absolute victory, but it was emphatic.[33] As if to confirm that victory, the Royal Bank which had previously declined to join the arbitration, later came into line with the other banks.[34]

J. F. Eager was later to note that the scale of the success of the IBOA was rooted in the unity of the Association and the willingness of its members to work for the greater good. He wrote: 'Each local representative, each local secretary, each member of the various local committees, and each individual member of the Association . . . can truthfully claim that were it not for his co-operation the victory would not have been so marked.'[35] It was also a great tactical triumph. The pursuit of recognition of the IBOA by the banks, the achievement of bringing the banks to arbitration, and the apparent moderation of the case presented by the IBOA created a momentum which proved unstoppable. The Association could claim a victory almost as its first act.

II

NEW CHALLENGES

The scale of the victory in arbitration enjoyed by bank officials ensured that the primary causes of dispute between bank officials and their employers were largely removed for the remainder of the 1920s. Naturally, there were matters of tension from time to time, but no deep-seated sense of injustice to provoke a major dispute. It was not, of course, the case that the lot of bank officials was without its strains; it was more the case that the extent of the advance in their working conditions as agreed in 1920 underpinned a decade of harmony in the workplace. The restoration of this harmony, however, was not merely the fruit of arbitration; it was also related to the innate conservatism of bank officials. Having achieved their objectives, there was a tendency to retreat to this conservatism. The simple fact was that, although the IBOA had won their victory by adopting the organisation of a union and by manifesting a willingness to strike, this was not how the IBOA wished to be perceived. The actions of the Association may have been rooted in those of trade unionism, but in their language they disavowed such a connection. The members of the IBOA had, after all, declined at every turn to countenance registering as a trade union.

Throughout the 1920s, the IBOA never again came close to industrial action. To the contrary, it made much of its own moderation. Its one-time honorary secretary and president J. F. Eager wrote in 1930:

> Since the Association was formally recognised by the banks the utmost harmony and friendship has existed between it and the directors. The policy of the Association has been to ask for nothing unreasonable, and any request made by it has been, invariably, very fairly met. The loyalty of officials to their respective banks – which loyalty has always been a by-word – was at no time disturbed by the Association and is now just as strong as ever.[36]

There were, of course, issues which required resolution. These included issues around weekday half-holidays, holidays, bonuses and the treatment of women. First amongst these issues was the position of temporary 'lady clerks'. One such clerk, signing herself 'A Demented Clerkette', wrote to the *Irish Banking Magazine* almost immediately after the arbitration agreement was signed. She asked simply:

> Is it not unjust that our needs should have been passed over? . . . When managers, accountants and other 'seasoned' members of staff were hedging and in doubt

as to whether they should have anything to do with the Association, we boldly came forward to swell the ranks . . . As a result of our endeavours, what do we receive? A crushing blow – while the 'lie-lows' and cowards step in to carry off the booty and live on the fatted calf of life for the remainder of their banking career . . . Oh, for a rational salary, a decent bonus and a good old spend.[37]

The IBOA moved immediately to clarify that its position was to secure permanent status for temporary clerks. It said that it understood the disappointment of 'lady clerks', but that they were working towards finding a solution. And some progress was made. In November 1920, the Provincial Bank placed its temporary clerks on the same footing as its permanent ones.[38] There was evidence, however, that many men held jaundiced views of the women they worked with. In that same month, November 1920, the *Irish Banking Magazine* published a number of essays from members condemning the performance and behaviour of 'lady clerks'. Then in the following month, December 1920, the *Irish Banking Magazine* published a letter from a bank official called A. H. Reid, who lamented the continued employment of 'girls' by banks, saying that although they had helped the banks to carry on functioning during the war, their employment was now having 'a detrimental effect on our banks'. Reid claimed that 'girls' spent too long talking on the telephone, were usually inefficient, and were unable to keep business books as they did not write in the appropriate columns. More than that, their general attitude was unsuited to the banking environment as if a 'girl' was spoken to firmly at work, 'she uses the greatest of all weapons against man, "tears"'. On top of that, wrote Reid, 'there is absolutely no doubt that girls cannot work as well together as men. Two men may have a quarrel and yet work side by side without the work suffering, Could two girls do likewise? And, all the while, their desire to get married hinders the bank: A man, the longer he is in the bank the greater is his interest in its prosperity. The average girl, and rightly so, hopes every year that it will be her last within its walls.'[39]

This brought a reply from a sub-agent of the Bank of Ireland who condemned Reid's sentiments as 'untrue and unjust' and that 'I do not consider them in any way inferior . . . This alleged chattering of women is all nonsense. My experience anyway in banks has been that men gossip more and waste more valuable time in futile chatter than any women . . . They can tot just as well as most men, and their handwriting and work is generally far neater than that of the average man . . . Women work as hard as men. I have never seen them in tears or near it. They are just as polite to clients as men are, and in every way just as keen, if not keener, on their work as their male colleagues on theirs, and with less incentive.' Even this defender of 'lady clerks', however, was of the view that: 'I do not consider them in any way inferior – on the contrary – but I do consider that for them bank work is unsuitable.'[40]

Correspondence on the matter grew in the editions that followed. In January 1921 a 'lady clerk' wrote in and laughingly referred to male critics as 'overgrown schoolboys'. She continued: 'I have yet to meet the man with whom I cannot compete on equal footing . . . I have met male clerks several years my senior in the office whose helplessness in their daily work was quite appalling. I am afraid many of those gentlemen are suffering from exaggerated ego . . . I quite agree with the point that a woman is seen to best advantage in the home, but that does not alter the fact that she is capable of performing excellent work in the clerical departments of life.'[41] The IBOA set up a Ladies' Committee to promote the position of its female members, yet there proved to be no straightforward solution to the problems of pay and pensions. Women working in Irish banks continued to work under conditions which were much inferior to that of their male counterparts and this treatment was something which surfaced repeatedly in the decades that followed.

If discrimination against women in banks was reflective of wider views in Irish society, the lives of bank officials were also shaped by other events, sometimes violently so. The Anglo-Irish War, for example, brought frequent raids on banks, and references to the 'nerve strain imposed on our staffs by those raids and robberies, holds up and other menaces to life and limb which a decade ago would have been read only in youthful "penny dreadfuls" or Wild West news, and which are now normal news in our morning and evening papers'.[42] There was correspondence in the pages of the *Irish Banking Magazine* on the best way to protect bank staff, including comparisons from Canada.[43] There was also praise for bank officials who resisted the raiders. R. H. Stevens, the manager of the Ulster Bank in Carrigallen, County Leitrim, refused to give money to a group of six men who fired shots and even threw a small bomb, and there were several other acts of resistance which led the *Irish Banking Magazine* to note that 'much latent bravery' lurked in Irish banks.[44] The reality of the revolution that brought into being the Irish Free State meant, however, that bank robberies became something of a commonplace. In February 1922, the Head Office of the Hibernian Bank sent a circular to its staff, which noted that directors had decided that 'special steps should be taken to protect their banks from armed robbery'. This decision instructed bank officials that unless armed guards had been provided, they should contact the local officer of the IRA to obtain an armed guard for duty at the bank.[45]

Bank raids continued despite all attempts to resist them. Branches of the Bank of Ireland at Kilbeggan, County Westmeath and Bagenalstown, County Carlow, were robbed in November 1922 of the sums of £1,329 and £1,155, respectively.[46] The Bank of Ireland at Mountbellew, County Galway, was robbed by armed men in October 1923 'who took away between £700/800 under threats of violence'.[47] When the Bank of Ireland branch in Kilkenny city was robbed, its manager F. Mulcahy was 'away abroad on a long spell of sick leave, owing to a breakdown suffered from overwork', while his wife 'was also absent in delicate health . . .' Furniture in their rooms above the bank was destroyed. Worse, when Mrs Mulcahy returned, she noticed women in Kilkenny walking round in clothes that had been stolen from her wardrobe.[48]

The Kilcock branch of the Munster and Leinster Bank in County Kildare, was robbed on three occasions between April and June 1921. Later, on 14 December 1921, five armed men called at lodgings of officials of the Munster and Leinster Bank in Newtownbarry, County Wexford. They seized the keys to the branch and took more than £2,000. At the Munster and Leinster Bank at Enniscorthy, County Wexford, four armed men moved in and robbed more than

£2,100 at 10.30 a.m. They were subsequently arrested, tried and found 'not guilty', even though they had been identified by the manager and staff of the bank. Solicitors for the bank also wrote to the provisional government of the Irish Free State to report a further robbery: 'On Sunday 7th May 1922, shortly after 1am, a ladder was put up to the Manager's bedroom window, he was ordered down to open the door in the name of the IRA; three armed men came into the house and demanded the keys. They had already secured the Teller's keys. The total taken was £2521.7.1.' All the banks sought compensation from the new Free State for money lost in these raids.[49]

Banks were also involved in the 'Belfast boycott'. This boycott had originated in a decision by the provisional government to boycott Belfast-based banks and insurance companies, before evolving into

During the Anglo-Irish War, the business of banking in Ireland was routinely disrupted by raids, and robberies were said to have imposed 'nerve strain' on the staff of various banks. As if to illustrate the risks associated with working in banking, this photograph shows soldiers guarding the Ormond Quay branch of the Bank of Ireland in 1920. *(Getty Images)*

44

a wider campaign against goods from Northern Ireland being sold in the south. The immediate motivation for the boycott was attacks on Catholics in Belfast, as well as mass expulsions from the city's shipyards and engineering works. The impact on banks varied from place to place. In October 1921, IRA men in Ballymote, County Sligo, fined local people who continued to bank with Ulster Bank in the town.[50] After the establishment of the Irish Free State a solicitor representing those fined wrote to the government looking to recoup the money taken in fines. This amounted to between £10 and £30 per person.[51]

The drawing of a border across the island presented less dramatic but nonetheless important challenges for the members of the IBOA. For example, the Irish Bank Officials' Health Insurance Society which had initially operated on an all-Ireland basis, was now confined to the Irish Free State. Following partition, a Banks' Health Insurance Society was established to operate in Northern Ireland. The funds of both societies were actually the property of both governments and were simply administered by the respective societies for the benefit of their members. Bank officials who crossed the border were obliged to transfer their contribution to whichever state they moved to, in order to continue to be qualified to receive sickness benefit, maternity benefit, and dental and ophthalmic care. It was a practical demonstration of the impact of the border on the lives of bank officials.[52] And yet the Association did not itself divide. In part, this was a reflection of the fact that the banking industry in Ireland remained an all-Ireland enterprise; it is also rooted in the sense that the instincts of many leading members of the IBOA were at that point unionist in orientation.

III

SOCIAL LIFE

After the initial euphoria of the victory in arbitration, there was a much-repeated concern in the years that followed that the Association was drifting and that its members were increasingly apathetic.[53] There were fears, too, that complacency would set like a rot into the IBOA and that young officials would not take the place of older ones. The debate was a little overwrought. It did not often allow for the inevitable lull that might be expected to follow a major victory, or for the fact that interest in the Association's activities would inevitably rise and fall over time and from place to place.

Indeed, what actually is apparent is that the 1920s were a decade of steady progression. The figure of 2,400 members at the end of 1919 increased to 4,844 by 1931. This was partly explained by the expansion in banking services offered in Ireland and the consequent employment of greater numbers of bank officials. It was also a consequence of the fact that more than 90 per cent of all bank officials joined the Association. The result was that 'for all practical purposes the IBOA represented and held in membership the staffs of all Irish banks'.[54] The growth of the IBOA was also rooted in the soundness of structure that characterised its organisation. Crucially, the partition of Ireland was not reflected in the partition of the IBOA, which continued to represent bank officials, north and south. Across the island, there was also coherence to the endeavour of the IBOA. In 1918, the Association had established as its base rented rooms at 16 South Frederick Street in Dublin. At the end of 1920, it moved to 93 St Stephen's Green, initially in office space provided by the Institute of Bankers in Ireland, and then in complete possession from March 1921. The IBOA paid £1,300 for the premises and its furniture.[55] It was from these rooms that C. H. Denroche, as secretary, directed the development of the Association under the guidance of a central Executive Committee. That Denroche remained in his position of secretary until 1932 gave the Association a continuity of leadership which facilitated its progress.

Outside Dublin, the IBOA had quickly established itself as a vital presence in the lives of bank officials. In Belfast, for example, the IBOA had made immediate and powerful strides. By 9 April 1919, the local committee had established new offices and this progressive attitude was retained through the 1920s and replicated in many parts of Ireland. The key to this strength lay in the proposition set out in a letter to the *Irish Banking Magazine* by an official who signed himself simply as 'Progressive'. Written in April 1920, the letter said: 'Now that we have secured a decent scale, however, we must realise that this organisation is not merely a piece of material-istic machinery. It has got an intellect and it has got a soul, and we have got to develop the whole as a living organism vital to our very existence as bank officials and as citizens.'[56]

One way to do this was through entertainment. From its inception, the IBOA had sought to provide a social outlet for its members. The very first issue of the *Irish Banking Magazine* lauded the achievement in bringing together bank officials for various social functions.[57] In the summer of 1919, for example, bank officials in Dublin had travelled out to Tallaght for a picnic, complete with egg-and-spoon races, weight-throwing competitions, relay races and sprints. After a tea on the grass, the 80-strong picnic party retired to a local ballroom for music and song.[58] A similar picnic in Cork saw 34 bank officials head out from the city to Ringabella on the last Sunday in August 1919. Along the beach, they played cricket, while others took to the water to swim. There was also the hint of romance in the air: a report of the outing in the *Irish Banking Magazine* remarked that some members 'went on what appeared to be a voyage of discovery, judging from the length of time they were absent from the main party'.[59]

In towns across Ireland, the IBOA established itself as a genuine presence, running picnics and car-drives, and holding dances. The next step was the establishment of its own premises for socialising. On 9 May 1921, a meeting was held at IBOA headquarters to 'ascertain the feeling of members on the subject of a club' and this brought general agreement to establish the Irish Bankers' Club.[60] By October 1921 the club was up and running, having had 250 expressions of interest from Dublin-based members and 100 from those in country areas. The club opened on 19 November 1921 with a smoking concert. At that point, the club consisted of a bar, a billiards room, a card room, a dining room and a reading room.[61] The regular entertainments put on at the club drew in large crowds of officials. In December 1922, for example, a conjuror called 'Presto' made packs of cards and an egg disappear, on a night which also saw performances from the Rathmines Choral and Musical

An excursion to Tallaght was organised by the Dublin Social Committee of the IBOA in June 1919. A programme of events, including various sports activities, was arranged for the day-tripping bankers. That same evening, the bankers adjourned to a local ballroom where they danced and sang their way through the evening. This photograph of the travelling group was reproduced in the *Irish Banking Magazine* in July 1919. *(IBOA Archive)*

Society.[62] For several years the club made a loss, but this had been rectified by the end of the 1920s and it was deemed 'an important and necessary part of the Association's fabric'.[63]

While dances, concerts and card-playing were the staples of the IBOA's winter activities, sport came to the fore during the summer. In Belfast, for example, sporting activities between bank officials had grown steadily since the war.[64] Teams were established and represented bank officials in league and cup competitions in Ulster and beyond. In time, this led to the establishment of a whole range of inter-bank competitions in sport, notably in rugby. It became a matter of great pride that a bank should win the inter-bank cup competition established in 1923. In June 1924, the *Irish Banking*

Magazine published a picture of the Ulster Bank Football Team, who won the Institute of Bankers Rugby Cup in 1924.[65] Usually, seven or eight banks entered teams in this competition.[66] The final was played in Lansdowne Road and ended with a city centre dinner and presentation night.[67]

In provincial towns such as Wexford, bank officials formed prominent elements of hockey and rugby teams.[68] There were proposals to hold chess competitions and an annual bank sports day.[69] Social outings of bank officials were timed to coincide with wider sporting events. The Tralee branch went on an outing to the annual regatta at Fenit in the summer of 1919 and its members won several of the swimming competitions that were staged there.[70] Throughout the 1920s, there was great interest in the competition played for the Denroche Golf Cup. C. H. Denroche had, in 1923,

The Ulster Bank rugby football team, winners of the Institute of Bankers' Rugby Cup in 1924. The final of the competition had been played at Lansdowne Road and was followed by a dinner and presentation in the city centre. *(IBOA Archive)*

announced that he was donating a valuable cup in his name to be played for by golf teams of bankers from country towns across Ireland. Initially, it was proposed that teams would play off in their own county, before progressing to national competition.[71] Eventually, though, it was changed to create a competition won by individual golfers and the annual entry ran to dozens.[72] This was a measure of the interest in golf in the banks, many of which had golfing societies.[73]

An inter-bank Lawn Tennis Competition was run from 1926. Amongst the banks which entered teams was the National Bank, which already had an active tennis club. Around its sporting activities, that club ràn a variety of social events. In December 1925, for instance, the club ran a Masked Carnival Ball at the Metropole Ballroom on O'Connell Street. Tickets were priced at half-a-guinea apiece and included a buffet and music by the nine-man Adelaide Orpheus Band. Patrons were advised to wear fancy or evening dress, and that special trams would run at 1.30 a.m. from Nelson's Pillar to Dalkey, Donnybrook, Clonskeagh and Terenure.[74]

From 1927, the list of inter-bank competitions was extended to cricket with the establishment of the Irish Bankers' Club Cricket Challenge Cup. The *Irish Banking Magazine* heralded the establishment of this competition by expressing the hope that this competition would inspire 'a great revival of the grand old summer game in the long evenings'.[75]

In general, the sporting world of the IBOA in the 1920s belonged very much within that of the sporting world of the empire with its diet of cricket, tennis, rugby, golf and hockey. This revolved around inter-bank activities, but also around the prospects for bankers of selection on the Irish international teams. G. C. Higginbotham was praised for his efforts on behalf of the Irish water polo team.[76] When M. J. Dunne of the Hibernian Bank played brilliantly for Ireland against England at Twickenham, there was praise that in so doing he had 'shed lustre on his profession'.[77] There were also occasional glimpses of a shift in interest, however, not least in the establishment by 1929 of a Dublin Bankers' Cup in soccer.

By 1928, the *Irish Banking Magazine* had added a report of the Munster Hurling Final to its coverage. In that same year, the magazine also congratulated the one banker who secured a medal at the Tailteann Games – a vast sporting and cultural festival run in 1924, 1928 and 1932 to celebrate the achievement of Irish independence and which restricted itself to 'native sports'. That banker was William T. Britton, the manager of the Munster and Leinster Bank in Cavan. Britton was deemed to be a hammer-thrower second only in prowess to Pat O'Callaghan who won gold in the 1928 and 1932 Olympics.[78] He was born in Kilmallock, County Limerick, and through his career won 71 major medals. Britton was not simply an Irish athlete, however. In 1930, he was the manager of the British Empire Team in athletics.[79]

The extension in the range of sporting activities enjoyed by bankers led to a proposal to establish an 'Irish Bankers' Sports Ground'.[80] This appeal was led by the new columnist in the magazine, 'Spectator', who provided a weekly overview of the sporting activities of members of the IBOA. It was repeated regularly. Momentum grew to the point where in September 1929 a meeting was called in the Irish Bankers' Club on the last Friday of that month to discuss the establishment of the sports ground. A committee was established to promote the endeavour and the hope was expressed that the whole enterprise would be supported by the directors of the banks. That such support should be sought was an eloquent statement of how far relations between bank officials and their employers had improved in the space of a decade.

3

The 1930s

The 1930s were a remarkable decade in Ireland. In politics, Éamon de Valera, who had led opposition to the establishment of the Irish Free State under the terms of the Anglo-Irish Treaty, became President of that Free State when the Fianna Fáil party he had founded won the 1932 general election. In the years that followed, de Valera set about reordering the constitutional structure of the Irish Free State and its relationship with the United Kingdom. That process stopped short of declaring Ireland a republic, but only in name. On top of that, a whole raft of policy initiatives – ranging from land and language to industrialisation – sought to re-imagine the social and cultural landscape of the south of Ireland. That all of this took place against the international backdrop of the Great Depression and the rise of fascism served only to highlight the momentum towards change.

Throughout the decade, Irish bank officials could not expect to remain immune, and they did not. There was much comment through letters and articles on current affairs in the 1930s. There was concern about the state of the Irish economy and the conflict with Britain, dismay at the enduring global economic slump, and a clear insight into the international politics of the era. For example, in the autumn of 1936, a most prescient editorial in the *Irish Banking*

52

Magazine, warned against the rise of fascism and communism. It noted:

> the vast political struggle convulsing the Continent of Europe which may have far-reaching effects on the future of representative government, and not improbably will lead to a disturbance in the balance of power between European states. This is the challenge that has materialised between the principles of democracy on the one hand, and those of Fascism and Communism on the other. While the latter two forces follow ideals differing ostensibly, they are united in the sense that both are based on the conception of a denial of personal liberty and an intolerant political philosophy of violence. The form of authority may be Fascist in Italy, Bolshevist in Russia, or Nazi in Germany, but each has the common feature that it relies upon a reign of force in which the State, generally personified in a single leader, is conceived as infallible and as the absolute source of authority.

According to the editorial, the battle between democracy and absolutism was being played out in Spain, which was then in the throes of civil war, and it would be disastrous if it should end in the overthrow of the democratically elected Spanish government by fascist General Franco-led armed forces. As an insight into the politics of the era, it is a piece of journalism remarkable for its clarity of insight and the accuracy of its prognosis, as well as being at odds with much of mainstream Irish sentiment.[1] After all, the Fine Gael TD Paddy Belton snr told the Dáil on 19 February 1937: '99.9 per cent of the Irish people stand for the recognition of General Franco, and there should be no equivocation about it . . . There is no need to paint the lily any further. Full proofs have been adduced here as to the real issues in the Spanish conflict . . . They have all indicated that this is a war between Christ and anti-Christ in Spain, and I do not think anybody here will attempt to deny that . . . I urged that . . . we should recognise the Franco government.'[2]

I

BANKS AND THE IRISH ECONOMY

Through all of the turmoil of the 1930s, Irish bank officials clung tightly to the Arbitration Agreement that had been struck with the banks in 1920. This agreement sheltered bank officials from the worst of the economic downturn and was sufficient to underpin a decade of industrial peace. The Irish banks were not, of course, a monolithic entity, devoid of characteristics peculiar from one to the next. There was, for example, the suggestion that different banks were suited to people from different walks of Irish life. As Cormac Ó Gráda has written, the various Irish banks 'served rather different clienteles. The Munster and Leinster's close links with the farming community and the rural co-operative movement meant that it found it easier to adapt to the conditions in the new Free State than banks with a heavily unionist ethos such as the Provincial or the Bank of Ireland, while the Royal's clientele earned it the soubriquet of "home for distressed Protestants".'[3] For banks operating north of the border, there was less sense of change in the decades which followed the partition in Ireland. In general, the reality of partition and of operating in two different legislative frameworks brought inevitable divergence between north and south.

Nonetheless, regardless of the wider politics of the island, the banks maintained a structure which saw them united in a common approach to their trade. This common approach had emerged in the midst of the dispute with the IBOA which had led to the arbitration court of 1920. It was then that Irish banks had banded together to form the Irish Banks' Standing Committee. This committee subsequently met quarterly and gave an institutional frame to increasing cooperation between the banks operating across Ireland. The purpose of the committee was 'to agree on rates for overdrafts, loans, and discounts, and to discuss other matters of common concern'.[4] The committee agreed, for example, in May 1920 to an annual charge of one guinea on current accounts. They also fixed interest charges which ensured Irish borrowers paid greater interest than those in England.[5] The Banks' Standing Committee allowed the operation of a cartel. For example, individual banks were not always granted permission to open branches in certain areas because it might bring 'unrestricted competition of a harmful nature to the offices already in or near these areas . . .'[6]

The increased cooperation between the banks' managements had implications for officials. In the mid-1930s, a new scale was introduced by all the banks for new entrants. This was essentially a reduction in the pay of new entrants and was to apply from 1 January 1934. The Irish Bankers' Joint Committee was of the view that it found the existing scales of pay too onerous and was obliged to introduce the change; the IBOA opposed but was relatively powerless to resist. The ultimate weapon was to go on strike, but there did not seem to be any appetite for that course of action. Ultimately, though, disillusion over the scale for new entrants was the fount of great dissatisfaction from the 1940s.[7]

Through all of this, 'the banking sector was in the doldrums in the 1930s' and this fostered a tendency to err on the side of caution. The caution so associated with Irish banks regularly drew complaints from those who wished the Irish economy to pursue a more dynamic approach. The scale of the caution was demonstrated by data supplied by the banks to the 'Commission of Inquiry on Banking, Currency and Credit', which had been established by Fianna Fáil in 1934 and which reported in 1938. The data revealed that 'only 8.5% of all bank advances in the Irish Free State went to manufacturers, builders, and railway and other transport concerns, as against 27 per cent to farmers, and another 22 per cent to wholesalers and retailers'.[8] Against that, there is evidence that the image of Irish banking in this as entirely conservative and averse to risk is overstated. Indeed, it is argued that, while Irish banks were indeed cautious in their activities, they could also be 'flexible and resourceful' and were adequate to the role of providing short-term credit. Their adequacy was rooted primarily in the reality that demand for loans by prospective entre-preneurs was limited.[9]

The upshot was that the Irish economy remained primarily an agrarian one. Joe Redmond, an official who spent three years working in the Roscommon branch of the National Bank in the mid-1930s, recalled a world where most of the customers of the bank were livestock farmers.[10] Another official, Jim A. McGann, recalled working in a midlands town in the same decade where the livelihood of the entire community was wrapped around the cattle export trade. As well as business which revolved around that trade during the year, a huge annual event in the town was the big cattle fair which lasted three days. In advance of that fair, held on the main street of the town where publicans and shopkeepers would have arranged beer barrels and wooden boxes, to protect their windows from straying bullocks, the bank ordered large amounts of money from head office. Cattle buyers would have already organised 'fair advices' – advice to honour cheques – from their own home banks. As McGann put it, 'the additional stock of money came like a great tidal wave that flowed through the town redistributing the community's wealth and discharging its many debts and contractual obligations. When the town had been cleaned-up, the normal restful rhythm of rural life returned.'[11]

This rhythm was shattered in the 1930s when an 'economic war' began between the British government and the new Fianna Fáil-led government of the Irish Free State. That war, a six-year-long dispute, which involved financial, political and defence matters as well as economic ones, began in 1932. Éamon de Valera abolished the oath of allegiance and declined to pay land annuities to Britian; in response, the British government imposed special duties on Irish imports, notably cattle and dairy produce. The dispute was only ended in 1938 with the signing of Anglo-Irish agreements on defence, finance and trade. In the interim, however, the decline of the cattle trade had a severe impact on the Irish economy. Indeed, it was recorded that the value of cattle and cattle products had fallen from £54,600,000 in 1929–30 to £31,100,000 in 1935–6.[12] The impact of the 'economic war' was, as Jim McGann noted, immediately apparent in Irish banks, where there was a significant decrease in business. Staff numbers were reduced in areas where the livestock trade was central to commerce. The turnover and income of the cattle trade collapsed and farmers who had used temporary overdrafts to finance their operations were now unable to service this debt.[13]

The 'economic war' eventually gave way to world war, or the period of 'The Emergency' as it became known south of the border. This brought further economic hardship and, eventually, the introduction of rationing. The reality of the Irish economy was that the export of live cattle continued to dominate – and this remained the case until well after the Second World War.

North of the border, too, economic stagnation was undeniable; the northern economy was in deep trouble. The linen and ship-building industries which had driven the prosperity of Belfast in the nineteenth century had fallen into terminal decline. Unemployment

Crowds attend the launch of HMS *Belfast* at the city's famous Harland and Wolff shipyard in March 1938. Despite the apparent prosperity, the shipbuilding industry, once a driver of Belfast's economic development, had fallen into decline by the 1930s. Throughout the 1930s, north and south of the island stagnated economically. *(Getty Images)*

became a huge problem and by 1932 there were 76,000 men unemployed in the six counties. Disease and misery were rife. Just as in Dublin, children walked barefoot in the streets, pawnbrokers thrived, TB and pneumonia were widespread. The squalor of the slums of Belfast reduced the city to something approaching the slums of Dublin. Unemployed northern Catholics and Protestants came together in huge numbers in Belfast – as many as 60,000 – for a 'unity' strike in favour of greater relief for unemployed people.[14] According to one of the strike leaders, Thomas Geehan, 'what we have achieved gives the direct lie and contradiction to those who said the workers of Belfast could not be united and would not fight. They had seen Protestants and Catholics marching together and . . . fighting together.'[15] The strike ended in a victory of sorts with the Northern Ireland government – subsidised by the Treasury in London – agreeing to increase the level of relief paid to the unemployed. That such extensive relief was needed, however, bore eloquent testimony to the difficulties faced across the Irish economy through the 1930s.

II

NEW LEADERSHIP AND NEW CHALLENGES

Against the backdrop of a floundering economy, the IBOA continued to promote the cause of bank officials, though there was significant change at the head of the Association. C. H. Denroche, the Organising Secretary of the IBOA almost since its inception, died in 1932 and was replaced by J. T. Donovan.[16] Donovan was a 46-year-old barrister who had previously worked for the civil service in India. He had been educated at Clongowes Wood College, Queen's College Galway and Trinity College Dublin.[17] On assuming office in the IBOA, Donovan wrote an article in the *Irish Banking Magazine* in which he lauded his predecessor as a 'truly great man', 'a great leader', and 'a tower of associational strength, a source of inspiration, and a repository of tradition'.[18] Donovan made it clear that he saw his role as protecting and developing the victory won by

Denroche and the IBOA through the 1920 arbitration award; this award he described as 'the Magna Charta [*sic*]'.[19]

The structures of the Association inherited by Donovan were by now well established. The growth in banking brought an attendant growth in the number of officials being employed. Amidst this expansion, the IBOA maintained its capacity to attract around 90 per cent of all bank officials to join its ranks. The result of this was a steady increase in membership and by the end of the 1930s the IBOA membership had passed 5,300. Notes from officials in Cork record almost 100 per cent membership in most branches. New officials were all joining the IBOA, while old ones who had left for a whole range of different reasons were coming back in. The correspondent from Cork speculated that there was a simple motivation for this: 'Perhaps members are better aware of what a solid Association means in this age of mechanical progress and labour-saving devices.'[20]

The case for membership of the IBOA as set out in *Irish Banking Magazine* in July 1929. Throughout the 1930s, the Association worked hard to increase membership, stressing the benefits to those who joined their ranks. *(IBOA Archive)*

Why should you join the
Irish Bank Officials' Association ?

¶ Because it exists to protect your interests.

¶ Because the directorates have by agreement admitted its right to deal with them on behalf of its members.

¶ Because it has secured for you a satisfactory salary scale and in due time a legal right to an adequate pension.

¶ Because it has secured for you an annual vacation, or compensation for its loss.

¶ Because it has safeguarded you from unreasonable hours of work and secured for you a weekly half holiday.

¶ Because it entitles you to free advice in any personal difficulty arising out of your employment.

¶ Because it has improved the status of your profession and won for it the freedom to combine and to negotiate.

¶ Because over 90 per cent. of your colleagues are members, and amongst them officials in the highest positions in the services.

¶ Because membership of the Association does not mean disloyalty to your Employers.

¶ Because non-membership does mean disloyalty to your colleagues.

¶ Because directorates and staffs working in harmony are a guarantee of the continued protection and advancement of our admirable Irish banking system.

The growth of the IBOA and its criticism of bank officials who did not wish to join the Association irritated some bank officials. One such official – who signed himself 'Pro Tanto' – complained of 'the clap-trap orations' of IBOA members and asked: 'Surely the dignity of the Association is not enhanced by the incessant ranting against those members of the banking profession who have not, up to the present, availed themselves of the benefits of membership.'[21] The view of 'Pro Tanto' drew a sharp response from a range of members, one of whom said that he presented 'a somewhat amusing spectacle as he flounders through the morass of his pretentious rhetoric' and another who simply pointed out: 'I do not think that there exists one non-member who genuinely believes that the position of the average Irish bank official would not be greatly affected for the worse if the Association were to disappear.'[22]

Inevitably, not all these members were active in the Association, with many content simply to pay their subscription and leave that as the sum of their engagement. Just as in every voluntary association, there was a hard core of activists upon whom the burden fell. Occasionally, their exasperation at their fellow members was vented publicly. In November 1930, the *Irish Banking Magazine* published an article which it said would resonate with many of the secretaries of local IBOA branches:

Nine Don'ts which will kill any organisation:

1. Don't go to the meetings;

2. If you go, don't be in time;

3. If the weather is bad, don't think of going;

4. Whenever you go to a meeting, don't utter a word of praise or encouragement; find fault with what is done;

5. Don't, under any circumstances, accept an office; it is easier to sit back and criticise;

6. If you are appointed on a committee, don't go to the meetings; if you are not appointed, get annoyed about it;

7. When your opinion is asked, don't say anything, or
say that you have nothing to say; but after the
meeting tell everyone how things should be done;

8. Don't do anything more than is absolutely necessary;
when others do the lion's share tell everyone that the
organisation is run by a clique;

9. Don't bother about getting new members; let those
who do the other work do that also.[23]

The reality, of course, was that the great bulk of work in
running the IBOA rested on the shoulders of a few members and,
for them, there was a regular and sometimes onerous set of duties
to be fulfilled. On a formal level, there were annual district meetings
every January and February in advance of the annual general meeting
in March. It was a regular source of frustration for activists that the
wider membership did not attend even the annual meetings.[24] These
meetings were not always plain sailing as members of the Association
were entirely capable of fervent argument. In the early part of the
1930s, one issue above all others dominated meetings – the establishment of a Medical Benefits Fund for members. It was utterly
divisive. In the dying months of the 1930s, C. H. Denroche had
worked on a scheme to insure IBOA members against serious expense
arising out of illness and accident. The essential plan was that
members should continue to bear the first £5 of all medical expenses,
but would then be covered for all further medical fees and consul-
tations, X-rays and surgical operations, and nursing home fees, up to
a maximum of £50 in any one year. To cover full insurance was
beyond the means of the IBOA and, as it was, the estimated costs
would involve subscriptions of members rising by 15s. per year to
reach £1 16s. It was decided that involvement in the scheme was
obligatory for all male members; there would be no option of
remaining in the IBOA at a reduced subscription. Finally, there
were further limitations to the scheme: it was to apply only to male
members, although it was 'hoped, at a later date, to bring in an
optional scheme, for the insurance of female members and the wives

and children of members'.[25] The context of this scheme, of course, was the appalling state of health provision in Ireland.

The proposed scheme was announced in January 1930 and a circular detailing its particulars was sent to all members. There was broad support from many members, but from a significant minority there was immediate and deep-seated opposition.[26] There was resentment that the scheme was obligatory, that the benefits were too small, that expenses under £5 would not be covered, and that too little time was being allowed to discuss the merits or otherwise of the scheme. Denroche moved immediately to counter the criticism. He wrote that he had worked night and day for four months to develop the scheme and he was adamant that the terms upon which the scheme was proposed to operate were emphatically the best possible. He noted that the main objection to the scheme was that 'it is compulsory and that forcing it on a minority would probably mean the loss of many members. Every optional scheme that has been tried has been a complete failure and was discontinued by the Insurance Company, which paid in benefits many times the amount of the premiums received. Only one insurance company could be found willing to entertain our proposals at all, and then only with reluctance. That company is not willing even to consider an optional scheme.'[27]

A voting form was sent to all members of the IBOA asking whether they were supportive of the scheme. While Denroche proclaimed his confidence of the result, the *Irish Banking Magazine* was sufficiently concerned to appeal to the altruism of its members: 'It is not always by any means possible for a large body of persons to see eye to eye in matters bearing on the general welfare, but it is a fairly frequent experience, where such matters are designed to operate for the benefit of the greatest number, for the minority to sink its differences. We would ask members . . . to consent, at least, to the course of giving it a fair trial.'[28]

The minority saw things a little differently. A statement prepared on behalf of representatives of that minority argued against the scheme. It was argued that the scheme changed the basis of membership of the IBOA and that the only condition of membership should be that the individual in question is a bank official 'and not that he subscribes to any scheme'. It was further argued that C. H. Denroche had acted 'without a definite mandate' when he presented a completed scheme to the Executive Committee and that the Committee had then neglected its duty to consider that scheme at length. Finally, it was argued that the only way to preserve unity in the IBOA was to vote against the scheme: 'We consider that no external scheme, however good, would compensate the Association for the decrease in membership which we feel certain will result from the compulsory nature of the proposed scheme.'[29]

At the annual general meeting of the IBOA the divide in the Association was immediately apparent. A vote was taken on the issue of allowing a subscription increase in order to pay for the proposed medical scheme. The motion was carried by just two votes: 61 to 59. So tight was the result, however, that the meeting decided to place the entire matter to a paper ballot involving the full membership. That vote was completed by the end of April 1930 and its result was announced in a letter written by H. V. Batt, the honorary secretary of the IBOA. Batt wrote that 'considerably more than the necessary two-thirds majority was obtained'. The final vote showed that 3,119 of the 5,071 members of the IBOA voted, of which 2,330 were in favour, while 789 members were opposed. That result, in turn, was considered by the Executive Committee and it was decided to progress with the plans.[30] Forms in connection with the scheme were sent to 4,694 male members (there were a further 383 female members whose position seems almost never to have surfaced in the debate) in May 1930. The scheme came into force in July 1930. Before then, 302 existing members signalled their intention to leave the IBOA rather than accept the scheme.[31] By October 1930 the number of members refusing to pay the increased subscription fee was put at 260.[32]

One of the issues facing J. T. Donovan two years later in 1932 when he became Organising Secretary of the IBOA in succession to Denroche was the task of restoring unity to the IBOA. By then, some – though by no means all – of the several hundred members who had resigned from the Association over the introduction of the Medical Fund had returned to the fold.[33] At the IBOA's annual general meeting in 1933, Donovan was able to show members that practically the whole amount of premiums paid by members (97 per cent) was returned in the form of benefits. In its ordinary workings, the scheme proved to be a success. It offered valuable protection to members who suffered a whole range of medical problems from appendicitis to rheumatism, and from TB to injuries incurred in motorbike accidents.[34] A great change in the scheme occurred in 1934 when the annual general meeting decided to continue with the idea of the scheme but to administer it internally. What now became known as the Medical Benefits Provident Fund became operational from May 1934. As the decade progressed there was general acceptance that the Fund had been successful.[35] The editorial notes in the *Irish Banking Magazine* put forward the view that 'few will deny that, in the light of the valuable benefits the Fund has conferred upon a large section of the Association's membership, the project has been amply justified, and we are not surprised to be informed that during the year the membership figure stood higher than ever before'.[36]

That membership, however, still did not extend to women. Following its formation in the early months of 1938, the new Ladies' Committee of the IBOA urged the Executive Committee 'to consider the possibility of extending the Fund in some form to lady members'.[37] The notion was rejected until 1939 when the annual general meeting of the IBOA approved the creation of a separate Medical Benefits Fund for women. More than 300 'lady clerks' signalled their intention to join but by July 1939, 40 per cent of these had failed to send in their application forms. Warning that the 'experiment' with the Ladies' Medical Fund would collapse unless more application forms were received, the *Irish Banking Magazine*, called on women working in Irish banks to give the Fund a fair trial. The call went unheeded and, in August 1939, the Executive Committee announced that it was abandoning the introduction of the Ladies' Medical Fund as fewer than 200 members had supported it.[38]

While the responsibility for the failure of the Ladies' Medical Fund clearly lay with 'lady clerks', it remained the case that the position of such clerks within both the IBOA and the banks was not on a par with that of men. For example, the dispute over the payment of pensions to 'lady clerks' continued through the mid-1930s. In part, the longevity of the dispute was related to the fact that women had

yet to reach pensionable age in the banks, as they had only begun to
be employed by them during the Great War. In the summer of 1938,
the dispute over pensions for 'lady clerks' had largely been resolved
after the IBOA completed negotiations lasting two years with all the
Irish banks. The pensions agreed were much lower than those granted
to male employees. Commenting on the agreement, the editor of the
Irish Banking Magazine noted: 'The pensions will not provide rich
retirement for the ladies concerned, but they will at least give them
some small comfort for the years that lie ahead.'[39] Disappointment
over the pensions issue had been instrumental in 'lady clerks' establishing a Ladies' Committee in early 1938 and it should be remembered
at this stage that there were no women sitting on the Executive
Committee of the Association. Indeed, it was not until the 1950s that
women were represented on the Executive Committee when Eileen
Keogh and Emily Soffe took their places.[40] The fact that women were
paid less by banks meant that they were perceived as something of a
threat by men. By 1939, there were 464 women enlisted as members
of the IBOA out of a total membership of 5,310. This was enough
for the honorary secretary of the Association, H. V. Batt, to note
with relief: 'We are not being swamped by women; that point we are
watching carefully.'[41]

Even then, however, there were other employees of the banks
who were in a much worse position. Michael Laffan, a bank official
from Wicklow, remembered the role played by bank porters, noting
they were 'badly treated with no voice to speak for them'.[42] They
were often used by bank managers in country towns to run family
errands, to work the family garden and to do general household
chores. Their pay was miserly and yet they were dressed up in
elaborate jackets. A one-time bank porter in Wicklow was James
Everett. Working in the bank brought Everett into contact with a
huge number of people, something which facilitated his election as
an urban councillor and then as a Labour Party TD for Wicklow.
Everett later served as a cabinet minister in the first and second
inter-party governments in the 1940s and 1950s.[43] Bank porters did
not qualify for membership of the IBOA and were unionised only
much later in the twentieth century.

III

SOCIAL LIFE IN THE 1930s

Comments made by W. G. Bryant, a cashier who had just retired after working for 47 years in the Bank of England, somewhat exercised the minds of Irish bank officials. Bryant said: 'Banking is a most monotonous life. If you don't have some outside interest you become a cabbage.' In response to these comments, the editor of the *Irish Banking Magazine* observed that banking was no more monotonous a career than many others, though he did allow that the first ten years were 'a trying period'.[44] It was in those years, however, that routine work provided the foundation for a career in banking which became more interesting in later years. It was also agreed that the job facilitated the pursuit of other interests.[45]

Such pursuits sometimes brought a certain fame and, paradoxically, the means to leave the bank. In 1935, a bank official of the Hibernian Bank in Navan, Philip F. Rooney, won a short story competition organised by the Irish Hospitals Trust for which the first prize was £100. The prize coincided with the publication of *All Out to Win*, Rooney's first novel, which was published by the Talbot Press. This proved a notable success and Rooney subsequently gave up his job in the bank (though not until he had at least a second novel published in 1938) to concentrate on writing and on radio work for Radio Éireann and the BBC. Before leaving the bank, Rooney contributed a 1943 broadcast entitled 'The Bank Clerk' to Radio Éireann which painted a vivid picture of the life of bank officials. Rooney published at least six more novels, the most famous of which was *Captain Boycott*, an emotional story set on the estate at Lough Mask, County Mayo, where Captain Charles Boycott was the land agent for Lord Erne. The story was partly 'drawn from family memory of eyewitness accounts in the Cong area, where Rooney's parents were once teachers'. The book was subsequently made into a film with a star-studded cast in 1947.[46] Celebrating Rooney's success, another bank official, T. F. Feeney, wrote that the literary success of bank officials included such luminaries as P. G. Wodehouse, William Allingham and T. S. Eliot, 'so there is plenty of encouragement for some "mute inglorious Milton", now, perhaps, writing remittances, to defy his soul-destroying environment and burst forth into song!'[47]

In general, the range of social and cultural activities engaged in by Association members in the 1930s continued to broaden. The development of literary, dramatic, choral and debating societies was complemented by the establishment of a 'Question Time' competition between teams representing the various banks.[48] On a more exotic note, the last years of the decade saw the establishment of a Dublin Banks' Fencing Team. The *Irish Banking Magazine* noted that fencing had emerged as something of a craze in Dublin and this was to be welcomed as 'apart from its value as a form of physical training, there is the enjoyment of pitting one's brain and speed against that of another man, for fencing is both an art and a science'.[49] The by now established cup competitions played between banks in rugby, hockey,

As depicted in this cartoon from the *Irish Banking Magazine* in May 1937, sport was a core part of the social calendar that the IBOA laid on for its members. *(IBOA Archive)*

golf, cricket, soccer, tennis and other sports were an essential part of the social calendar. So, too, were the numerous dances and card-playing evenings organised across the country. There were regular trips organised by local committees.

The social life of some members of the IBOA was adversely affected by the fact that there was no standardised day across the country for the weekly half-holiday on which banks shut. It had long been the ambition of the IBOA to enshrine Saturday as the day on which banks would close for a half-day. There had been negotiations with the banks in this regard, but still no standardised day was chosen. That is not to say that all bank officials agreed with the idea of closing for a half-holiday on a Saturday. A bank official who signed himself simply as 'Senior' said that he was based in a town in the west of Ireland and Saturday was market day and the busiest trading day in the town. He lamented the fact that it seemed to him that the Saturday half-holiday was being promoted because rugby matches were played on that day. He believed that 'business is entitled to a prior claim and, moreover, a mid-week half-holiday affords a pleasant and beneficial break'.[50]

There was some sympathy for this viewpoint in the *Irish Banking Magazine*, whose editor noted that serving the interests of business was vital because 'with the spread of banking habits, banks are becoming more and more literally the servants of the people'.[51] On the whole, however, the magazine supported the notion of the Saturday half-holiday. In 1935, the Limerick Local Committee of the IBOA sent out a circular which called on the IBOA to lobby the government to introduce the half-holiday on a compulsory basis in the Irish Free State (it omitted to call for a similar campaign in Northern Ireland, but later amended its proposal to include that point). Writing on behalf of the Limerick Local Committee, W. T. R. Martin claimed such a move would be beneficial to health, sporting involvement, tourism and trade: 'It is universally admitted that periods of leisure are essential in the rush and bustle of the modern world.'[52] When the proposal of the Limerick Local Committee was debated at the annual general meeting in 1936, however, it was not put to a vote; rather, it was agreed that progressing the issue of the Saturday half-holiday should be left in the hands of the Executive Committee. There was no immediate resolution of the matter and it was an issue which dragged on well after the 1930s.

Compounding this problem was the enduring difficulty officials had in arranging their annual leave. There were restrictions on when they might take their leave. In the late 1930s, the banks agreed with suggestions that bank officials might be facilitated in taking their leave between May and September, but could offer no guarantee. A 1938 letter on behalf of the Irish Bankers' Joint Committee promised to 'issue instructions that in all branches leave lists are to be prepared, and that these should be adhered to, except where exceptional circumstances necessitate their alteration'.[53] Further to this was the ambition to have more days declared as bank holidays, including, for example, Easter Monday and 27 December.[54]

There were further reminders of the restrictions placed on the lives of Irish bankers when reports emerged of a Scottish banker who had been summarily dismissed by his employers because he intended to marry without the consent of the bank. The official had written to the Commercial Bank of Scotland Ltd in April 1934 asking for permission to marry his fiancée. The official had nine years' service with the bank and took home a salary of £160 per annum. The bank had a regulation which demanded that their employees earn £200 per annum before they should marry. The employee wrote that his father was agreed to make up the difference in his annual salary. The bank refused permission. The employee then asked for a transfer and a promotion that would bring him up to £200 per annum. In reply, the bank granted a transfer but allowed for a salary of just £180 per annum and instructed the official that he must not marry until the specified salary was reached. Soon afterwards, however, the employee wrote again to his employers saying that his father would make up the difference in his salary and that he intended on marrying the following Monday. The 'bank's reply was a summary dismissal'.[55]

The case brought discussion of two aspects of the 1920 Arbitration Agreement between the IBOA and the Irish banks which had not been settled to the satisfaction of the Association: the restrictions in respect of marriage and the ability of the banks to dismiss employees should they so choose. The power to dismiss was not frequently used, however, while the restrictions on marriage were more of a convention which was honoured by officials who did not dare cross their employers. Bank officials understood the reasons given by banks as being related to 'the great store set by appearance', but also noted the 'unjustified interference with personal liberties'.[56] The restrictions on marriage – as well as the right of summary dismissal – survived through the 1930s.

And yet the good relations between bank officials and their employers were evident for much of the 1930s. The President of the IBOA, J. Elliott Forde, claimed in 1933 that 'the closest co-operation existed between the Association and the directors of the banks'.[57] There were practical examples of this in the sporting life of bank officials. On 6 February 1939, a squash court was opened at the Bankers' Club on St Stephen's Green, with a series of exhibition matches involving players such as Judge Cahir Davitt (son of the Land Leaguer, Michael Davitt). The opening ceremony at the club was performed by H. Campbell, the managing director of the Hibernian Bank and Major W. N. Foster, the general manager of the Bank of Ireland, and the opening of the squash court had been facilitated by generous donations from the banks.[58] The expansion of the Bankers' Club had continued during the decade and it now included a reading room, a writing room, a library, a lounge, a bar, a billiards room, recreation and cards rooms, and a dining room.[59] It had been liberally decorated for the Eucharistic Congress in 1932.[60] Elsewhere, IBOA members in Belfast opened their own Bankers' Club at Donegall Place.[61] Just as in Dublin, there were rooms for reading and writing, for playing billiards, for cards and for table tennis, as well as a large hall for dances. The Club was a great success and there was dismay when, in the spring of 1937, it was destroyed by fire.[62] Within nine months, however, the club had been successfully renovated. There were developments in other cities and towns, too. In Cork, for example, the local committee received a grant to enable them to buy a table tennis set and a wireless.[63]

All told, the social world of Irish bank officials, as reported in the pages of the *Irish Banking Magazine*, seemed in many ways oblivious to the calamitous slide to world war which dominated the last years of the 1930s. And yet that magazine had ensured that its readers could be left in no doubt about the events that were unfolding across Europe. Even as the long-feared war was materialising in the autumn of 1939, an editorial of dark resignation was printed: 'That the incredible should come to pass, and another war be inflicted on a world which has scarcely yet recovered from the suffering and appalling social and economic consequences of the last, opens so bleak and negative a prospect that we feel every straw of hope will be clutched at so that the tragedy may yet be prevented.'[64] The despairing tone of the editorial was apt; by the time the magazine had been printed, the world was at war.

A view of Donegall Place in Belfast city centre in the early twentieth century. It was here that IBOA members opened a Bankers' Club in the 1930s. An Irish Bankers' Club had previously been established as a social centre for bank officials in Dublin in 1921. *(NLI, Lawrence Collection)*

The Bank of Ireland on College Green is decorated for the Eucharistic Congress, which was held in Dublin in 1932. The Congress saw a massive demonstration of popular Catholic piety in the south of Ireland and many of Dublin's major buildings, including the Bankers' Club on St Stephen's Green, were given a facelift for the occasion. *(NLI, Eason Collection)*

4

The 1940s

The First World War had brought profound change to Irish banking; the Second World War had a similar influence. As the *Irish Banking Magazine* noted in 1939, the Great War 'was hopefully deemed at the time – wrongly as it has unhappily proved – to be a "war to end war".' Equally, while everyone had considered that the 1920 Arbitration Agreement would offer a permanent framework for good relations between the banks and their employees, the magazine warned that 'it would be a mistake to rely too exclusively upon achievements which have been gained in the past . . . Any one of many eventualities may arise. The only safe course lies in preparation for all.'[1] This was wise counsel. During the Second World War good relations between the Irish banks and their officials slowly unwound and by the time the war had ended, the Irish banking world was hurtling towards its own form of turmoil. After the stability of the 1920s and 1930s, the 1940s brought deterioration to industrial relations in Irish banks; once again, world war had a dramatic local impact.

I

BANK OFFICIALS IN TIME OF WAR

For much of the 1920s and the 1930s, the fact that the IBOA operated equally north and south of the Irish border was of no great consequence. There were, of course, operational problems presented by the obligation to represent officials across two separate states; but none of these problems proved grave or insurmountable. The outbreak of the Second World War changed all that. It was now a simple truth that some members of the IBOA were living in a country that was engaged in the greatest war in history, while other members were living in a country that remained neutral throughout that war. This issue was addressed in the *Irish Banking Magazine* in June 1940: 'Though part of our country is neutral, we cannot escape the repercussions of such world-shaking events or their inevitable economic impacts.'[2] While this might mean privation and rationing in the south, it meant much more in the north. Indeed, the passing of emergency legislation saw the British government conscript the private services and property of individuals, and regulate wages and profits. Control of the banks in Britain and in Northern Ireland was now directed by the state; in essence, the British banks would now 'operate under Government orders'. Banks in the south of Ireland were to be affected only in so was far as their business in Northern Ireland was concerned. All of this was evidence of a new economic and social reality: 'Thus Britain, with the complete assent of Parliament and people, has suspended the liberties that have formed the essence of its constitution for nearly a thousand years – though only temporarily and with the sole object of winning the war.'[3]

A month later – in July 1940 – with France defeated and Britain isolated, the *Irish Banking Magazine* concluded in anguish:

> History holds no clue to the nature of the events that will now ensue from the almost complete subjugation of Western Europe by Nazi power. The creed of Nazism is total conquest . . . aggression, ruthlessness, and complete lack of tolerance and scruple. The coming battle for Britain will be much more than decisive of the largest-scale war yet known in history; it will decide the whole world's future and the nature of the forces that must henceforth determine the destinies of its civilisation. The issue is clear-cut – whether a new Dark Age is to emerge dominated by fear, or a new international system be

created through the liberation of conquered peoples and their reconstitution upon a basis of security, freedom and ordered peace.'[4]

The 'Battle for Britain' would 'provide for all time the supreme test of that nation's endurance and manhood', and a second question was what it all meant for the Southern Irish, their neutral stance and 'how long can they hope to remain so or avert the dangers of being drawn into the vortex of the stupendous conflict.'[5]

That the *Irish Banking Magazine* was suggesting to its readers that they enlist in the British army was ill disguised. Noting that every Irishman should give serious thought to how best they should assist their country, it was noted with approval that many IBOA members had responded to the call to go to war. This included men from both sides of the border. Others in the south had joined the Irish army or the Local Defence Force, and still more had joined their local branch of the Red Cross. This was commended and encouraged.[6] Bank officials across Ireland had new conditions to contend with and also developed new interests. The staff of the National Bank across Dublin came together under the direction of W. A. Collins and leased 65 acres of land, which were used to cultivate wheat.[7] Soon there was news of 'the first Irishman serving in the British Army in the present war to be awarded the Victoria Cross,' and he was Captain H. M. Ervine-Andrews, son of the manager of the Provincial Bank in New Ross, County Wexford. Captain Ervine-Andrews was honoured for his bravery in protecting the retreat from Dunkirk in the teeth of overwhelming enemy fire.[8]

The nature of the war – with bombs falling in urban areas far from what might previously have been considered the theatre of war – brought changes in the working lives of bank officials across the channel in Britain. Many members of staff had been evacuated from cities and were based now in schools, country houses, restaurants and dancehalls. Those who remained in the cities operated a skeleton service of much reduced opening hours and restricted service, while a great deal of work was now conducted through correspondence. By the summer of 1942, more than half of the 60,000 male bank

The scene in Belfast after it was bombed by the Luftwaffe in April 1941. Although Dublin would also suffer bombing when the North Strand was attacked, the realities of partition meant that the experience of war for IBOA members north and south was very different. The IBOA acknowledged as much, contrasting the fate of those 'cast in the zone of war-ravaged territory' with those who enjoyed the 'blessings of peace'. Even so, many bank officials across the country volunteered to serve in the British war effort. *(Getty Images)*

officials in England had left the bank, many to join the army. To cope with the loss of men to the army, the Bank of England had 'broken one of its most inflexible rules in permitting the employment of married women'. Many of these were women who had previously worked in the bank until marriage had forced them to leave their positions. The unique circumstances of war drove change that would otherwise not have occurred.[9]

It was clear, though, that it was not merely war but also 'the influence of the age' which was bringing more women to work in banks. The IBOA was critical of Irish banks, which did not seem to comprehend that 'lady clerks' were now an integral part of the banking system and not incidental to it. Yet, in all Irish banks, basic facilities for women were nonexistent or inadequate, and pay and pensions remained much below that of men. In the attitude of the banks, the presence of women in banking was construed as a temporary arrangement, one that would pass in time to allow men return to once more assume outright control.[10] And yet there were by the end of the war 936 women working as 'lady clerks' in Irish banks. These women were working on a scale of income much lower than that of men, running from £100 per annum on entry to reach £200 after fourteen years' service. While many women married and left the bank, there were many more who built a career there. For those women, there was no right to an increase in salary over the last twenty-one years of service. This, claimed the IBOA, was 'disastrous on the morale of the women staff'.[11]

In the south of Ireland, men and women alike saw the value of their wages shrink during the 'Emergency' – the euphemism by which the wartime era quickly became known in the south. Measures taken by the southern government during the war were partly responsible for this. Several government orders imposed restrictions on wages and salaries, one of which was the 'Standstill Order', which essentially meant that there was to be no rise in salaries (except where increments of scale were in place) and that there should be no increase in bonuses. The attempts to stabilise wages were condemned by the *Irish Banking Magazine*. In October 1942, it was somewhat bitterly noted that bank officials had agreed to salary and bonus ceilings, and had agreed to pay income tax. In the first years of the war, there had been an increasingly fraught set of negotiations between the banks and the IBOA. These negotiations had led to a change in the arrangement by which bank officials paid income tax.[12] That change meant that where bank officials had previously received the full amount of their net salary with the bank paying such income tax as was due to the state, now salaries would be higher by 6/- in the pound, but income tax would be the responsibility of the bank official. Increasing inflation in Ireland ensured that the cost of living in the country was growing, however, and bank officials were seeing their standard of living eroded significantly. What particularly irked the IBOA was 'the rather specious case' made by the banks that it could not afford the salaries paid to its officials, particularly because net profits and deposits were showing an annual increase in Irish banks even in the midst of war.[13] The IBOA continued to lobby for pay increases and an arbitration award was heard which directed that bank officials be given pay increases.[14] This award was rejected by the banks, who simply refused to pay. In peacetime, the next step would most probably have been to strike, but wartime legislation had outlawed the right to strike in Northern Ireland and severely restricted it in the south.[15]

Inevitably, of course, while fighting continued, the complaints of bank officials were lost beside the horrors of war and the infinitely greater suffering of others. When the Luftwaffe bombed Belfast in 1941, the IBOA donated 100 guineas for relief of distress in Belfast and a further £50 for the support of refugees from the city now domiciled in Dublin: 'Apart from the fact that there are no boundaries within our organisation, the call of humanity demands aid and succour for these unfortunate victims, and this is trebly reinforced by ties of race, neighbourhood and kinship. Our sympathy is extended to those of our own body whose lot, by unhappy circumstance, is cast in the zone of war-ravaged territory while we, their colleagues, more fortunate, enjoy the blessings of peace.'[16]

When peace finally arrived, the *Irish Banking Magazine* noted in June 1945 that over the previous four years censorship had restrained it from publishing details of the engagement of its members with the British forces. Now, however, it was at liberty to pay tribute 'to those who answered the call to conscience and in so many cases reflected lustre on their community and country'. The editorial continued:

> 'It is a matter of common knowledge that hundreds of bank officials in Ireland, North and South, answered the call to arms and flocked to the standards of the various services – land, air and sea – in Europe, Africa and the Far and Middle East. Many will return and we shall welcome them with pride and affection to their wonted places in our midst; but many have made the last sacrifice; others have been reported missing or wounded, and yet others have achieved the high distinction of mention in despatches or a decoration for some act of valour or noted service.[17]

This editorial drew criticism from some IBOA members who did not see it as appropriate and who noted that the editorial had failed to pay tribute to those bank officials who had joined the Irish army and the Local Defence Force during the 'Emergency'. One letter condemned the fact that no welcome home was paid to those who had 'answered the call to arms of our own country when she stood alone, threatened from all sides. Not one word of mention, much less one word of tribute, did you pay to that plucky band. Welcome back and all honour to those lads who answered the call of their own flag.'[18] The editor acknowledged that there were opposing currents of feeling on the course of action that Irishmen should have adopted in the war, but when it came to paying tribute to those who had fought against Hitler and Nazism he was not for turning. He wrote that the numerous bank officials who had served in the Irish forces during the war had been regularly, wholesomely and rightly commended for their efforts, but for members who joined the British forces 'we feel that a special tribute is due to each and all who registered coura-geously their conviction so to act . . . Many gave practical expression to a conviction that the call of duty was to a cause with issues stretching far beyond the limits of national borders.'[19]

80

Cast members from the National Bank Dramatic Society's production of *The Whiteheaded Boy*, the Lennox Robinson comedy which was first staged in the Abbey Theatre in 1916. The review of this production, which appeared in the *Irish Banking Magazine* in January 1940, was laudatory, but not uncritical. While the lead actor was said to have given a 'very sound performance', the reviewer would have preferred 'a little less restraint in his acting'. *(IBOA Archive)*

II

CHANGE IN IRISH BANKING

While war was being waged across the world, there was significant structural change undertaken in Irish banking through the formal establishment of the Central Bank of Ireland. The Central Bank Act, 1942 gave the new bank 'responsibility to guard the purchasing power of the currency and to control credit in the interest of the people as a whole'.[20] Over the decades that followed, the powers of the Central Bank were consistently extended. The establishment of the Central Bank came in the wake of a 1938 report, *Commission of Inquiry into Banking, Currency and Credit.* That report, consisting of a majority report, three minority reports and extensive appendices and supporting material, was conservative in tone and, as such, was given a warm welcome by the *Irish Banking Magazine.* Outlining the contents of the report, the magazine noted with approval the words of Lord Glenavy that 'nothing whatever is wrong with our system of currency, banking and credit . . . The steady frugal Irish citizen and the solid unpretentious Irish bank have, in co-operation, created all the conditions which even the most potent monetary wizards ever aspired to create through central banking in other countries.'[21]

That 1938 banking commission was actually the second commission on banking, which had reported since the establishment of the Irish Free State. The first commission had been established to examine what changes, if any, in the law relative to banking and note issue were considered necessary or desirable following independence. It had produced the 1927 report, *Commission of Inquiry into Banking and the Issue of Notes.* That report had led to a major Act, which affected the work of bank officials: the Currency Act, 1927. The essence of that Act involved the decision 'to reinstate legally the Irish pound . . . and to introduce into circulation a distinctive set of Irish notes and coins'.[22] The Irish pound was introduced on a one-for-one, no-margins exchange basis with the pound sterling. Long after the Act, the pound sterling continued to circulate freely south of the border. The new Irish currency, managed by the newly established Currency Commission, began to circulate in 1928. The design of the notes and coins had been undertaken by a committee chaired by W. B. Yeats.[23] The notes carried a painting of a woman, by Sir John Lavery, which is thought to be a portrait of his wife, Lady Hazel Lavery. The notes and coins also bore the legend, 'Saorstát Éireann' (this was later changed to 'Éire' in 1939) and in their design they were perceived, as Yeats wrote, as 'silent ambassadors of national taste'.[24] Overall, the immediate impact of the Act was that there were now two currencies circulating across Ireland from the late 1920s onwards. The Currency Act, 1927 also marked the 'gradual distancing of the management of Irish monetary affairs from that of Britain', which continued through the establishment of a Central Bank in 1943.[25]

In practical terms, the banking commissions on the 1920s and 1930s made relatively little difference to the daily working lives of bank officials. Nonetheless, throughout the years of the war, the frustrations endured by Irish bank officials were many and were leading to a steady erosion in relations with their employers. Pay was the most vital source of disgruntlement, but was far from the only one. The usual irritations in relation to such matters as inadequate opportunities to break for lunch and the denial of leave at the optimum moment lumbered along. The manner in which 'lady clerks' were treated was also a persistent cause of discontent.

Another issue was raised in an April 1940 article entitled 'Hope Deferred', in which the *Irish Banking Magazine*, spelled out the dissatisfaction that was 'daily growing greater and which will sap the vigour of the staffs as a working force if it is not remedied or removed'. The cause of this was the failure to secure promotion. Indeed, 'many men approaching forty years of age are to be found in every bank who have virtually abandoned all hope of promotion . . . Sterling material though they are, they will deteriorate; the loss of self-respect will lower them as human beings.' That such men were eager for responsibility and still more eager to show their mettle, made the situation all the worse; deprived of possibilities 'the result can only be evil both for them and for the banks'.[26]

Still another issue arising was the payment of overtime. Bank officials were not paid overtime and their working day began and ended at the whim of the local branch manager. In many cases this presented no problem or, at least, created only the occasional inconvenience; in other cases it led to bank officials working late into the evening on a regular basis without compensation.[27] The *Irish Banking Magazine* was adamant that this must change. Yet, for this change to come, it was deemed crucial that Irish bank officials adopt an approach that was entirely new to them. Whereas bank officials in years after the Great War had sought to increase their pay and conditions by emphasising that they were emphatically not of the same class as ordinary workers, it was now being suggested that they reverse this notion: 'If any of us still hold erroneous notions as to bank men being a class apart from any other group of workers, we must shed these profitless ideas and realise that it is not *infra dig* [beneath one's dignity] to cease work at a regular hour each day as do road-workers, railwaymen and bricklayers. These workers have long-ago been blessed with a realisation of the fact that overtime without pay is simply making to your employer a gift of labour with a definite cash value.'[28]

A work/life balance: A bank official from the 1940s presents for work after typically robust inter-bank rugby match. *(IBOA Archive)*

In strictly legal terms, the IBOA shifted from being essentially a professional association when it formalised its status as a registered trade union in May 1942. This move was made as a result of new legislation, which had made it a requirement that any organisation wishing to exercise powers as a negotiating body with employers must register as a trade union. The *Irish Banking Magazine* commented that 'the days when clerical workers could afford an attitude of prejudice or antagonism towards the trade union movement have faded into the remote and unrelated past . . . We feel that . . . Irish bankmen will in the future prove themselves to be as good trade unionists as in the past they have been staunch associationists.'[29] Naturally, of course, the prejudices of the past were not shed with facility. There were members of the IBOA who abhorred the idea of trade unionism; they did not perceive bankers as ordinary workers. The IBOA declined to join the Trade Union Congress (even if that was the wish of some of its membership), and there were many who resented that any change had been made. Inherited notions of superiority were not easily lost, but after the Second World War, the number of members who thought in that way passed from constituting the majority to being eventually an ever-dwindling minority. Nonetheless, in the years after the Second World War, no bank official in Ireland could stand apart from the industrial unrest that was to sweep the sector. And this meant strike. Once again, world war had presaged a new departure for Irish bank officials.

III

STRIKES NORTH AND SOUTH OF THE BORDER

Increased militancy amongst bank officials was paralleled in other sectors of the Irish economy. In the second half of the 1940s there was a dramatic collapse in industrial relations harmony in Ireland. This was the consequence of a range of different factors. In the years immediately after the Second World War, it was apparent that the entire project of an independent Irish state was mired in economic stagnation, unemployment, emigration and poverty. Northern Ireland was comparatively more prosperous but there, too, a certain disillusion was rife. The gathering power of trade unionism in the 1940s – coupled with the sense of national drift associated with enduring economic disappointment – culminated in considerable unrest in the second half of the 1940s. The weakness of trade unionism in the early years of the Irish Free State had been due, in part, to the failure of the unions to organise themselves properly. There was no united front. When James Larkin returned from America in 1923, he had fallen out with his colleagues in the ITGWU. The result was a bitter split and the establishment of the Workers' Union of Ireland (WUI) in 1924.[30] The 'Larkin split' contributed to a decline in ITGWU union membership from 100,000 members in 1921 to 15,453 in 1929, and was symbolic of the general decline in the strength of Irish trade unionism in the 1920s.[31]

The 1930s had brought increased vigour in the trade union movement and there were a number of serious strikes. One such strike, involving Dublin buses and trams, began on 3 March 1935. It went on to become the longest public transport strike in the history of the Irish state.[32] It originally started because of the perceived unfair dismissal of a bus driver by the Dublin United Tramways Company (of 1913 Lockout fame), but escalated – in many ways against the wishes of the union leaders – into a battle for improved wages and conditions on the part of the rank and file of the workers.[33] With public transport still at a standstill in Dublin nearly three weeks after the commencement of the strike, the government ordered the army to run buses in the city. In response, the IRA Army Council offered 'its willingness to assist the workers in their struggle' and army buses' tyres were slashed.[34] The strike finally ended on 17 May 1935 when the company offered the workers considerable wage increases.[35]

The willingness of the Irish state to take the part of employers in the 1935 dispute was no surprise. From the beginning, the Irish Free State had endured a fractious relationship with trade unions. In September 1922, a postal strike saw the Free State government dealing with its first real industrial dispute. After cutting postal workers' 'costs of living' bonus, the government determined that they could not strike. In the protests that followed, the police and military shot one striker on picket duty at Merchant Quay only for her suspender buckle to deflect the bullet.[36] On top of that, one of the first acts of senior civil servants in the Free State was to disallow arbitration for the Irish civil service; this stood in contrast to what occurred in Britain at the same time under the Whitley procedures.[37]

This combination of increased trade union militancy and determined state resistance gathered momentum in the 1940s. In February 1940, 2,000 Dublin Corporation workers went on strike looking for an increase of eight shillings a week. The strike lasted 20 days before being called off following the intervention of the Auxiliary Bishop of Dublin, Dr Wall.[38] During the Second World War, wage freezes were introduced by the government in 1941 and then, in the following year, strikes were outlawed.[39] There was similar state resistance to trade unions north of the border. When, in 1944, the British government introduced new arbitration procedures, the Northern Ireland government determined to retain restrictive measures – repealed in Britain – relating to strikes.[40]

Peace in Europe was the signal for industrial strife in Ireland. Diarmaid Ferriter has noted: 'Strikes by farm labourers were common after the war and the newly emergent Federation of Rural Workers also had to endure red-scare tactics by Fianna Fáil and the *Standard* newspaper. After initial strike action in Kildare, by the summer of 1947 the Federation had a membership of about 17,000 in 21 counties, and they managed to get four of their members elected to the Dáil in 1948.'[41] The growing militancy of unions was evident in a growth in membership: between 1945 and 1950 trade union membership in Ireland rose from 172,000 to 285,000.[42]

What was critical for bank officials is that it was not now 'working men' alone who went on strike. When members of the Irish National Teachers' Organisation (INTO) in the Dublin area went on strike on 20 March 1946, it represented 'the first outright use of the strike weapon by a professional group in Ireland'.[43] In November 1944, 26,000 civil and local authority servants received significant increases in their ordinary cost-of-living bonuses, but teachers received an increase that they considered 'contemptuous and insulting'.[44] A further deal offered to teachers in late 1945 proved equally unacceptable and a series of votes followed on whether to strike before action began in March. Crucially, the Catholic Church, through the Archbishop of Dublin, Charles McQuaid, waded in behind the teachers, writing that 'the religious superiors have full sympathy with the ideal of a salary in keeping with the dignity and responsibility of your profession as teachers'.[45] By September 1946 the issue had become, in the words of Louie Bennett, the General Secretary of the Irish Women Workers' Union, 'the spearhead of a struggle between Government and people', and 'a moral issue'.[46] In October, 70 teachers in black coats invaded the pitch at Croke Park during the All-Ireland football final between Kerry and Roscommon without the approval of the INTO.[47] Although the strike ended in defeat in late October, after seven months of protest, 'it laid much of the groundwork for the INTO's emergence as an increasingly powerful force in the educational sphere in the 1950s'.[48]

During the teachers' strike, the IBOA had passed on its good wishes in what it termed a 'fight for fair and adequate salaries'.[49] At the IBOA annual general meeting, a resolution was unanimously passed promising any assistance which could possibly be given. A meeting of the newly founded Irish Conference of Professional and Service Associations (ICPSA) in February 1946, saw the IBOA share a platform with INTO leaders, as well as with leaders of the Irish Local Government Officials' Union and the Railway Clerks' Association.[50] The formation of the ICPSA was supported by the IBOA, which bought into its ambition to secure a 'fair deal for the salaried and professional classes in this country and the provision of means through which they may speak with a single voice for the amelioration of their conditions and preservation of their economic rights. It is a body for mutual aid, without any aggressive or revolutionary designs save that of voicing the claims of a single, by no means insignificant, section of the community.'[51] Indeed, joining the ICPSA was in many ways the ideal scenario for the IBOA; it offered the potential of support from other organisations without compelling involvement with elements of the wider trade union movement for which bank officials clearly retained a certain distaste: the IBOA might now be a trade union, but it did not wish to be seen as one.

Whatever the formal constitution and allegiances of the representative body, bank officials were growing increasingly militant. Complaints from bank officials about their pay and conditions had been rising throughout the 1930s; those concerns were sharpened during the war and were sharpened still further almost immediately upon the cessation of the war. There was no headlong rush to confrontation, however. When the annual general meeting discussed the range of grievances held by bank officials, the IBOA's Organising Secretary, J. T. Donovan, urged caution, positing the view that any strike action would be both against the law and tactically inadvisable. In respect of the pension problems of retiring 'lady clerks', for example, he said: 'I want to say here and now that the best way of dealing with this case is by negotiation. I say, too, that no useful purpose is served by using intemperate language about Directors in this connection or in any other connection. I have heard language . . . intemperate language about Directors, which I can only characterise as scurrilous. Directors are men like ourselves, and they are not inhuman. I have known of very many cases of humanity in the acts of Directors towards bank officials.' Donovan was not, however, blind to the gathering resentment of bank officials. He laid out a path which recognised that bank officials might have to take a step which they had never taken before: 'If we have a case we have to convince our opponents of its justice, and we may even have in the long run to take the extreme step of striking, but let us do it decently.'[52]

Despite Donovan's emollient words, within four months 'the extreme step of striking' had actually been taken. Towards the end of the IBOA annual general meeting in March 1946, a motion from the Portadown branch proposed that the pay of bank officials be substantially increased to a starting salary of a minimum of £150, rising to a minimum of £800 on promotion to the position of manager. In the debate that ensued a divide emerged between north and south. This divide saw the northern delegates assume a much more militant stance, one partly rooted in the fact that higher rates of income tax in the north left bank officials there worse off than in the south. Indeed, it was suggested that bank officials who moved north of the border as part of their duties could forfeit as much as £100. A Mr Johnson from Portadown concluded: 'We say that when demanding these scales of salaries, that the Directors be given the minimum time to reply, and if the reply be not what we want, that we go out on strike.' The motion from Portadown was eventually amended to allow the Executive Committee to draw up a new scale of salaries. This marked something of a compromise, but there was no disguising the feeling of the meeting. As a Belfast delegate put it (and as was generally agreed): 'The whole agreement of 1919 between the Association and the banks is out of date.'[53] The logic of that statement led inevitably to confrontation.

What was delaying that confrontation was the clear reluctance of the Executive Committee to go down the road of strike action despite the obvious demands of its membership. The Executive Committee had long tied itself to the policy of negotiation. It had done so particularly since a 1941 agreement with the banks where a formal Negotiating Committee was established, comprising six members of the banks and six members of the IBOA. This committee was charged with resolving matters of dispute around pay and conditions. Time and again, the Executive Committee had looked to this Negotiating Committee to resolve disputes, but to little avail. As one Northern bank official wrote: 'We have arbitrated and negotiated, but have never obtained to the full that which we were seeking; like the few efficient fleas on the back of an elephant, we annoy but never hurt . . . There is hardly a Junior or Senior Official in Northern Ireland who is not crippled by income tax or by debt. Let the Executive Committee put aside their "some-future-date and time-is-not-ripe" policy and demand for us a living wage. Let us strike for it if necessary.'[54]

The militancy of northern officials forced the hand of the Executive Committee. At a meeting on 26 April 1946 the Irish Banks' Joint Committee informed the IBOA that it was rejecting claims of bank officials in Northern Ireland to have their pay increased to the same level as staff in the rest of Ireland.[55] On top of that, the banks' proposals of improved terms for 'lady clerks' were deemed wholly inadequate. The clear signal from the banks was that they were unprepared to offer any concessions worthy of the name to bank officials. The response was decisive. A ballot of northern members resulted in almost every member there supporting a proposal to strike; of 1,407 ballot papers returned, just 30 opposed the proposal. Under advice from J. T. Donovan, the Organising Secretary, the Executive Committee voted unanimously to serve notice of strike on 11 June 1946 in Northern Ireland. A 5 July 1946 meeting at Stormont Castle between the representatives of the banks, the IBOA and the Ministry of Labour ended in collapse. On 10 July and on the morning of 11 July 1946, there were last-ditch negotiations at which some progress was made and it appeared concessions were forthcoming from directors to avert the strike. The IBOA deemed the final offer of the banks to be quite unacceptable and the talks ended in failure. Strike notice was to expire on 12 July 1946. On the afternoon of 11 July 1946, led by the IBOA's newly formed Strike Committee of Northern Ireland, bank officials in the north took the momentous decision to go on strike on 13 July 1946. Telegrams were sent to bank officials around Northern Ireland informing them of what was to happen.[56] The following morning – 12 July 1946 – banks across Northern Ireland did not open their doors. This was something that 'the public believed could never have taken place.'[57] But it was also something which bank officials in the IBOA did not imagine would take place. Many imagined instead that 'strike notice would be a trumpet blast before which the walls of the opposing citadel would collapse'.[58]

Not alone did collapse not come immediately, the dispute actually dragged on for five weeks.[59] Across those five weeks the IBOA professed its pride in the organisation, discipline and unity of its northern members, all bar three of whom went on strike. The Association also said it particularly deplored two aspects of the dispute. The first was 'the lowering of an ancient and honourable profession like banking to the level of an arena for the waging of industrial strife'. The second was 'the inconvenience inflicted on the public', and the hope that that public understood that bank officials had been left without other options.[60] The Ministry of Labour intervened and a meeting between representatives of all sides was called for 18 July 1946. At that meeting, which lasted until 2 a.m., the Ministry of Labour proposed the establishment of a committee with plenary powers and containing independent members as well as representatives of both sides to resolve the dispute. The banks agreed to the proposal, but as it was a condition that the strike be abandoned immediately, the IBOA wished to consult with its members on how it should proceed. At a mass meeting in Grosvenor Hall in

Belfast, the proposal was unanimously rejected and the strike continued.[61]

There was support for the strikers from Stormont. The unionist politician J. W. Nixon blamed the government of Northern Ireland for not doing more to resolve the strike, and said that his sympathies lay entirely with the bank officials who were not being paid as they should be. He was supported by a fellow unionist politician Nat Minford, who said the pay of starting bank officials was akin to that of farm labourers, and was not appropriate for young men of education. Labour politicians in Stormont were also supportive, including Robert Getgood who said that 'the banks have no case at all. They had declared war on the officials . . .'[62]

The strike was run by the Northern Strike Committee from a room at the IBOA Bankers' Club in Donegall Place. It was there that the committee – which included one woman – met in almost continuous session: 'Private considerations ceased to have any weight. Homes were deserted. Meals were neglected. Sleep was scanty – and troubled. Rest was almost unknown. Holidays were interrupted and cancelled. Gardens and hedges became wild. Wives and children were strangers.'[63] A daily strike bulletin was published and was ended with the words: 'Our cause is just. Stand firm.'

There was the repeated suggestion that bank officials in the south would come out in support of their northern colleagues.[64] This was ultimately decided against and, instead, subscriptions were collected to support the financial needs of strikers as the dispute rolled into a third and then a fourth week. As public disquiet rose in the north over the impact of the strike, the Ministry of Labour organised a National Arbitration Tribunal to review the case on 1 and 2 August 1946. A day later, the proposed award to be made to bank officials was announced. It was much less than desired; another mass meeting of 1,000 strikers rejected the award and refused to return to work after a meeting which lasted almost three hours.[65] Leaving the meeting, J. T. Donovan said: 'Town and country members were unanimous in instructing me to tell the Minister that they will not go back to work . . . We are on strike and will be so until this matter is settled.'[66]

The next step was taken by the government of Northern

Ireland. On 9 August 1946 summonses were served on three bank officials – A. W. Connor, T. H. Daly and W. J. H. North. In response to the summonses, the *Strike Bulletin* reported: 'We have just heard that legal proceedings are to be taken against certain bank officials. The fight is really on now.'[67] Essentially, the state was deciding to test the legality of the strike. On Tuesday 13 August 1946 the case was dismissed by the Magistrate presiding at the Magistrate's Court and costs of 75 guineas were awarded to each of the three defendants. A further impasse had clearly been reached. The following day, however, the Northern Ireland government brought together both sides to the dispute and informed them that unless a settlement was reached by Friday evening, the state would take action to reopen the banks on the following Monday. Eventually, at 9.45 p.m. on Friday evening, 16 August 1946, a settlement was reached and the strike was ended.[68]

In reporting the outcome of the settlement – which granted improved pension entitlements for female members, a new conciliation machinery to resolve further disputes and raised the pay of entrants to the bank to £130 per annum rising to £644 in the twenty-second year for men (£135 to £320 in their eighteenth year for women) – the *Strike Bulletin* accepted that it was less than what they had fought for, but 'every member may be assured that in no known circumstances could anything better have been obtained'.[69] To the IBOA, it 'was brought to an end only when it was obvious that harm might result incommensurate with any further benefit that could ensue from its continuation'.[70] The following morning – Saturday 17 August 1946 – bank officials returned to their desks to prepare for public opening on the following Monday morning. Commenting on the outcome of the strike, the *Irish Banking Magazine* noted that not everything sought had been won, but sufficient had been gained to ensure the strike could only be considered a victory: 'To our northern colleagues, and the inspiring leadership they have had from their local organisation – and from the Organising Secretary in person – must be paid full tribute for an achievement which will undoubtedly stand as a landmark in Associational history . . . Great expectations had been aroused by the strike, and these were naturally disappointed in the settlement.

In many ways, certainly, the settlement is unsatisfactory; no-one will deny that. But such things as strikes invariably end in compromise. It is only the fanatic that pursues his course to disaster; and even the victor, if he be wise, will not push his triumph too far.'[71]

The question was now: what would happen in the south? The reality of operating across two jurisdictions brought complications. The differing rates of income tax on either side of the border had left less acute demand for strike action in the south. Nonetheless, there were serious grievances that the rate of pay was now such that bank officials were retreating to conditions that had existed after the Great War because of the persistent rise in the cost of living. There was, on top of that, disillusion with the approach of the banks and their perceived failure to pay adequate wages even while their own profits rose. The view of the IBOA was that the approach of the banks was to adopt 'an ostrich policy that deceives nobody but themselves'.[72] A certain twist was put on the tale, however, by the publication in the summer of 1946 of a Bill to establish a Labour Court in the south of Ireland. The Industrial Relations Bill, 1946 proposed the establishment of a full-time body which would transform the management of industrial relations in the state. Immediately upon the publication of this Bill there was speculation that the dispute between bank officials and their employers was headed for the Labour Court, almost as soon as that court was established.[73]

That remained in the future when the banks approached the IBOA in October 1946 with the proposal that the agreement struck in the north should now be applied to the south. In a letter to the IBOA on 3 October 1946, the banks argued for such a move to facilitate 'workable uniformity' across the island. The letter called for a conference to be held on the matter. The IBOA met on 25 October 1946 and agreed to the idea of the conference. When that conference took place, the IBOA told the banks that a further increase in the 'cost of living bonus' paid to southern bank officials would be required to meet the problems caused by inflation. Following the conference with the banks, the deputation that had represented the IBOA reported back to a meeting but there was deep division in the organisation on what to do next. Some wished to postpone agreement in the belief that a better deal would be achieved once the scale of the banks' profits became public in 1947; others wished to accept the proposals under protest.[74] For several months, bank officials disagreed – and did so publicly – on the appropriate course of action. In the course of the dispute, at least three members of the Executive Committee resigned and the Organising Secretary, J. T. Donovan, expressed a willingness to leave.[75] The Executive Committee had eventually decided to accept the banks' offers, but was roundly condemned by the membership at various meetings for doing so. In response – in December 1946 – the Executive decided to take a ballot of all members, which was essentially a vote of confidence in their position. That vote was won, but was won so narrowly as not to constitute a victory at all. What was apparent was that the membership was not of any mind to accept the offer of the banks. It was equally apparent that no further decisive steps would be taken until the IBOA's annual general meeting in the Royal Hibernian Hotel in Dublin on St Patrick's Day, 1947.[76]

The mood at the annual general meeting was definite and was perhaps best demonstrated by the election of 'a new and more militant executive committee'.[77] As the *Irish Banking Magazine* put it, there was an accession of new blood to the Executive 'to take over the task of deciding upon future policy and action in the firmly declared object of repairing the shaken fortunes of bank officials in Ireland through the catastrophic fall in the real value of their remuneration'. These 'new bloods' now carried the hopes of the 'large section of the Association, which desires that a more militant policy should be followed'.[78] Further correspondence with the banks in the wake of the meeting demonstrated the gulf which had emerged between the two sides and what had for quite a while seemed inevitable came to pass when the matter went before the Labour Court on 22 May 1947.[79] In an opening statement to that court, J. T. Donovan referred to the 'dangerous mood' of the IBOA, which was caused by the banks which had an 'unyielding attitude' which had 'financially crippled many of its members'.[80] There was also the stirring development of J. T. Donovan calling on the Labour Court to grant equal pay to women, through the slogan: 'Equal pay for equal work.'[81] That is not to say that the IBOA was now uniformly bent on strike. Indeed, there was ongoing division amongst the Executive Committee on whether strike was the appropriate action and even those who favoured strike were worried that it might cause damage to the economy.[82]

Further hearings of the Court on the matter took place on 30 May, 2 July and 28 July 1947, at which both the IBOA and the banks presented their respective cases. Then, on 8 August 1947, the Labour Court issued its recommendations. These came as a profound shock to IBOA members and were immediately rejected by the Executive Committee. Commenting on the recommendations, the *Irish Banking Magazine* agreed with the proposition that it was part of a 'Government-inspired trend to wipe out the middle classes'. Indeed, it was claimed that there should be no surprise 'if these classes – the forgotten men, as they might be called, who bear the burden and the heat of the day but are usually lost to view in the dust of the economic conflict – will in future regard the operations of the Labour Court with the deepest suspicion'.[83]

This view was rooted, partly, in the comments made in the course of the recommendations issued by the Labour Court. Noting the lack of 'mutual understanding and comprehension', and the presence of 'constant friction' between the nine Irish banks and their 3,900 officials working in the south, the Labour Court recommended the establishment of a standing committee to resolve all matters of dispute from that point on. It also set out a revised scale of salaries that it deemed appropriate for the work of bank officials. The Court refused to involve itself in issues relating to the payment of overtime and the provision of a lunch interval. In delivering these recommendations, the Labour Court observed: 'The Association, in its presentation of its case, was not very helpful and appears to have an unduly high opinion of the responsibilities borne by bank officials of all grades as compared with those of workers in other employments.'[84] It was a quietly brutal appraisal of the IBOA's case and one which piqued the IBOA into commenting: 'A generalisation of this kind leads nowhere, as well as being derogatory.'[85]

Ten days after the Labour Court recommendations were issued, 1,300 members of the IBOA met at the Metropolitan Hall on Lower Abbey Street in Dublin. E. H. Flint, the then president of the IBOA, told the meeting of the 'contemptuous tone and treatment' endured at the hands of the Labour Court. He spoke of 'injustice' and of a 'lack of courtesy'. The militancy of the meeting was confirmed as the Organising Secretary, J. T. Donovan, repeated that the unanimous view of the Executive Committee was that the recommendations be rejected and that a strike ballot be taken. The feeling of the meeting was one of agreement, just as it was when similar meetings were held in towns across Ireland on 22 and 23 August 1947.[86] The result of the strike ballot was clear cut: 3,351 voted in favour, 143 voted against, and 27 votes were spoiled.[87] By then, bank officials had already decided to restrict the hours that they would work, starting at 9.30 a.m. and finishing at 4.30 p.m.[88] A strike became increasingly inevitable.

When that strike did eventually take place, it did not do so in quite the manner expected. On Saturday 4 October 1947 the banks took the initiative and – with the support of the government – closed the banks. In a statement, the Irish Bankers' Joint Committee said they were shutting the banks because the IBOA had 'unilaterally reduced the working hours, with the result that the discharge by the Banks of their obligations has fallen into arrears'.[89] Essentially, the banks had convinced the government that there would be chaos in banking in Ireland unless they were allowed to close their doors.[90] Furthermore, the banks ordered that each official should sign an undertaking to 'comply with such instructions as the due discharge of business requires'. Those who did not sign would be deemed to have broken their contract, 'leaving the Bank no alternative save to terminate his or her employment'.[91] When the matter was raised in the Dáil, it was apparent that the Fianna Fáil government was supportive of the banks, and not of their officials.[92] As the *Nenagh Guardian* reported, 'The Government for once showed its hand, and sided with the employers.'[93]

The Executive Committee went into emergency session through the weekend, but there was no meaningful course of action open to the Association, except to advise its members to resist signing the undertaking and to turn up for work as usual.[94] All through the week that followed the banks remained closed.[95] Having been shut for a little over a week, bankers and their officials were essentially pushed into a negotiation by government, who were coming under pressure in the Dáil from the Opposition, which accused them of overstepping their powers and from businesses across the country who were complaining of inconvenience. [96] *The Irish Press* reported that both sides had agreed to a 'conference without conditions'. To underpin the compromise, bank officials would return to working normal hours and the banks would withdraw their request that an undertaking on such hours be signed by their officials.[97]

Pictured at an emergency session of the Executive Committee of the IBOA in October 1947 are (l–r): W. H. K. Peard, Honorary Secretary of the Dublin District; E. M. Flint, the President of the IBOA; and P. S. Foley, Assistant Honorary Secretary of the IBOA. *(IBOA Archive)*

Those talks continued through late October and early November, until, on 7 November 1947, representatives of the banks and the IBOA met in Dublin from early morning until midnight. The discussions ended in agreement that bank officials would receive a rate of pay in advance of that proposed by the Labour Court.[98] It was also agreed that bank officials would now be provided with an hour for lunch. To facilitate this, banks would close their doors from 12.30 to 1.30 p.m. from 1 January 1947. The annual leave period was fixed from 1 April to 1 October. Relief duty and transfer expenses would now be allowed, and the working week would effectively be set at 42½ hours. Finally, negotiation mechanisms to resolve disputes were established on the lines of those previously agreed in Northern Ireland.[99]

When the proposed settlement was put to bank officials, the resulting ballot saw 3,453 vote in favour, with just 166 opposed. The scale of the margin of victory might suggest that bank officials now had pay and conditions of an order that would guarantee a measure of contentment for the foreseeable future. This was not the case. J. T. Donovan said the settlement was 'not a perfect one, of course, but a settlement without dishonour'.[100] Even as it reported the results of the vote, the *Irish Banking Magazine* was cautioning that the result was merely 'a considerable step towards declared objectives' and that the years of 'interminable clash and conflict played its part in securing the favourable vote, for there are many indications that the agreement on remuneration, both in its immediate and longterm aspects is by no means favourably viewed by so large a majority'.[101] The unhappy truth was that this 'strike' – and its resolution – did not mark the end of 'clash and conflict', but, instead, proved a stepping stone to more bitter division.

5

1950s

The 1950s is one of the key decades of modern Irish history. It was in this decade that the guiding principles that had underpinned the project of political independence in the south of Ireland came unstuck. Unemployment, emigration, population decline, political instability, renewed IRA violence and the slow demise of the generation of leaders who had emerged in the War of Independence forced a radical rethink of policy. Even at the start of the 1950s, agriculture was the bedrock of the Irish economy; by the end of the decade, agriculture remained vital, but there had been a discernible shift towards industry and services. This shift was rooted in the bleak performance which saw the Irish economy slide towards collapse even as the economies of almost all the rest of Western Europe and America passed through the greatest boom in their history. Economic woe was not, of course, the full story of the decade. No decade is simply one thing or another; rather it is a complex of overlapping ideas, experiences and processes. After all, a letter sent to the *Irish Banking Magazine* in 1953 carried a simple question: 'Could you find out for me if I am the only Pensioner left who served in the Boer War? There can't be many left?'[1] And, yet, the 1950s was also the decade when television was installed in the Irish Bankers' Club. The reality is that, even in the midst of turmoil,

Irish people continued to live out their lives, driven by the usual impulses, and this meant woe was just one experience of the 1950s. This was as true for bank officials as it was for any other section of society.

I

STRIKES

Any hope that the agreements which emerged from the strikes of 1946 in Northern Ireland and 1947 in the south of Ireland might bring stability to the relations between bank managements and bank officials soon evaporated. At the annual general meetings of the IBOA in 1948 and 1949, it was apparent that bank officials remained disgruntled with their levels of pay and with enduring work practices such as the non-payment of overtime, the obligation to sleep on the bank premises during the absence of the normally resident official, and the convention of receiving the consent of the bank in order to marry. That the lives of bank officials continued to be intruded upon in a variety of ways was underlined in a dispute which arose when a young bank official returned from his holidays sporting the makings of a beard. He was summarily sent home by the bank manager who ordered that he remove the beard. The official obliged despite the belief that the manager was invading his private rights and exceeding his own authority. A letter writer to the *Irish Banking Magazine* noted that doctors, architects and 'other professional men wear beards, or not, as the spirit moves them'. Ensuing correspondence in the magazine suggested that a moustache was acceptable, but not a beard.[2]

In general, there was a feeling that the strikes of 1946 and 1947 had left much unfinished business. They had brought some advances to bank officials, but had also left many hopes unfulfilled. Those strikes were crucial, though, not in what they achieved, but in the very fact that they took place at all. The idea of bank officials going on strike was now no longer notional; it was something real and something that would most likely happen again. When he addressed his last annual general meeting as Organising Secretary in March

'How to succeed in the Bank' – the *Irish Banking Magazine* offers some tips in January 1954. *(IBOA Archive)*

1948, J. T. Donovan told delegates: 'There are hard days before the Association, but its course is set in the right direction and the tide has turned.'[3] It was clear from Donovan's last address that he was pleased that he was leaving the position which he had held for sixteen years; the last three years of his tenure had been particularly trying. Donovan's successor was John Titterington. He started work in November 1948 and quickly established a formidable reputation for himself. Described later as 'irascible, charismatic and resourceful, he was what the IBOA wanted at the time'.[4] More than that, 'the combination of his talents with the will of the members to accept the type of leadership he was so qualified to provide, initiated a period in which time after time the impossible became possible'.[5]

John Titterington, pictured in September 1948, shortly before his appointment as Organising Secretary of the IBOA. He succeeded J. T. Donovan who had held the post for the previous sixteen years. *(IBOA Archive)*

Titterington was at the helm of the IBOA when a dramatic strike was called at Christmas 1952. Leading IBOA member W. K. Peard was clear that the origin of the new strike lay in the agreements which had been made with the banks in the aftermath of the strikes in the 1940s and eventually signed on 31 December 1948. They were, wrote Peard, 'at best a covenanted truce'.[6] The possibilities of making permanent that truce were rooted in the application of the spirit of the 1948 Agreement to particular sets of circumstances and in the smooth operation of the machinery designed to sort out disagreements between the banks and their officials. There was optimism when the first negotiations took place under the new machinery in March 1949. There were fifteen matters on the agenda for discussion and five were dealt with immediately. There was careful consideration of ten further items, including issues around pensioners. Eventually, the banks refused to discuss this matter further, saying it lay outside the scope of the 1948 Agreement. They were technically correct in this interpretation, though it irked the IBOA.[7] Throughout 1950, further claims on the pay and position of 'lady clerks', on the block on promotion that had emerged and on basic salaries had produced a groundswell of annoyance at the attitude of the banks. The simple belief was that the banks' attitude to negotiation and arbitration was 'quite scandalous'.[8]

As annoyance grew, so did demands for action. A meeting of the

Dublin district of the IBOA drew 1,000 members to the Round Room at the Mansion House on 24 November 1950.[9] John Titterington told the meeting that it was now clear that the rise in the cost of living had destroyed the lives of bank officials who could 'no longer continue to house, clothe, feed themselves, or educate their children' to a decent degree.[10] He noted that the IBOA had attempted to operate the machinery justly, but the banks had 'always opposed a

Mr J. P. Mannick counts out cash in the National Bank in Listowel, 1944. The work of bank officials at the time was often characterised by drudgery. Speaking of his experience in the Bank of Ireland in Belfast in the 1950s, another official remarked that the 'daily routine was never-ending. The ledgers were hand-posted. Columns were totted and accounts balanced. Passbooks, in those pre-statement days, were written up and woe-betide you if you did not keep them up to date. Interest was calculated manually and double-checked.' *(Irish Picture Library/Fr F. M. Browne Collection)*

104

fair settlement'.[11] He noted that the IBOA had accepted an award made for women members, not because it was just but because it was a step towards equal pay. What was clear, though, was that the failure to address the general issue of rates of pay was pushing both sides towards confrontation. It was apparent from speeches at the meeting that the mood amongst bank officials was to strike if necessary.[12]

Just three days later – having held a series of Executive Committee meetings to confirm that there was sufficient support for strike – on 27 November 1950 the IBOA served notice of strike on the banks.[13] The response of the banks was 'a blank wall of negation'. Indeed, the directors of the banks did not come to a meeting held under the machinery in December, which was supposed to be directed towards resolving the strike. Instead, they sent representatives who did not have sufficient powers to negotiate.[14] The banks did pay a Christmas bonus to staff, but this was viewed as mere tokenism when set against the refusal to deal with substantive issues. On Christmas Eve 1950, a last-ditch effort was made to avert the strike when both sides came together at Jury's Hotel in Dublin under the auspices of the Chief Conciliation Officer of the Labour Court. The representatives of the banks again said they had no powers to negotiate. The talks collapsed and bank officials went on strike in the Republic of Ireland. On Christmas Eve, £10,800 was drawn from the IBOA's strike fund and distributed across the Association. On 27 December 1950, the banks of the Republic of Ireland did not open.[15] The *Irish Banking Magazine* claimed that the response to the call to strike was supported by almost 100 per cent of members.[16]

The following day, 28 December 1950, the inter-party government, which then held power, made an order authorising the banks to stay closed until 1 January 1951. In a related development, the Labour Court announced its intention to intervene. The IBOA announced that it would attend the Labour Court only if subpoenaed to do so. It made this announcement because it insisted that the banks must meet the IBOA with full negotiating powers in direct talks as this was the only way in which the matters at dispute could be resolved. For its part, the Irish Bankers' Joint Committee announced that it would be prepared to enter into negotiations, but on condition that the strike was abandoned. The result was a deadlock, which was only broken when the Labour Court used its legal powers to call witnesses from the IBOA, led by John Titterington.[17]

The fact that the banks had decided to attend the Labour Court placed the IBOA on the defensive and created the perception of intransigence. Even as the Labour Court was preparing to open negotiations, the *Irish Banking Magazine* was struggling to explain the stance:

> It wishes to imply no contempt of the Labour Court . . .
> Sad experience shows that arbitration by outside bodies
> or persons, where it has been resorted to in our industry,
> invariably seems to produce results which bring the
> parties no nearer to a satisfactory settlement of their
> differences. The reason probably is that outside bodies,
> no matter how closely they question witnesses, cannot
> be expected to have knowledge of the problems, or
> appreciation of the background, that govern conditions
> in a professional calling like banking and are auto-
> matically taken into account in direct negotiation. The
> latter, however, requires one important condition for
> success, namely that each party comes to it with a will
> to facilitate a settlement. It is the absence of this on the
> employers' side that has led to the present strife and
> confusion in the banking profession.[18]

This apparent absence of trust left it impossible for the negotiations conducted by the Labour Court to prosper. No solution was found. The banks did not open in the Republic of Ireland throughout the whole of January 1951. Writing in his 'Cruiskeen Lawn' column in *The Irish Times*, Myles na gCopaleen, parodied what he claimed happened next:

> This bank row is getting interesting. The public has
> made the discovery that there is no real need for banks
> at all. *The Irish Times* summarised the whole monetary
> puzzle in a report of a few weeks ago. It explained that
> there was a lot of loose cash floating around after the
> Christmas. These deposits were in pubs, drapery shops
> and cinemas. The proprietors of these establishments
> kindly gave various industrial undertakings sufficient
> cash to pay wages. Within a week, all this cash got back
> into the hands of pubs, drapery shops and cinemas. It

was redistributed in wages. It did the rounds again. There appears to be no necessity for any other arrangement. Why have these banks?[19]

Naturally, there was a general public outcry at the strike. Amidst this was significant criticism of the IBOA. In Cork, the *Southern Star* wrote an editorial that was critical of the failure to engage with the Labour Court.[20] The *Munster Express* noted that the sudden strike 'came as a bombshell to the general public' and that, were it to be prolonged, it would 'precipitate a crisis of the first magnitude'.[21] For their part, the IBOA took out advertisements in the newspapers which asked: 'Why are we on strike?' The answer provided was that it was because of 'an 83% rise in the cost of living, set off so far by only 36% increase in remuneration. This is the simple issue . . . After all the directors have recognised the difficulty of the times by increasing their fees by 100% or more since 1939.'[22] Both sides of the dispute were condemned by many. A letter published in the *Irish Independent* bitterly noted: 'These gentlemen, both directors and officials, seem to forget that there would not be any local banks to provide fat salaries, pensions, warm offices, short hours, and half-holidays, for them if was not for the hard-earned money left in their charge by the small farmers out working in all weathers, night often as well as day and Sundays, and the small farmers have to stand any loss they may suffer, and get no pensions.'[23]

The Labour Court was in no doubt who was primarily to blame for the strike, however. It issued a statement which was trenchant in its criticism of the IBOA: 'The Court can find no justification for the course taken by the Officials' Association . . . The Court is obliged to say that it finds the Association guilty of a breach of faith all the more reprehensible because committed by a body of officials who have claimed that they occupy positions of trust and responsibility and who must have known that their action would result in dislocation of the ordinary course of business and grave inconvenience to the community.'[24] Wild rumours swept the city of Dublin as bank officials came under pressure to end the strike. John Titterington told a meeting of 2,000 strikers in the Mansion House on 17 January 1951: 'I am not a communist. I am not a member of any political party, either here or in Great Britain or elsewhere. I am not an imperialist, as was suggested by someone last week. I am not anything other than a man who is trying to do his job conscientiously, and that is the job of Organising Secretary of the IBOA . . . It is disgraceful that certain people are trying to create dissent and split the Association.'[25]

It was not merely the IBOA which was under pressure from the strike, of course. The *Tuam Herald* noted that there was 'sharp criticism of the Government for allowing the situation to go to such an extreme.'[26] With no end to the strike in sight, the inter-party government moved to intervene. The Taoiseach, John A. Costello, noted the 'great public inconvenience and loss to commerce and business'.[27] On 24 January 1951, Costello met, separately, with a delegation of the IBOA and with Arthur Cox, solicitor to the Irish Banks' Joint Committee, and tried to broker an agreement. Insufficient common ground could be established and the strike continued. Bank officials in Northern Ireland raised £5,300 to support the strikers. This gesture was, according to the *Irish Banking Magazine*, 'a truly inspiring proof of the bond of union in which the Association is joined together and of the spirit of self-sacrifice that fires it in a common cause'.[28] It was also necessary. It was reported that various members of the IBOA were in dire straits and in desperate need of financial assistance.[29]

With no apparent end in sight, the inter-party government moved again to find a solution. Taoiseach John A. Costello (Fine Gael) and Tánaiste William Norton (Labour Party) took charge of the situation and invited the banks and the IBOA to a meeting in Government Buildings in Dublin on 2 and 3 February 1951.[30] For more than twelve hours the negotiations continued under the chairmanship of the Taoiseach.[31] On several occasions, the talks seemed on the verge of collapse, until finally agreement was reached on the terms of reference under which arbitration could be conducted. That arbitration took place between 5 and 7 February 1951 with the high court judge, Cahir Davitt, and two lawyers, Alexander Bayne and Francis Vaughan Buckley, as arbitrators. On 8 February 1951, the findings and award of the arbitrators were announced. This offered a modest increase in pay to male bank officials and clarified the position in respect of the payment of the cost-of-living bonus, rank allowances and overtime.[32] The award was immediately put to a vote of the membership of the IBOA and secured a relatively narrow majority in favour – 2,437 in favour and 1,537 against.[33] The banks duly reopened on 16 February, seven weeks after they had closed.[34] Two weeks later – on 22 February 1951 – representatives of the banks and the IBOA met in Belfast in search of an agreement for bank officials based in Northern Ireland and one was arrived at which accepted the same minimum salary scales as in the south.[35]

Commenting on the resolution of the dispute, the *Irish Banking Magazine* said it was 'more than a pyrrhic victory' and something which had left the IBOA 'stronger than ever before . . . Possibly it marks no very great advance, but gaps have been filled in and some injustices removed'. This was particularly seen to be the case in respect of senior bank officials, who would now benefit from changes to the scale. Against that, the *Irish Banking Magazine* allowed that there would be a good deal of sympathy for 'the ladies' who had got a 'rather poor deal', with no increase at all in their basic pay and only a minimal increase in scale payments.[36] In the wider Association, there was an obvious divide over acceptance of the award. This was made clear by one bank official in a letter which he signed as 'Disgusted Junior': 'This is no time for the trumpets of victory. Let there be no doubt about it, we have been defeated by nothing less than the treachery of all those members of the Association who voted "yes" in the final ballot. . . . We all know what happened: 2,500 officials, refusing to exercise their common intelligence, or perhaps selfishly following sectional interests, let down the whole Association in general, and the junior members and ladies in particular. It was an appalling debacle.' Most damagingly, 'Disgusted Junior' claimed that the final Arbitration Award was 'no better, and in some respects worse', than the final offer which the banks had made to the IBOA in their last-ditch attempt to avert the strike.[37] This letter drew support from other correspondents who avowed the 'disappointment, disgust and despair' of junior officials who, 'having gone on strike, now feel we have gained nothing from it'.[38]

When the strike was reviewed at the annual general meeting of the IBOA – held on 5 May 1951 in the Abbey Lecture Hall, Lower

Abbey Street in Dublin – it was claimed that the arbitration award was accepted only because 'we felt that if we did not agree to it, certain members would resume work'.[39] This, of course, was a statement that was impossible to prove or disprove, but it was clear from the address of the Organising Secretary, John Titterington, that the strike had left a bitter aftertaste. Titterington did claim that 'the strike was justified by events' and that it had been 'widely said that it was the best organised strike in the history of trade unionism'. Nonetheless, in the next breath he acknowledged: 'Whether we got all that we wanted is a different matter.'[40] Most pointedly, he noted the continued failure of the banks to pay to 'lady clerks' the 5 per cent pre-Christmas bonus, which had been paid to male officials south of the border and to all officials north of the border. Titterington told the meeting: 'There is no justification at all for this discrimination . . . Still the banks refuse. I can't understand their brand of logic.'[41]

Indeed, it was this gulf of understanding between banks and their employees that was the kernel of the problem. And the gulf was widening. More than simply the disappointment felt by some officials at not getting such increases in pay as they believed they merited, what was actually most worrying for future relations between the IBOA and the banks was the apparent collapse of trust. The leadership of the IBOA simply did not believe that the Irish banks were willing to treat with them or their members in good faith. This is evident in the discussions which ran through 1951 and 1952 and which were supposed to deal with contentious issues and ensure that there should be no future strike. The truth of it was that there was no meaningful, sustained attempt at compromise between the two sides. Dispute became the watchword of their relationship as relatively minor matters were quickly inflated to matters of supreme importance.

At one point in the summer of 1951, the IBOA requested a meeting with Éamon de Valera, who had been returned as Taoiseach, but this was denied. De Valera's reply was that the dispute should be sorted out between employers and their employees.[42] By the autumn of 1951, the *Irish Banking Magazine* was warning of increasing tension and that strike was once more a possibility. The issue at hand was the belief in the IBOA that the banks simply wished to neuter the Association rather than actually negotiate with it. This was because, in attempting to establish a new machinery to allow for the resolution of grievances and disputes, the banks wished the IBOA to promise to provide a month's notice on the date on which a strike would actually start and to agree to exempt from membership of the IBOA enough officials as to ensure that in the event of a strike banking operations would not be entirely suspended. The *Irish Banking Magazine* viewed this as characteristic of the banks' determination 'to maintain their ill-disposed attitude of no compromise . . . From the day on which the staffs returned to work, after an arbitrated settlement of the strike, the Directors have shown in various ways that they are determined to break the officials' union.'[43]

Month after month – and then year after year – disagreements between the banks and the IBOA lingered. Intemperate language was standard on both sides, in private letter and in public statement. Pensions, overtime payments, appropriate salaries, scales of pay, annual leave, the Saturday half-day, opening hours, the block in promotion, bonus payments and discrimination against 'lady clerks' were recurring points of argument. Strike was only narrowly averted on several occasions in 1952 and 1953. Then, in December 1954, renewed industrial action began when bank officials started working restricted hours, which essentially amounted to a working week of 30½ hours.[44] There were appeals from government ministers to resolve the dispute. Gerald Sweetman, the Minister for Finance, wrote: 'As such patriotic Irish men and Irishwomen, I would ask them in all sincerity to avoid anything that might injure the nation, to come together and develop the terms and conditions of arbitration machinery which will not merely get over the present impasse but will serve as a lasting basis of that just peace which is so desirable in the administration of banking and other public service.'[45]

The appeals fell on deaf ears. Restrictive working lasted until March 1955, when a conference was held between representatives of the banks and the IBOA at the Mansion House in Dublin.[46] The conference lasted for five days under the chairmanship of the high court judge, J. C. Conroy.[47] It was actually the third such conference to be held across the three months of the dispute and on this occasion agreement was reached. The conference agreed an improved rate of pay for male officials and a revised scale of pay related to the Consumer Price Index. It did not deliver on the IBOA's demand for equal pay for women, however, with Judge Conroy saying that he was 'not satisfied from the representations made to us that the duties of male and female bank officials are analogous'. Crucially, it also established a tightly regulated Machinery for Conciliation and Arbitration.[48] Judge Conroy's proposals were accepted by the IBOA in the south and this was quickly followed by the signing of a similar agreement in Northern Ireland.

In the round, the result of the conference was a favourable one for the IBOA. It was not that everything they wished for had been conceded; indeed, there was significant disillusion at the decisions on equal pay for women, on pensions and on overtime, but the single most important development was the establishment of the Machinery for Conciliation and Arbitration. This machinery was used time and again by the IBOA to promote the working conditions of their members, particularly in relation to improved basic salaries. Other achievements related to conditions of employment such as the removal of the duty to sleep on bank premises and of the convention of seeking consent from the bank to marry. It also facilitated adequate notice of transfer, improved expenses, improvements in sick leave pay, an optional retirement scheme, improved office conditions, new systems for annual leave, improved Christmas leave and *pro rata* leave for new entrants. There were, of course, many matters – not least equal pay for women – which remained unresolved, but what made the achievements all the more striking was the backdrop against which they were achieved. For Ireland in the 1950s was not a prosperous place.[49]

II

A CONSERVATIVE PEOPLE?

For much of the 1950s there was little cause for optimism in Ireland. Amongst many causes for dismay was a renewed campaign of violence as the IRA attempted to rejuvenate itself and to make a military assault on the Northern Ireland state. After a number of skirmishes in 1955, the IRA moved to a full offensive in December 1956. The offensive lasted for just over five years until it was abandoned in the spring of 1962. In that period there had been around 600 incidents, ranging from murder to minor civil offences. Almost all incidents took place in 1957 and 1958, and after that the campaign fizzled out, but not before twelve Republicans and six police officers lost their lives. That Northern Ireland remained a divided society was underlined by the emergence of a new generation of Unionist politicians. This generation was marked by a populist rhetoric, which reinforced the Protestantism of the northern state and eschewed consensual gestures towards Catholics. Throughout the 1950s, the voices of unionists who sought a more conciliatory approach to the position of Catholics in the state were drowned out. Between violent republicanism on the one hand and uncompromising unionism on the other, Northern Ireland was divided unto itself.

Meanwhile, in the south, there was the looming sense that the entire project of Irish independence was on the verge of falling to pieces. On more than one occasion, the state almost ran out of money. It was also running out of people. Alone in Western Europe, the population of Ireland declined in the 1950s. In general, the pessimism of the 1950s was rooted in persistent economic failures. But it was also rooted in the sense that there were no new ideas coming to the fore and that there was, instead, a return again and again to policies which had already been tried and had already failed. The sense of dismay in the south of Ireland was evident in the words of the Minister for Industry and Commerce, Seán Lemass, when he said: 'I did not relish the prospect of coming back into government in the conditions of 1951 at all . . . We had not really got down to clearing our minds on post-war development.'

In its own way that was a savage indictment of the failure of Irish politics. Six years after the ending of the Second World War there was still no clarity on how best to advance the future of the Republic of Ireland (the south of Ireland had finally been declared a Republic in 1948). No clear vision emerged of what the future might be. The result was an inability to construct anything approaching a coherent programme for economic development. In 1952, the Fianna Fáil Minister for Finance, Seán MacEntee described the finances of the country as 'difficult almost to the verge of desperation'. The Republic was buffeted by the inflation which affected the global economy after war broke out in Korea. Prices rose, taxes rose, wages fell and the standard of living declined. The *Irish Banking Magazine* noted that the Budget in 1952 'fulfils all the worst expectations that could be entertained of economic harshness and severity, and appears indeed almost savage in its attack upon the earnings and resources of the community.'[50]

A General Election was called in May 1954. Fianna Fáil lost enough seats to allow the formation of a second inter-party government. Just as they had done in 1948, the opposition parties combined to form a government with John A. Costello as Taoiseach. On this occasion, however, just Fine Gael, Labour and Clann na Talmhan members served as ministers. Three Clann na Poblachta members and five independents were prepared to support the government from the outside – but were not prepared to serve in ministerial office. It was the most fragile of arrangements.

The government was not a success. It was divided as to how to meet the challenges it faced and only unprecedented taxes prevented national bankruptcy in the spring of 1956. The measures which the government took to attempt to stabilise the economy undercut its popularity and it lost office in March 1957. The big surprise was that it had survived the best part of three years. Fianna Fáil was returned to office and Éamon de Valera was returned as Taoiseach. De Valera was now seventy-six years of age. It was apparent that the successive governments of Ireland in the 1950s were divided not by policy, but by history and by personality. These were men who shared a broadly similar vision of Ireland, who when in power implemented broadly the same social and economic policies, and who, in truth, were separated usually by the fact that there had been a civil war in Ireland in the 1920s.

On top of this political stagnation, the power of the Catholic Church appeared to have reached new heights. Successive governments entered into negotiations with members of the Catholic hierarchy in advance of the construction of policy. Not alone did the Church control effectively much of the education system and the health system, entire areas of the social policy of the state were also left in its control. For example, it was in the 1950s that the control exercised by the Catholic religious orders over the Reformatory and Industrial schools was at its greatest. It was to be several decades before the implications of that secession of power were laid bare, but when it eventually happened the consequences were shocking in their depravity.

Against this backdrop of political stagnation and clerical power, two things – both of which were wrapped up in the same parcel – happened: the Irish economy collapsed and emigration reached heights unwitnessed since the famine of the 1840s. The contrast between, on the one hand, the booming consumerist economies of Britain and America, and on the other hand, the stagnation of Ireland was stark. The result was a mass exodus of the unemployed and the underemployed from Ireland. The scale of the exodus was staggering. In second half of the 1940s, about 150,000 Irish people emigrated. Then, during the 1950s, the floodgates truly opened and almost 500,000 Irish people emigrated. That was equivalent to almost one in six of the population.

Amongst those leaving were people who actually had jobs, including bank officials. In 1957, for example, month after month of the *Irish Banking Magazine* was filled with letters from junior bank officials who were emigrating. On one level, this was a reflection of the gloom enveloping the country. On another level, it was a reflection of the pay and conditions of junior officials. One letter writer who signed himself as 'Emigrating Junior' wrote: 'Is there any other branch of the white collar workers so poorly paid? Whom do we work for – a bank or a pawnshop?'[51] Tension over emigration also revealed generational antipathy. When a letter writer signing himself 'Manager Member' wrote lamenting the defeatist attitude of junior bank officials who did not understand quite how good they had it, 'Emigrating Junior' replied by asking why anyone would want to work under such a man whose 'grey hairs bristle with self-righteous indignation at any signs of ambition or initiative in their junior staff'.[52] The view of the *Irish Banking Magazine* was that married bank officials would love to join the ranks of juniors leaving the country, but 'the banks know that they have the vast majority of married officials locked as tightly as the cash in the strong-rooms, as it takes a great deal of courage for a man to uproot his wife and family and set out for foreign parts. But desperation may take the place of courage very soon.'[53] Either way, the population of Ireland fell and fell, to reach just 2.9 million in 1961.

An unemployment meeting in Dublin, 3 April 1957. This demonstration, held within a month of the fall of the Republic's second inter-party government, took place against an economic backdrop of high unemployment and mass emigration. Over the course of the decade, almost half a million Irish people left the southern state to make new lives in the cities of Britain and the United States. Among those who left were many junior bank officials. *(Lensmen)*

The broader conservatism of Irish society was reflected in the stagnation in its banks. As John Donnelly recollected in his contribution to Des Smyth and Éilis O'Brien's *Golden Guineas: Tales of Irish Bankers, 1920–1970*, there was an innate conservatism which underpinned decision-making: 'I never met a bank manager who was losing sleep because his deposit figures were not growing fast enough, but I saw a few lose their jobs because of the condition of their loan book. The loss incurred in bad debt is tangible . . . Realism is never more at home than in a bank debt that has a stale smell.' And yet, while the impulse was often to say 'no', actually delivering the news was not straightforward:

> Even when a decision is easy, saying 'no' is not easy . . . I found that the more bizarre the proposition, the greater the reluctance to accept rejection. I have, over the years, declined strange ideas ranging from pub purchase in what I was assured was the upmarket area of Rio de Janeiro, to the provision of countless beehives some-where in Russia. The instigators of such schemes shared common characteristics: unbridled imagination that gave them confidence and made them allergic to the word 'no', and a distinct lack of money of their own.[54]

On a more serious note, Donnelly remembered: 'The most difficult time to say "no" is when faced with a marginal proposal from a very good customer. A refusal may often mean losing business.'[55] Donnelly's recollections were confirmed by those of Bill Finn. He wrote of his time in Bank of Ireland at the end of the 1940s and into the 1950s. The ethos of the bank was, according to Finn, arch-conservatism, in its approach: 'The inherited wisdom went like this: "We have the Government accounts, which provide the bulk of our profits. So, keep your head down, obey the rules, avoid blotting your copybook and you will eventually attain the exalted position of agent." It was not surprising then that there was less emphasis on new business. Fresh ideas were rarely entertained.'[56]

In this, there was caution, but there also was duty. When an agreement was struck in 1958 between the National Farmers' Association and the banks to finance a TB-eradication scheme, it was opposed by one banker who wrote that 'the mere spraying of money through the farming community' was a dubious policy. The question posed, however, was what should a banker do when faced with a policy handed down from head office which he opposed?

118

Was there a duty to resist, or 'do we sit dumb in the face of startling changes of banking policy?' These questions went unanswered, though there was concern about 'the invidious position we now find ourselves placed in'.[57]

Another bank official, also writing in 1958, was stark in his description of what he considered to be the greatest problem for bank officials: 'At the moment, Irish banking is in the doldrums. The industry has ceased to expand, and, like any other industry which is not expanding or seeking to expand, it must inevitably begin to stagnate.' The reason for this stagnation was clear: 'Initiative, progress and imagination has been continuously discouraged and, in this stifled atmosphere, stagnation has begun.' More than that, significant innovation at every level was needed to 'lessen staff discontent and dissatisfaction, and to brighten the life of many a frustrated banker'.[58]

III

SOCIAL LIFE IN THE 1950s

The social world of the Irish banks was rooted in old traditions and new recruits to the banks recalled that those old traditions were not easily shifted. Lauri MacDermott, from Killeshandra, County Cavan, remembered his first day at the Bank of Ireland on College Green in Dublin as something of a culture shock. MacDermott entered the bank in 1950 and recalled how his official name now became: 'L. P. P. MacDermott'. He referred to his 'rather strange banking colleagues', none of whom spoke with a Cavan, Mayo or Kerry accent, and none of whom 'even played Gaelic football'. For all that there was initial culture shock, though, there was a ready acclimatisation: 'I came to enjoy their new world of golf, rugby, and even cricket, and their shouts of "Come on Bank" on the sidelines of sporting clashes with our arch-rivals the Munster & Leinster.' More than that, MacDermott recalled the fact that several of the 'serious, middle-aged cashiers' had another side, one which

119

IBOA members pictured at the annual district dinner in Clonmel, 1958.
(IBOA Archive)

revolved around music, song, mime and the playing of practical jokes. After six years, when he left College Green and was transferred to Shannon, he had built 'lifelong friendships'.[59]

Throughout the 1950s, the sporting world described by McDermott remained largely intact. The wider divides of the Irish sporting world also manifested themselves in bank sports. The Gaelic Athletic Association (GAA) continued to impose its ban on GAA members playing rugby, hockey, cricket and golf. That ban was widely defied, however, and not least, it would seem, by GAA men who worked in banks. For example, in the summer of 1955, the annual cricket match between teams representing the married and single men of the Bank of Ireland was played in the grounds of the Pembroke Cricket Club. One of the stars of the show was a 'former star of the GAA' who was credited with some 'lusty batting'. The *Irish Banking Magazine* teasingly gave his name as 'Dxn Bxcxlxy', presumably to ensure he was not the subject of ban-related controversy.[60]

The banks' sporting world was, itself, undergoing change. The existing sporting competitions continued to thrive and remained the most important by a considerable distance, but were now joined by new ones with the establishment of an inter-bank Gaelic Football Cup in 1950. This became an annual event, which quickly gathered significance. In December 1955, for example, the National Bank beat the Bank of Ireland in the final of the competition at Belfield. The 'ban rules' operated by the GAA also prohibited GAA members attending dances organised by 'foreign games' clubs but this seems to have been ignored by the banks. The Gaelic footballers were feted after the match at a dinner in the Bankers' Club and then at a dance organised by the National Bank Ladies' Hockey Club. The *Irish Banking Magazine* lamented: 'There is no report to hand of the winners at these functions.'[61]

What is clear from the recollections of the social life of Irish bank officials is that the vision of a backward, priest-ridden society is far too simplistic. The reality was much more complex than that. The idea that any country can be only one thing at any given time is, of course, a nonsense. For all that the 1950s were suffused with misery and cataclysm, people also had to live. And, in the midst of that living, a lot of people had an awful lot of fun, and many of them were bank officials. Much of that fun revolved around music. This was the era of bands such as The Clipper Carlton, The Dixies, Brendan Bowyer and others. The showbands offered a heady mix of rock-and-roll hits, country-and-western sentimentality, novelty numbers and routines. It was an extraordinary phenomenon. At their peak, there were an estimated 700 showbands touring the country and playing in more than 1,100 ballrooms and dancehalls. The showbands also gave a start in various lines of business to men who later became famous internationally. Van Morrison, for example, started his career in a showband, while the future Taoiseach Albert Reynolds first came to prominence as a promoter of showbands all across the midlands.

Lauri McDermott recalled dipping his toes in this world, alongside the men he worked with or shared digs with: 'My first dance in the Adelaide Ballroom was not an experience I recall with any degree of fondness. Standing at the back of this long narrow hall, fists clenched, I kept promising myself I'd go out for the next dance. Jimmy Masson's band was playing at the other end, but I never got to see him because I never took to the floor. However, I persevered and eventually my limited success led to nerve-racking first dates at the Met or under the clock at Clery's, always hoping she'd turn up!'[62]

The Bankers' Club in Dublin continued to run its repertoire of musical recitals, Sunday afternoon dances, bridge nights, and billiards, snooker, table tennis and squash competitions. To this were added public speaking nights, through the newly formed Hellfire Toastmasters Club.[63] There was also a Gramophone Club with more than 100 members.[64] Soon, traditional entertainments were being put under pressure by the spread of television. The 1950s saw the installation of a television set in the Bankers' Club in Belfast. In November 1955, it was announced that 'subject to reception being satisfactory over a trial period, it is intended to install a television set in the Dublin club'.[65] This was still six years in advance of the establishment of RTÉ, so the club depended on reception from the BBC. The new TV room quickly became a popular aspect of the club, the novelty of watching television drawing in many members. When the BBC broadcast from London an amateur boxing international between Ireland and England in March 1957, the Bankers' Club TV room 'was packed with a cheering sporty crowd egging on the Irish team'.[66] When dry rot was discovered in the club at the end of the 1950s, the bars were overhauled, with new lighting and decor installed.[67]

The great change in the Bankers' Club lay not in technological innovation or in renovations, but in the admittance of female members. The IBOA, throughout the 1950s, pursued a policy which amounted to the slogan 'equal pay for equal work'. Women were elected to the Executive Committee, including Maureen Collins, who was first elected in 1951. Then, in 1958, Collins became the first woman to be elected as an officer of the Association, when she was voted in as Assistant Honorary Secretary and Treasurer.[68] All of this marked the IBOA out as being progressive on matters of equality. It does not, however, tell the full story. The sexism that lay at the heart of Irish banking – and, indeed, of Irish society – was also eloquently displayed in the manner in which the Bankers' Club was run. Before the 1950s, no 'lady clerk' qualified for membership of the Club, which was restricted to men. Finally, at the annual

A large crowd gathers at the Dublin Bankers' Club in November 1953 for 'Question time', organised by the Association's Literary and Debating Society. The breadth of social activity laid on for IBOA members was truly impressive and included musical recitals, Sunday afternoon dances, bridge nights, billiards, snooker, table tennis and squash competitions. In addition, public speaking nights were organised through a newly formed Hellfire Toastmasters. *(IBOA Archive)*

general meeting of the IBOA in March 1952, it was agreed that women would now be admitted to the Bankers' Club. The form of their admittance was nonetheless segregationist. It was agreed that 'special facilities be provided', and to this end 'a room separated from the rest of the premises is to be set aside for their exclusive use'.[69] A special committee was established to run the room as a club for women. In the room would be magazines and newspapers, cards and card tables would be supplied, and the squash court would be available for use on every second Saturday.[70]

The Club Room for women opened on 1 December 1952. Reporting on that event, Ethne Stephens, secretary to the new Ladies' Club, wrote in the *Irish Banking Magazine*: 'The ghosts of ancient misogynists must have clanked dismally outside the Bankers' Club on the evening of December 1st last. For the unheard of had happened – one of their fortresses had capitulated and the women were in. The hallowed, purely masculine stronghold, guarded so long and jealously from female intrusion, had traitorously let down its portcullis to admit the hordes of women of every age, description, category and bank.' On opening night, one 'lady clerk' played music, others served 'toothsome sandwiches and cakes of superlative lusciousness', and there was general approval of the way the women had transformed their new room with a 'froth of femininity'. Also present were 'semi-submerged dark splotches, which on closer examination proved to be men – ten of them'. These men offered fulsome welcome to the women and urged them to make their presence felt throughout the building. It is clear that not all men were joyous at the new development. As Ethne Stephens triumphantly concluded: 'At this enormity, the moping shades outside tucked their heads under their arms and, with eldritch shrieks, departed into the night.'[71] Momentum means much in history, of course, and once the door had been opened to 'lady clerks' the world of the Irish Bankers' Club was entirely changed; to the extent, indeed, that by the end of 1958, a 'mixed lounge' was also opened in the Club.[72] The decades that followed heralded even greater change.

6

The 1960s

The 1960s brought significant social and economic change in Ireland. This change was rooted, of course, in the economic woes which had bedevilled Ireland in the 1950s and which had seen the country almost slide into bankruptcy. The 1960s, by contrast, brought much more optimism. It is not the case that Ireland was redrawn overnight, but there was a genuine sense of a new beginning. This sense of a new beginning was compounded by the departure of Éamon de Valera from the office of Taoiseach in the summer of 1959. De Valera had been in failing health in the 1950s. More particularly, he had passed months on end in the Netherlands being operated on and receiving care for his eyes; he was essentially blind by the end of the decade. He was replaced as Taoiseach by his long-time deputy, Seán Lemass. Although Lemass was, like de Valera, a veteran of the 1916 Rising, the fact that he was actually seventeen years younger lent credence to the idea that this was a new beginning.

I

A NEW BEGINNING FOR IRELAND

Even before Seán Lemass had assumed the mantle of Taoiseach, there had been a significant shift in government policy. In the early months of 1957, a civil servant, T. K. Whitaker, who had been appointed Secretary of the Department of Finance in 1956, assembled a team of fellow civil servants to work in small groups to produce a report which would analyse the state of the Irish economy and which would look at ways to make that economy grow. The result was the publication in May 1958 of a 250-page report, which was simply called 'Economic Development'. This report stimulated a whole range of departmental and governmental contributions in the intervening months and formed the core of a new government white paper, which was called the *Programme for Economic Expansion*. It was published in November 1958 and was intended to act as a blueprint for the economy from 1958 to 1963. The *Programme* still stressed that agriculture should drive economic development, most notably through increased export of cattle and beef. All the key investments in the *Programme*, however, were targeted at promoting industry. Systems were set up to allow better access to loans and the courting of foreign investment, as well as improved grants to new industries and tax reliefs for manufactured exports. Across the five years of the *Programme for Economic Expansion* it was proposed to invest some £53.4 million – less than £14 million of that was to go to agriculture.

A new Act – the Industrial Development (Encouragement of External Investment) Act – was passed. The ambition of this new Act was to attract investment from foreign companies to come and set up in Ireland and to use the country as a base from which to export. And all of this made an almost immediate difference. By 1965, 80 per cent of all investment in Irish industry came from foreign capital and during the 1960s 350 new foreign companies were established in Ireland. In general, foreign investment facilitated major advances in the industrial sector, which was largely responsible for overall economic growth during the course of the *Programme for Economic Expansion*. Agricultural output remained frustratingly low, but Irish industry finally took off. And, with this, the Irish economy took a great leap forwards. From having had the slowest growth rate of any European economy in the 1950s, economic growth in Ireland reached 4 per cent per year in the years between 1958 and 1963.

Closely associated with this wider economic development were dramatic changes to the structures of banking in Ireland, north and south. These changes were designed to resist the threat of external takeover and of increased competition from abroad, as well as being designed to pursue economies of scale.[1] At the heart of this lay an unprecedented amalgamation of banks. The process had commenced in 1958 when the Bank of Ireland took over the Hibernian Bank. In 1966, the National Bank was also taken over by the Bank of Ireland. Alongside, an expanded Bank of Ireland a new banking force was constructed – Allied Irish Banks. This bank was created with the merger of three existing banks: the Munster and Leinster Bank, the Provincial Bank, and the Royal Bank. Further banking change, whose impact was felt largely north of the border, came in 1970 when Northern Bank (already part of the British-owned Midland Bank) absorbed the Belfast Bank. Increased competition in banking came with the emergence of banks from North America and Europe in the late 1960s and early 1970s; these captured more than 10 per cent of the banking market in this time.[2]

From the beginning of this process, the IBOA adopted the rationale that it could not do anything to prevent the consolidation process, nor should it. It welcomed the progressive aspects of the development and understood that it was in the interests of the better operation of banking in Ireland. There was concern at the potential for redundancies, reduced promotional opportunities and the safe-guarding of the welfare of bank officials. Assuaged on these points, the IBOA generally supported the bank mergers. There was concern that the two new powerful groupings of Bank of Ireland and Allied Irish Banks were going to fill senior executive positions from outside the banking profession.[3] All concerns were tempered by the reality that ultimately there was little that the IBOA could do.

In tandem with the consolidation process, there came a rapid extension of banking services through the establishment of sub-offices. In July 1962, the *Irish Banking Magazine* reported on this development: 'Traditionally, the banks were used by business, professional and white collared classes. The changing face of society has seen the increased numbers and prosperity of the industrial workers, the well-paid operatives, an entire class who knew not Caesar. So, it became necessary, for the good of both of them, that Caesar show his wares. The sub-offices are part of the effort to do this. There is now scarcely an industrial area, or an area where industrial workers live, into which some Bank has not found its way.'[4]

Analysing this development, a senior bank official and later Honorary Secretary of the IBOA, Brendan O'Donoghue, wrote in 1967 that this effort to expand was not straightforward:

> The Banks still project an image of remoteness which constitutes a formidable barrier . . . It is indeed a fact that Banks up to quite recent times were not that terribly interested in the man in the street. Consequently, an accurate and valid image of remoteness was given to many people. Fortunately, this attitude has changed. The Banks are now anxious to deal with everybody but the man in the street is hardly aware of the change; the image of remoteness remains and undoubtedly will remain unless a conscious policy to dislodge that image is undertaken.'[5]

O'Donoghue acknowledged that the service provided by bank officials was vital to attracting new customers to banks, but that there was a limit to what this might achieve. He called instead for the banks to adopt a more progressive approach to advertising. The banks, he noted, had so far made no connection between their 'image' and their 'advertising', to the point where 'the two words have scarcely reached the courtship stage, not to talk of their marriage being consummated into an intelligent publicity campaign'. O'Donoghue described the current attempts of the banks to advertise as providing sufficient material for a work entitled 'How not to advertise!' Finally, he called on the reorganised banking system to entirely overhaul its image through advertising: 'What is needed to do this is the full symphonic treatment of the modern mass media.'[6]

While banking change presented new difficulties for the Irish banks, it also presented significant challenges to the IBOA. In October 1968 an editorial in the *Irish Banking Magazine* welcomed the emergence of two big groups in southern Irish banking, the 'girding of their loins' by the northern banks and the plethora of foreign and merchant banks, but expressed concern that 'pressures never before experienced by the staffs of the Irish banks have resulted'.[7] The editorial agreed that banking on the island had needed a shake-up, but worried about the impact it might have on officials: 'For too long, all policy has been dictated by precedents written with quill pens. A change was indisputably needed. When the winds of change began to blow few expected them to be so far reaching or to have gathered such momentum so quickly. But it was inevitable that once the pace was set all the banks would set about outdoing the other as fast as their resources would permit.'[8] In the longer term, these words were to prove bitterly prophetic.

II

BEING A BANK OFFICIAL IN THE 1960s

Throughout the 1960s, women who worked in Irish banks continued to be paid considerably less than their male counterparts. During the 1950s, the IBOA had adopted the position that women who worked in Irish banks should be given equal pay to that of men who did the same work. On top of that, the idea that the normal promotion structure as applied to men should also be applied to women was supported by the Association. At successive Arbitration meetings with the banks in the 1950s and the 1960s, the IBOA argued for the position of women with regard to pay, promotion, special allowances and bonuses, to be improved. These arguments were usually rejected by Arbitrators who, according to the IBOA, did not understand that the duties of men and women in the banks were interchangeable, even if women were denied formal promotion. During this time there were some breakthroughs. In 1961 the Ulster Bank appointed a number of women to work as Mechanisation Supervisors, Assistant Mechanisation Supervisors and Ledger Clerks, and in doing so also increased their pay.[9]

As well as occasional breakthroughs, there were also occasional matters of dispute. In the summer of 1963, it was reported that some banks had begun to train what were now being called 'lady officials' as tellers. This presented a dilemma for the IBOA. While it might welcome the advance of 'lady officials', it sought also to protect the rights of its men. In this instance, the essential problem was that 'lady officials' would now be doing the work of men, but doing it at a much reduced rate of pay. Why then would the banks not prefer to promote from amongst the 1,500 'lady officials' rather from the men, when it would be less expensive for them to do so. And, with the number of women employed by the banks climbing and climbing, the potential outcome here was obvious. The Organising Secretary of the IBOA, John Titterington, wrote to the Irish Bankers' Joint Committee on 22 July 1963 to say that 'unless the Banks paid lady cashiers the male scale, plus the rank allowance, strict measures would be taken even to the extent of the withdrawal of labour . . . The Executive Committee are not prepared to allow the Banks to cheapen this important position.'[10] In the event the matter was the subject of negotiations between the banks and the IBOA through 1964 and 1965. There was no resolution and discontent on this matter was influential in provoking strike in 1966.

The plight of underpaid women bank officials as portrayed by the *Irish Banking Magazine* in March 1963. With little success, the IBOA routinely pressed the interests of so-called 'lady officials' at Arbitration meetings with the banks throughout the 1950s and 1960s. *(IBOA Archive)*

Thank heaven for little girls, without them what would little boys do?

276

March, 1963

130

Discrepancies between the amount of money paid by the Irish banks to men and to women was not by any means the only matter of division between bank officials. The idea that bank officials were a single, homogenous entity, struggling together for their common prosperity, is not an accurate one. It is clear that there continued to be serious differences between junior and senior bank officials. In previous decades, junior officials affiliated to the IBOA had occasionally alleged that the Association had been willing to sacrifice the interests of junior members at the altar of providing for the needs of seniors. This allegation was overstated but there was, nonetheless, a tension between juniors and seniors which surfaced even in the pages of the *Irish Banking Magazine*. In April 1961, for example, the magazine had published a poem written by a junior, which included the lines:

A word in favour of the junior clerk,
So subject to the raucous senior clerk,
Just fresh from school he comes, a sitting duck
For ill-considered spleen; with the bad luck
To have, perhaps, to spend his better years
In some outlandish village, where he fears
Almost to raise his voice in case he might
Infringe the sacred code that holds him tight,
While his own brother as a student finds
The life of Reilly's his – and no-one minds
So let the higher ups on him go slow,
For they were juniors not so long ago.

The frustration of junior bank officials was rooted, at least partially, in the nature of their employment. Brendan Smith recalled the tedium of work in the Bank of Ireland on the Falls Road in Belfast: 'The daily routine was never-ending. The ledgers were hand-posted. Columns were totted and accounts balanced. Passbooks, in those pre-statement days, were written up and woe-betide you if you did not keep them up to date. Interest was calculated manually and double-checked. Cheques, lodged by customers, were sorted into individual banks and sent to London or Dublin after they were balanced with the teller. It was a rare occasion when both parties agreed. If they did not, a lengthy call-off of all cheques followed until the error was found.'[11] Brendan Fullam also noted the relentless aspect of the work: 'Your accuracy with figures was constantly put to the test. The real marathon took place once a month when the thrift accounts had to be balanced. There were pages and pages consisting of fifty lines to the page to be extracted and totted. And to make matters more difficult, it was the era of L-S-D [pounds, shillings and pence].'[12]

Bank officials at work in the Ulster Bank on College Green, 1 February 1968.
(RTÉ Stills Library)

There were other issues. Two-handed branches were considered the 'scourge of the service'. If either the manager or the cashier was absent for even a day, he had to be replaced. Stories survive of people unable to take a day off to attend even a family funeral when no replacement could be found.[13] The facilities in the environment where bank officials worked were rudimentary. Fullam recalled how, when he first arrived to work in Killorglin, County Kerry, in January 1953, the branch had only the bare necessities. There wasn't even a telephone . . . In the winter a turf fire burned in the office and gave the place a homely atmosphere. But the overall office appearance was like a scene from Dickens. Only the quill pen was missing. On every desk there was an ink well and what we called an ordinary pen which consisted of a wooden handle, a holder and a nib. Biros were banned. If you wanted to use a fountain pen you bought your own. The men of Sparta would have felt at home. I also served in a branch in those early days where there was no office typewriter. The manager had a small portable one and when he went on holidays letters had to be written by hand.'[14]

It was the tedium of this world which people such as Bunny Carr and Christy Moore sought to escape. There was change, however. At least since the late 1920s, members of the IBOA had speculated on what impact increased mechanisation might have on the work of bankers. There was fear that it would undermine the position of officials and even see them displaced by machines; there was also optimism that such mechanisation would remove the worst of the drudgery from their daily work. By the 1960s, bankers were getting the opportunity to find out. A bank official wrote that it was 'heartening to note that more and more branches are being equipped with accounting machines'. This machine inherited the role of the old-time ledger clerk with his steel pen. It was enough to bring the bank official to dream 'that the day is not far distant when the stacks of notes and bundles of cheques may be safely left in the capable hands of streamlined machines, and our abilities devoted to the many interesting and complex problems presented by banking today'.[15]

Mechanisation could not, of course, deflect from the truism that work was still work. And the escape from work at the bank in the evenings and at weekends provided the opportunity for a vibrant social life. The 1960s saw the Dublin Bankers' Club flourish. In January 1961, the writer Brendan Behan came to the club and spoke for 90 minutes on 'The present state of Irish theatre'. A huge

Staff in the Munster and Leinster Bank in Tralee, 1966. This modern office environment contrasted favourably with much of what had gone before. Recalling his
experience of arriving as a bank official in Killorglin in January 1953, Brendan
Fullam remarked that 'the branch had only the bare necessities. There wasn't even
a telephone . . . In the winter a turf fire burned in the office and gave the place a
homely atmosphere. But the overall office appearance was like a scene from
Dickens.' *(Kennelly Archive)*

crowd turned up on the night and were wooed by a masterful performance.[16] In general, the increased numbers of bank staff hired in the late 1950s and into the early 1960s helped boost attendance at events. Amidst a boom in revenue, facilities in the club were renovated. A Volkswagen was raffled in 1968 to help pay for renovations and, in 1969, it was agreed to develop another new bar; this opened for business in December 1970.[17] The diverse activities in the club throughout the decade were critical to ensuring its ongoing success. From squash and table tennis to debating and social events, the club proved adept at drawing in bank officials. Several hundred people regularly attended cheese-and-wine or cocktail parties. The Honorary Secretary of the Bankers' Club, M. P. Hartnett was moved to remark that the atmosphere on such nights 'after the initial intake of alcohol proved what a sociable group bankers can be'.[18]

Sociability extended beyond the confines of the island. On 6 June 1969 a party of seventeen soccer players, six tennis players and two officials flew out from Dublin airport to Madrid where they competed in the Sixth International Banking Games, organised by the Club Banesto, the sports club of Banco Espanol de Credito. The

Bank officials by night: Michael Chambers and Anita Begley do the 'twist' at the Munster and Leinster dance in Dublin in early 1962. *(IBOA Archive)*

135

officials were drawn from AIB, but they endured a series of defeats. The soccer team lost all three matches to French, Italian and Spanish opposition. Of the tennis players, only Diane Rowell prospered to reach the semi-finals. For all that the results on the field may have disappointed there seems to have been much fun off it, not least at an 'Irish night' reception thrown at the Irish Embassy.[19]

In general, sporting interests were a central part of the social life of bankers. The sportsmen and women who were employed by the banks in the 1960s demonstrated the extent to which the profile of officials had diversified since the establishment of the IBOA. Men such as an official of the Royal Bank in Dublin, Billy Walsh, continued very much in the established tradition of play, which dated from the late nineteenth century. Walsh was a hockey star who had played for the Leinster Schools team against a touring British Army team in 1948. He later won numerous Leinster senior medals and pushed for a place in the Irish team. Walsh also played rugby, soccer and golf for his bank's teams, in competitions, which had now been established for several decades.[20] Sport in the banks had been transformed after the Second World War through the adoption of Gaelic games. There was, for example, the establishment of an Inter-Bank Hurling Competition in the summer of 1961. Four banks entered teams and the final was played at Islandbridge in Dublin. A National Bank team, spearheaded by the Kilkenny hurler Seán Clohessy, comfortably defeated a team from the Provincial Bank, amongst whose stars was Eddie Keher, another Kilkenny hurler who went on to become a legend of the game.[21]

III

THE THREE-MONTH STRIKE

Although the 1960s are remembered as a time of considerable change in Irish banking, there were also serious echoes of previous decades with the emergence of more industrial unrest. In 1964, 'strike notice was served in Northern Ireland, postponed, served again in the Republic of Ireland and finally the strike was averted at the eleventh hour by the institution of new dispute machinery in the form of a Joint Industrial Council'.[22] One Council operated for the Republic of Ireland, while a second operated in Northern Ireland. Initially, these Councils operated relatively smoothly. Under the system, in the autumn of 1965 claims by the IBOA for the revision of the overtime system and for increased payment of weekend and bank holiday rates were agreed by the banks. Ominously, however, these claims had initially been refused by the banks at Council meetings and were only conceded when bank officials north and south informed the banks that they would no longer work overtime until their requests were acceded to.[23] The question now would be what would happen when the IBOA pushed for salary increases.

Increased wage demands were a regular feature of Irish life in the mid-1960s. The IBOA still did not wish to be associated with the wider trade union movement, however. When the Irish Congress of Trade Unions recommended in early 1966 to its affiliate unions that they should seek a flat £1 per week increase in the coming round of negotiations, the IBOA was displeased. Such a measure, it believed, might be 'suitable for the lower paid unskilled worker but certainly it is not appropriate for the craft unions and unions, such as ours, catering for white-collared workers on incremental salary scales'.[24] In part, this attitude reflects the tradition of the IBOA standing apart from mainstream trade unionism. Instead of joining the ICTU, for twenty years the IBOA had been affiliated to the Irish Conference of Professional and Service Associations. The other affiliated bodies included the Irish National Teachers' Organisation, the Guild of Assurance Officials, and the Civil Service Executive and Higher Officers' Association.

This attitude manifested itself when some members of the IBOA voiced criticism of the Executive Committee at meetings in Dublin in December 1965.[25] The view of some members, it would appear, was that the IBOA was behaving too much like a trade union. John Titterington was not impressed with this view. As the *Irish Banking Magazine* reported, he 'emphasised at each and every meeting that our only method of securing increased remuneration was by Trade Union action'. The magazine continued: 'It is now apparent that should the Executive Committee decide to place a Salary Claim before the Joint Industrial Council, a determined and united Association must be prepared to follow the Claim through with a strike if necessary. Should any member or group of members feel otherwise, now is the time to declare their hand to the Executive Committee and not as previously happened in the middle of the crisis.'[26]

This was a reference to the dispute over salaries at the end of 1964. In 1962 the IBOA had sought a salary increase of 15 per cent for its members, citing the rising cost of living and the increased salaries being enjoyed by workers in other sections of the economy. In response, the matter went to arbitration in 1964, but the claims of the IBOA were largely rejected.[27] The *Irish Banking Magazine* railed against the behaviour of the banks, who argued that bank officials were merely ordinary clerical workers and, as such, were actually overpaid: 'This deliberate belittling of our members has angered the Association . . . What has developed in the past few weeks . . . has very regrettably created the very worst relations ever known between the two parties.'[28] But the magazine also looked closer to home when apportioning blame. It was clearly of the view that higher salaries could have been achieved had it not been for the actions of some of its own membership: 'The Executive were embarrassed and impeded by disloyal proposals and views expressed by a handful of members in Dublin and in Northern Ireland . . . That the Association was not fully successful in securing a universally acceptable salary settlement is largely attributable to the delinquency of this minority of members whose motives must remain as suspect as those of the people who resigned from the Association in previous disputes.'[29]

Where once the Executive Committee and the *Irish Banking Magazine* were voices of restraint holding back the more radical of its membership, there was now a stridency associated with the demands that were being made and this stridency was the inevitable consequence of the repeated feeling of being hard done by.[30] As it turned out, strike was only narrowly averted in 1964, but there was no such escape in 1966. In March 1966, the IBOA balloted the membership and the result of that ballot was to give an over-whelming mandate for strike action. The reason for strike was straightforward: the belief that it was essential to fight for a proper and just salary structure for Irish banking. Wrapped around the desire for higher salaries was exasperation at what the IBOA believed was the unending desire of the banks to deny them their rights. The editorial in the *Irish Banking Magazine* noted in April 1966: 'The members are fed up! Their patience has been tried too far. They now realise that only a grim and bitter struggle can win justice. They now realise that talking will not provide a solution to their problems. And this time they are not bluffing!'

When the annual general meeting of the IBOA was held at the Crofton Airport Hotel in Dublin on Saturday 23 April 1966, the mood of militancy was apparent. The difficulty for the banks was how they might respond. Now bound into the policy of the Federated Union of Employers, they were restricted to offer an increase of 3 per cent for bank officials in the Republic of Ireland and 3½ per cent in Northern Ireland. This was viewed as derisory by the IBOA (seeking an additional 7 per cent in the south and 11 per cent in the north), not least because of the soaring profits made by the banks. It was pointed out that 'the Bank of Ireland were able to find £12,200,000 the other day to buy the National Bank during a credit squeeze! The offers made by the banks would cost them £185,000 in the Republic and £90,000 in Northern Ireland. This cost would be shared by ten banks. One after another again this year the Banks announced hugely increased profits. The Ulster Bank's profits went up by 58 per cent! Why then are the Banks resisting the payment of a few paltry thousand to their staff?'[31]

The strike, which for months had seemed inevitable, began when banks closed their doors at 5 p.m. on 5 May 1966. North and south of the border, 10 head offices and 900 branches ceased to function. In the days before the strike, many businesses began to withdraw large amounts of money for their staffs and for general company use. Indeed, the day before the strike started was deemed one of the busiest days in years as thousands of private individuals also sought to make withdrawals and complete other transactions.[32] It had been agreed that 3,400 junior bank officials should go on strike in support of their pay increase. Senior bank officials were not to strike, as it was planned to use their salaries to contribute to the strikers' pay. The banks issued protective notice, however, and laid off 4,000 senior bank officials. Senior bank officials turned up for work and sought injunctions from the high court to restrain the banks from dismissing them.[33] The banks also launched a public relations campaign to undermine further the position of the IBOA. Donal Carroll, chairman of the Banks' Staff Relations Committee, held a press conference in Dublin on 20 May 1966 in which he lamented the campaign mounted by the IBOA 'to disable the banks'.

As the strike gathered momentum, hundreds of the younger bank officials went to England to work for the duration of the strike.[34] The women went to work in secretarial positions, usually in London. The men took up temporary jobs in pubs and factories. A few went to France and Germany, and others even went picking tomatoes in Jersey.[35] Seventy of the bank officials who had moved to London during the strike met on Sunday 22 May 1966 at Speakers' Corner in Hyde Park. They stood around in groups discussing the situation in Ireland. Many were based in branches in small-town Ireland and viewed the transition to London as an exciting adventure. They arranged to meet again to organise a welfare fund for any hardship cases. The following Wednesday night a dance and bacon-and-cabbage dinner was organised for the bank officials in the Irish Centre in Camden Town.[36]

Within a week of the strike starting, J. H. Scott of the Industrial Relations Branch of the Northern Ireland Ministry of Health and Social Services was presiding over talks at Stormont between both parties. The speculation was that bank officials in the north were not as committed to the strike as their southern counterparts. The talks rumbled on for several weeks until, finally, an offer from the banks to pay bank officials in Northern Ireland an immediate increase of 3½ per cent, followed by a further 3½ per cent in January 1967 was put to a ballot of northern members. They voted acceptance.[37] Banks in Northern Ireland reopened on 20 June 1966, having been closed for six weeks.[38]

Talks in Dublin to resolve the strike in the Republic of Ireland were considered cordial, but were fruitless.[39] The talking continued week after week, but to no end. An *Irish Times* editorial lambasted the bank officials: 'On the face of it, a bank strike is crazy. Crazy in economic terms; crazy in terms of how bank people behave elsewhere and were expected to behave here until they proved the contrary in 1951, when they struck for seven weeks, made a loud noise in public, but failed really to disrupt the country . . . Perhaps it went only to show that even bank clerks are not indispensable. Whatever the reason, the country enjoyed the spectacle of a body of men who in London would be bowler-hatted, well-umbrellaed and impeccably shoe-shined, parading the streets with placards.' The editorial concluded that the IBOA was pursuing a 'fantastic claim' of 'lunatic nature', that nothing had been done to substantiate the claim which seemed to have 'little basis in justice', and that the strike was injurious to the national interest.[40]

The *Irish Banking Magazine* responded that the article was a 'morass of irrational nonsensical statements'.[41] On the whole, the reaction of press and public to the strike was restrained. For example, J. R. Dick, president of the Dublin Chamber of Commerce downplayed the impact of the strike, even as it entered its third month: 'Everyone seems to have worked out his own salvation. There are no major problems at all.'[42] By July 1966, John Titterington was estimating that most of the junior officials in the Republic of Ireland were now working in England. Money was collected to alleviate the needs of those who remained. The IBOA received assistance from banking unions across the world as it dealt with the impact of the strike on its members. For instance, a letter was received from the South African Society of Bank Officials and enclosed was a cheque for £100 to 'alleviate hardship resulting from the strike'.[43]

At some point, of course, a solution had to be found and at the beginning of July 1966, both sides met again at the Labour Court. Negotiations lasted seven days and there seemed to be considerable progress made, before the talks collapsed on 8 July 1966, with IBOA representatives unhappy at the level of increase secured for junior officials. Just before the talks collapsed, it had appeared that a deal was imminent. Banks had offered to pay significant compensation to senior bank officials (80 per cent of their salary over the period) whom they had locked out of work. The IBOA agreed to this offer, but would accept it only on condition of junior officials receiving additional money. When the banks refused this, the deal fell apart.[44]

On 11 July 1966 further efforts were made by Dermot McDermott, the Labour Court's Chief Conciliation Officer, to re-establish negotiations. Renewed meetings took place between the banks and the IBOA at which it became apparent that no additional money would be provided for junior officials. The IBOA negotiators were in a quandary. They were left with a situation where they were essentially being offered much the same 3 per cent that had been refused before the strike. There were also on offer some improvements to structures and scales of pay, a revised approach to pensions and overtime. Further, a job evaluation was to be undertaken to assess future pay scales for women. When the Labour Court made recommendations which basically supported the position of the banks, the IBOA was in still greater difficulty. After eleven weeks, the strike was clearly going nowhere.[45]

These matters were considered at length by the 32-person Executive Committee of the IBOA on 18, 19 and 20 July 1966. The outcome, as John Titterington explained, was that 'the Executive Committee have unanimously decided that a stage has been reached where the members must be given the opportunity to express their opinions by secret ballot'.[46] Titterington acknowledged the disappointment that nothing meaningful had been achieved for junior officials: 'The Executive Committee have been very conscious that no immediate benefits were being given to junior officials and we have fought every day of the negotiations to bring home to the Banks that a denial of concessions and improvements to those on strike will result in bitterness and severely strain the loyalty of those on whom the future of the service will depend.'[47]

Ballot papers were immediately circulated and returned by 28 July 1966. The decision was to accept the terms and to return to work. After three months – or 84 days – Irish banks opened once more.[48] The fallout from the strike was recriminatory, however. There was overwhelming disgust from some junior and female officials who believed that once again they had been let down or, worse still, sacrificed. More than that, there was disgust that senior officials were to be compensated for their time on strike, while

142

In an effort to bring an end to a strike that was then into its third month, IBOA negotiators – (l–r) T. E. Meade, Executive Committee member, John Titterington, Organising Secretary, and P. F. O'Grady-Walshe, Honorary Secretary – arrive at the Labour Court in July 1966. The strike would ultimately end with a ballot of IBOA members at the end of July. *(IBOA Archive)*

juniors were to be left without anything. Two employees, who signed themselves as 'Two Junior Ladies', were bitter in their criticism of the deal struck by the Executive Committee in a letter written to John Titterington. They decried their efforts as 'ludicrous' and 'all bluff':

> It seems to us that we would gain more by spending the
> £10 p.a. which we contribute to the IBOA on masses in
> the hope that by some miracle [we receive] the fair play
> and equal share which both the Executive Committee

and the Banks have denied us . . . We would like a detailed statement of what yourself and your 'brilliant' Executive Committee have in store for us in the future. If your plans are to take any course parallel to your last fiasco then you may cancel our membership forthwith as we realise we have been the sacrificial lambs so far.[49]

In the aftermath of the strike, it was hoped to make further progress through the Joint Industrial Council. Throughout 1967 and then into 1968 there were attempts to advance the position of bank officials. None was successful in any meaningful sense. Then, in the south, preliminary meetings between the banks and the IBOA on the introduction of a new salary scale began on 18 May 1968. Full meetings of the Joint Industrial Council took place in Dublin on 6 and 7 June 1968 and in Belfast on 14 June 1968. Further meetings took place in July in Dublin and an agreement was reached which was swiftly put to a vote of IBOA members. The *Irish Banking Magazine* was able to report in August 1968 that the agreement had been endorsed by a substantial majority of IBOA members and that 'the milestone of a negotiated salary settlement has been passed and the new salary scales have already been implemented'. Agreement in Belfast came more slowly, not because the banks and the IBOA disagreed, but because the Department of Employment and Productivity at Westminster was required to sign off on the deal to ensure that it complied with the United Kingdom's prices and incomes policy.[50] Even in agreement, however, there were serious concerns for the future. There was an acknowledgement that a significant minority of what were called 'dissidents' were not satisfied and regarded the agreement as inadequate. The great majority of these dissidents lay in the ranks of junior bank officials. Their discontent was treated with a degree of dismissiveness within the IBOA: 'The younger member, like youth everywhere, is continually striving for improvement and probably could never be satisfied.'[51] The discontent was real, however, and was soon to flare up with considerable force. The salary agreement of 1968 was soon in considerable difficulty; the disputes of the 1960s continued long into the 1970s.

7

1970s

The 1970s were a decade of discord. By the start of the decade, the optimism that had attended the conclusion of the 1968 Agreement had entirely evaporated and the IBOA was setting itself on a path of growing militancy. On 23 January 1970, a mass meeting of members of the Association was held at the Metropole Hotel on Dublin's O'Connell Street. A resolution was passed promising support for any action the Executive Committee considered necessary to restore the standard of living of members.[1] The Metropole meeting was only one of many. Throughout the months of January and February 1970, more meetings were held in towns and cities across the country. They drew huge crowds: nearly 4,000 members attended the five major gatherings, many of them travelling long distances to participate in an impressive show of strength.[2] These mass meetings were held in an atmosphere that was highly charged and occasionally intemperate,[3] yet the message to emerge from each was consistent and unequivocal: the Executive Committee were to take whatever steps were necessary to bring about an immediate and 'realistic' increase in the salaries of members.[4]

The root cause of this frenzy of popular activism was the steep rise in the cost of living. Inflation soared in Ireland, just as it had in many European countries in the late 1960s, an international trend driven by, amongst other things, increased American-led demand.[5]

145

John Titterington addresses a mass meeting of IBOA members in Dublin's Metropole Hotel on 23 January 1970. *(IBOA Archive)*

From 1968 until 1972, the Consumer Price Index in the Republic spiralled upwards at an average annual rate of 8.3 per cent.[6] The response of trade unions was to press for wage increases to negate the loss to their purchasing power. The pacesetters on the issue were not the IBOA, but a group of maintenance craft workers, who embarked on strike action in 1969.[7] The controversial strike lasted for nine weeks and ended with the employers acquiescing to their demands. The maintenance workers achieved a 20 per cent increase in their wages and they were followed shortly afterwards by building workers who achieved a similar rise.[8] For trade unions, as much as anyone else, there were clear lessons to be drawn from these triumphs. The IBOA certainly drew them. On 9 October

1969, in the wake of a motion unanimously passed at the previous April's Annual Delegates Meeting, John Titterington wrote to E. Grace of the Banks' Staff Relations Commission setting out a demand on the part of all bank officials – junior and senior, male and female – for a 'substantial general increase in salaries'. Other claims were made for a revision of differentials, for automatic promotion for men and women to the Senior Bank Official scale and for a variety of adjustments to the provisions relating to pensions, fringe benefits, overtime and hours of opening. Despite the menu of demands, there was clarity as to the primacy of pay.[9] It had already been publicly acknowledged, John Titterington observed, 'that lower position workers are entitled to increases because of their position in the community' and bank officials were entitled to at least the same.[10] Perhaps even more so: in a throwback to an argument which had been used in the very first months of the existence of the

A section of the large attendance at an IBOA meeting, 23 January 1970. *(IBOA Archive)*

IBOA it was claimed that the erosion of earnings hit bank officials more heavily than others because of the necessity to 'maintain a good social status to "live up to" their high responsibilities'.[11] The speed at which prices rose undoubtedly played to old anxieties about societal roles, but it also struck hard at the officials' sense of financial security. It placed bank officials in a predicament that the pages of the *Irish Banking Magazine* presented in the starkest of terms. 'Never before', the magazine's editorial declared in January 1970, 'has there been such hardship imposed on the lives of bank officials and their families'.[12]

I

WAR OR FAMINE

Alleviating this hardship and pressing the claim for a salary increase necessitated a revisiting by the bank managements and bank officials of the terms of the June 1968 Agreement. Intended to run for a period of two years ending in June 1970, the Agreement had begun to unravel almost before the ink on it had dried. As inflation began to climb, a trend aggravated by the government's mini-budget of November 1968, attention came to centre on a clause in the Agreement which held that it could be reconsidered in the event of 'extraordinary circumstances'. For the IBOA, the rapid escalation in the cost of living constituted just such circumstances. The banks took a radically different view. One employer expressed the view that extraordinary circumstances excluded almost everything short of the extremes of 'war or famine'. Indeed, the banks as a whole clung to the narrowest of interpretations of the clause, using it first as a device not to engage in meeting with the Association and then as a means to avoid addressing their core concerns. At meetings of the Joint Industrial Council in November and December 1969, the banks maintained their denial of 'extraordinary circumstances', but agreed to have the clause, if not the claim, put to arbitration.

It was against this backdrop that the series of mass meetings were held in the early months of 1970. In the vacuum that existed, mistrust between the two sides deepened and the IBOA, emboldened by the mandate it received at the meetings, began to prepare itself for industrial action. Circulars were issued to members stressing the need for unity and discipline. Members were impressed as to the importance of 'rigid observance' of fixed hours of work and in towns where more than one bank existed and where no local committees were already in place, it advised the establishment of a Town Committee to monitor the enforcement of the Association's instructions and report any infringements that took place. Established local committees were to do the same.[13] This was all by way of preparation for the action taken by the bank officials on 2 March to work restricted hours and to curtail the services of the banks, including opening hours to the public.

From that moment, events moved rapidly. The following day, the Labour Court appointed Trinity College academic and future government minister, Professor Martin O'Donoghue, as chairman of the arbitration tribunal. His finding, issued eight days later, rejected IBOA claims to 'extraordinary circumstances'.[14] The IBOA, in turn, rebuffed by way of a ballot the finding of the Tribunal and by the end of March, the banks had informed the Association that salaries, far from being increased, would actually be reduced by 25 per cent to take account of the reduced hours being worked.[15] The escalation of the dispute continued through the month of April 1970. When the banks sought to transfer staff to the Clearing House to deal with a backlog of work created by the restriction on working hours, the IBOA instructed its members to reduce its hours further so that the total number of hours worked would not exceed that being done before the transfers. The banks reacted by suspending all staff working in the Clearing House and followed by closing their doors to the public.

The banks stayed shut from 30 April until 17 November 1970.[16] There were several attempts to break the impasse in the intervening months, all of them unsuccessful. The government, which had advocated the capping of salary increases to a maximum of 7 per cent, placed the blame for the logjam flatly at the door of the IBOA. The Minister for Labour, Joseph Brennan, criticised the Association for failing to enter negotiations unconditionally.[17] This was a reference to the Association's insistence on a cash payment or retrospective salary increase for the period before June 1970 (when the 1968 Agreement was due to elapse) and the need for negotiations on the restoration of the 25 per cent salary that had been cut by the banks following the restriction on working hours in March 1970.[18] As far as the IBOA was concerned, its members were not seeking payment for going on strike, but for being effectively 'locked out' by their employers.[19] Indeed, they insisted that the action of the banks in cutting salaries was unprecedented, contrasting greatly with their reaction in 1955 when, during a similar dispute, staff worked restricted hours.[20] The IBOA was undeterred by the opposition of government, insisting that the campaign of restricted hours was justified on the grounds that, ultimately, it was about survival – 'Survival for the members as people; Survival for the Association as a members' trade union; Survival of the dignity of bank officials.'[21]

In many ways, the hard-line approach of the bank officials ran counter to their own instincts. They still perceived themselves to be an essentially conservative force in society and they continued to prize loyalty to the banks against which they had set themselves.[22] Against that, there was a belief that some elements within the banks were bent on the destruction of the Association. This was bolstered by reports that managements at Ulster Bank and the Bank of Ireland Group had been pressurised to distance themselves from their colleagues and resign from the Association.[23] One ex-bank official, incensed by the behaviour of the banks, felt moved to write to the Taoiseach Jack Lynch at the outset of the strike: 'Bank directors are natural born bullies of their staffs', she wrote. They were men without scruple, who had no qualms about 'holding up the public in Ireland to ransom and causing chaos in business and economic circles using the country as a pawn and a weapon to break the strike'.[24]

Efforts to isolate or divide bank workers were doomed to failure, however. Despite occasional tensions between radical younger members and their cautious elders, as well as between members from different banks, John Titterington later reflected that the IBOA had one major advantage over their adversaries.[25] 'The Banks were divided and always would be', he said. 'They were in competition with each other. Members of the IBOA were one solid unit.'[26] In truth, for much of the strike, this unit was more scattered than solid. As the dispute became more entrenched and the banks remained closed, many officials left the country. By early May 1970, an estimated 3,000 of them had left to take up temporary work in England, while the remainder sought out replacement jobs at home.[27] The majority succeeded in finding alternative employment. The importance of this cannot be underestimated: by limiting the financial hardship on members, it enabled the Executive Committee of the Association to dig in heels and to stick firm to their demand for increased pay secure in the support of their members.[28]

After rejecting proposals from the Labour Court (to which the dispute had been referred by the Minister for Labour) in July 1970 and declining a fresh offer from the banks in an August ballot of members, the Executive Committee pushed out the negotiations long enough to secure concessions from the banks that would warrant a return to work. The point at which the two sides finally agreed terms came in October 1970. The IBOA claimed it as a triumph.[29] The headline gains were the achievement of a 36 per cent hike in salary for officials in their first six years of service and a 23 per cent increase for more senior officials.[30] Not everybody saw the outcome in the same light as the IBOA. A report into the bank dispute, carried out by Professor Michael Fogarty at the request of the Minister for Labour, remarked that the most arresting feature of the eventual settlement was how unremarkable it was. For certain, it had put 'impressive amounts of money into the pockets of officials', but when set against what was happening in other occupations – the Civil Service and the ESB, for example – at a time of price and pay inflation, bank officials did not end up substantially better off than other white-collar workers.[31] Fogarty, indeed, wondered what it was all for: He wrote colourfully: 'The mountain has laboured and out has come this ridiculous mouse.' [32]

The IBOA emerged from the dispute at once strengthened and drained. The Association had demonstrated a remarkable resilience and unity of purpose, but the protracted nature of the dispute had left them isolated. The Association and its members found themselves 'pilloried' by the public, the press, the television, the government and, of course, the banks.[33] What united all sides at the end was the understanding that there should be no repetition of the dispute. It was for that very reason that Joseph Brennan, the Minister for Labour, commissioned the investigation by Professor Fogarty. When published in 1971, his report was unflinching in its criticism of both banks and bank officials. Both sides were deemed guilty of acting in a manner which served only to prolong the dispute. In industrial relations terms, the biggest problem was the deep-rooted mistrust between the two sides. As Fogarty saw it, caricatures had become cast as reality. He wrote, for instance, of the persistence of 'a mythology of the IBOA as slippery customers and of bank directors as flinty-hearted capitalists and bureaucrats'.[34] And yet, alongside such analysis lay words of advice. For the IBOA, Fogarty advocated a more professional organisation including better-trained and more local representatives, more full-time officials and the possibility of a full-time – as opposed to a voluntary – Executive Committee. As it happened, the IBOA was already thinking along these lines. It fully acknowledged the need to reorganise and to strengthen its structures at headquarters. As if to symbolise the wider set of responsibilities it intended to take on, a decision was also taken to amend the title of Organising Secretary, deemed anachronistic, to the more appropriate General Secretary.[35]

One of the Association's key activists throughout the 1960s and the early 1970s was Paddy O'Grady Walshe. As the IBOA's Honorary Secretary, he formed a formidable partnership with Titterington as the highly respected voice of the serving bank official. The extent of his influence can be gleaned from the tribute in *IBOA News* which followed his death in January 2004,[36] where it was recorded that 'no one member of IBOA, whether as an Executive Committee Member or an Honorary Officer, made a greater contribution to the improvement of the terms and conditions of employment of Bank Officials than he'. His obituary in *The Irish Times*[37] went even further, noting that 'during some of the most turbulent years in the association's history Paddy, together with the late John Titterington, provided the charismatic leadership which proved decisive in the struggle for better terms of employment for the members. Many of today's bankers probably don't know it, but they owe a great debt of gratitude to Paddy O'Grady Walshe, whose efforts not only improved working conditions for his fellow bankers but also set a headline for other white-collar occupations.'

II

EQUALITY FOR ALL

The Fogarty Report was essentially an anatomy of the most prolonged and comprehensive stoppage ever recorded in banking in Ireland.[38] But it also offered a fascinating snapshot of banking at a time when the entire business was in the midst of massive change. Irish banking had transformed more in the previous decade than it had done in the century previously. The mergers of the 1960s had led to the creation of more large-scale operations and increased the levels of competition.[39] The system that was still taking shape in the early 1970s was one at odds with the old structure where small operations were run by managers and staff and where matters of promotion were decided simply on the basis of seniority.[40] By the early 1970s, there were more players in the Irish market, but the Associated Banks – the Bank of Ireland Group, Allied Irish Banks, Ulster Bank and Northern Bank – still dominated. These were also the largest employers: in January 1971, the four big banks boasted a staff of just under 8,000. Almost as striking as this number was its composition. Men comprised the majority of staff, but women accounted for a vastly increased number, 3,405 of all employees.[41] In the three years from 1968 to 1971, there had been a 60 per cent increase in the number of women taking up employment at entry grade level and their numbers helped swell the ranks of the IBOA.[42]

The movement of women into the IBOA mirrored their wider participation in Irish trade unionism. Throughout the 1960s there had been a sharp increase in female membership of trade unions, especially among those in white-collar employment. Despite this, women remained significantly unrepresented in the world of Irish work. In the Republic, by the mid-1960s, women constituted only 25.5 per cent of the workforce – a statistic alarmingly similar to that from fifty years earlier.[43] What had changed for Irish women, however, was the type of work in which they were engaged. There was sharp decline in the numbers involved in agriculture and domestic service and this was offset by increases elsewhere. For girls without a secondary education, working opportunities arose as factory operatives, shop assistants, waitresses or servants. For those with secondary education, jobs were taken up in offices, in nursing and teaching. Less than 1 per cent of women entered the so-called 'higher professions'.[44] Given such circumstances, it is little wonder that the feminist writer Mary Maher remarked of the 1960s that the term 'career' had yet to become part of the vocabulary of Irish girls.[45] For a young woman entering employment in a bank at the time there was certainly little prospect, or expectation, of forging a lengthy career. Entry requirements for women were largely the same as men, as was the pay (though it was slightly lower for women) – for the first five or six years. Thereafter, the experiences of male and female bank officials diverged. The big impediment to the advancement of women was the marriage ban. Just as elsewhere, women in banks were obliged to resign their jobs when they married. The upshot, as the Fogarty report demonstrated, was that female bank officials, in the main, had shorter working lives and were concentrated among the lower grades where they mostly operated machinery and acted as secretaries to managers.[46] The monotony of the work and the circumscribing of opportunity created a degree of despondency among female bank employees.[47] It was simply demoralising, one female official remarked, to watch male colleagues gain promotion for no other reason than that similar opportunities were closed to women.[48]

The IBOA supported women's claims for better treatment. And progress, albeit limited, had been made. In 1966 a new promotional scale – Scale 3 – was introduced for women while the old Scale 2 – the 'Unpromoted Ladies Scale' – was phased out in the early 1970s.[49] In addition, the 1970 Bank dispute had delivered an automatic right of promotion to Senior Bank Official (SBO) grade for women after twelve years.[50] John Titterington considered such developments as key stepping stones towards eventual acceptance of the principle of equal pay for equal work, yet the slow pace of change remained a source of frustration.[51] In June 1971, for instance, the *Irish Independent* ran an article which stated that that while 'a girl's chances of flying high in a banking job are improving, it would probably be better for her not to be too ambitious'. The point was backed up by a startling comparison of male and female promotions: by January of that year, only 5 of the 3,405 women employed by the banks had risen as high as Assistant Manager level; in contrast, 1,788 of the 4,415 male officials had reached this grade. Time did nothing to diminish such disparities. Among men with 22 years service, it was claimed that 94 per cent had been promoted; the figure for women stood at a mere 2 per cent.[52] The promotion of women was bound up inextricably with that of marriage. The link was underlined in the promotional literature used by the Bank of Ireland Group which, in an effort to attract young women employees, posed the question, 'A career in banking or a stepping stone to marriage?', before outlining the various gratuities that were available to them on marrying.[53] In contrast, young men were seduced with the promise of management positions, with all the trappings of salary and status, by their early thirties. Mary McCutchan, the women's editor of the *Irish Independent,* declared that it was time for women bank officials to act. The Fogarty report, she wrote, had brought the grievance of female bank officials into the light, now it was up to the women themselves 'to ensure they are put right'.[54]

Putting matters right is what women across Irish society were attempting to do in a more organised manner in the early 1970s. Building on the traditions of older self-help groups like the Irish Countrywomen's Association and the Irish Housewives Association, the early 1970s witnessed an explosion of new, more radical women's groups.[55] They came with a panoply of demands, the most significant of which, for working women, was the ending of the marriage restriction on employment and the right to equal pay. Although the Fogarty report claimed that the IBOA was intent on retaining the marriage ban against the wishes of the banks, the two sides reached an agreement to have it removed in June 1973, a move that coincided with its abolition in the public service.[56] The principle of equal pay followed: from the 1 January 1976, female bank officials were entitled to automatic promotion to the Senior Bank Official (SBO) level on the same basis as their male colleagues.[57]

None of this happened in isolation. The transformation in the working landscape of women north and south was underpinned by new legislation. In the Republic of Ireland, the Anti-Discrimination (Pay) Act 1974 was followed by the Employment Equality Act 1977. In Northern Ireland, meanwhile, the standard was set by the Equal Pay Act (Northern Ireland) 1970.[58] These advances, liberating and significant as they were, did not relieve the pressure on women bank officials to effect change both in their terms of work and their role within their representative Association.

As their number increased as a proportion of the total number of bank officials, the clamour for greater representation on the IBOA Executive Committee grew louder. By the mid 1970s, they accounted for the majority of all members and at Annual Delegate Meetings, motions were put recommending more places for women on the Committee. 'I feel that our ladies would do far better if they had a little more experience on the Executive', the Ladies' Social Representative for Bank of Ireland in Dublin, Ms Margaret Kearns, told delegates in April 1972, adding cautiously that they had no wish to 'oust' men from any positions they held.[59] The odds were stacked against women within and without the IBOA. It is a measure indeed of how deeply entrenched the discrimination had become that the bar in the IBOA's own social headquarters, the Bankers' Club on St Stephen's Green, remained a male preserve until 1974.[60] The opening of the doors of the bar to women was not simply a succumbing to the equality agenda – though it was a major factor – it was also an acknowledgement of the sheer volume of female membership within the IBOA. The weight of numbers ensured a greater visibility for women in banking life: the pages of the *Irish Banking Magazine* began to fill with features on the lives, likes and concerns of female officials. Reflecting the multifaceted nature of their lives, this covered a multitude, from their sporting and holiday habits to their campaigns for maternity leave and equality of access to staff home loans.[61]

The 1970s was certainly a watershed decade for Irish working women. And if, across the banking sector, the barriers that held women back from top positions did not exactly collapse, they were more regularly breached. Nuala McNamara, working with the Bank of Ireland Group, became the country's 'first lady manager' in 1972 and in 1976 Pat Quigley became the 'first lady Council Member' of the Institute of Bankers in Ireland.[62] For all that such appointments were markers of progress, the simple truth was that they were conspicuously rare. As the 1970s drew to a close, the gap between the professional ambitions of men and women in banking was still vast. Indicative of this gulf in career expectation was that the fact that some 7,000 female officials were, by 1978, still not members of the Institute of Bankers, a body which facilitated the professional education of bank employees. The IBOA pushed for women to become involved, but stressed that the solution lay with women themselves. The *Irish Banking Magazine* summarised the argument: 'One can only influence an organisation by participating in it and if the Institute does not appear relevant to the ladies at present then the solution lies in their joining in big numbers . . . and thereby influencing the future development of that body.[63] The logic of this is difficult to question, but if there were lessons to be drawn from the experience of women in the IBOA in the 1970s, it might have been that influence did not automatically flow from participation or numerical strength.

III

EUROPE, TECHNOLOGY & 'THE TROUBLES'

The story of the extension of the legal rights of Irish women in the early to mid-1970s is inseparable from that of Ireland's accession to the European Economic Community (EEC) in 1973. In legislating change, Irish politicians were, after all, not simply responding to a determined women's movement, but to a series of European equality directives. Moves towards closer European integration extended beyond the political, however. Simultaneous with the steps that Ireland and the United Kingdom began to take towards EEC membership in the early 1960s were the efforts of various groups and organisations, including bank officials, to explore opportunities for greater international cooperation. The IBOA had always looked beyond the island for a wider framework of reference, but up to the late 1960s, the Association's contact with counterparts in other countries had been on an individual basis. The relationships were more casual and ad hoc than formal and organised. The founding of the European Union of Bank Employees (UEB) changed that.

The setting up of the organisation – which was non-political and non-sectarian – grew out of recognition of the increasing inter-dependence of economies and financial institutions, particularly in an era of large bank mergers and multinational finance. At a meeting held in Berne in 1967 to consider the establishment of a supranational body, a representative of Britain's National Union of Bank Employees (NUBE) stated that the benefits of membership should be seen not so much 'for what we can get out of it but for what we can contribute to the general well-being of bank workers wherever they ply their skills'.[64] Ireland was not represented at that Berne meeting, but it joined the new organisation shortly afterwards, in early 1968. At that time, the Union covered six countries, France, Germany, Britain, Ireland, Italy and Switzerland, but during the 1970s it was enlarged to encompass additional European countries.

From the beginning, the IBOA looked to play full part in the UEB. In 1971, they hosted for the first time a gathering of delegates in Dublin, winning praise for their organisation and hospitality.[65] The following year, the IBOA's veteran General Secretary, John Titterington, was chosen unanimously as President of the UEB. In taking up this new role, Titterington relinquished his old one.[66] For the IBOA, the departure of Titterington was genuinely momentous. As Professor Fogarty acknowledged, there was no figure of comparable stature across the Irish banking sector. Unlike any bank director, he observed, Titterington was a 'real and known persona-lity, attracting enthusiasm from long service staff and respect and support from younger people'.[67] A fierce negotiator, he had not alone held the post of Organising Secretary for over twenty years and led the IBOA through five major disputes, he had, in the words of one commentator, succeeded in putting 'steel' into a once 'genteel' organisation.[68] As it turned out, Titterington would return to the

IBOA on a caretaker basis in March 1973 after his replacement, British trade unionist John Nelson, unexpectedly stepped down after only eighteen months in the job.[69]

Given the brevity of Nelson's tenure, it is perhaps fair to say that Titterington's true successor was Job Stott. Appointed in October 1973, the Tralee native came to the IBOA after serving as General Secretary of the ESB Officers Association.[70] On taking the role, Stott set about expanding the Association. Membership ballooned in the 1970s, partly in response to the growth of the banking sector, but partly too as a result of decisions by the Executive Committee itself. One such decision was taken in 1974 when staff of the Belfast Savings Bank were accepted into the Association.[71] This extension in numbers went hand in hand with the introduction of new methods of working. Indicative of this changing world of work was an application for membership of the IBOA made earlier in the decade by the Computer Department ('non-bankers') of the Bank of Ireland, which was also accepted.[72] Indeed, the IBOA embraced computerisation in the belief that it would ease the 'drudgery' of their members' work. That much was certainly true. In 1972, when the first electronic cheque-cashing machine was installed in the Ulster Bank on College Green, it was said to eliminate most of the physical handling of money by a bank clerk.[73] There were no serious concerns at this point that the use of computers might threaten jobs. Rather, the IBOA was confident that the use of computers would create more opportunities for promotions.[74] By the end of the decade, however, this optimism had already begun to soften. The sheer speed of technological change proved unsettling. In June 1979, for instance, the *IBOA Newssheet* complained of the manner at which new services and systems were 'constantly imposed from on-high on branches demanding the acquisition of ever-increasing skill by staff. One need only look around to see the promotional block now firmly entrenched in the system. It is a recipe for unrest.'[75]

In Northern Ireland, the situation had moved well beyond unrest. It is somewhat paradoxical that the modernisation of banking was pursued against the backdrop of a slide into violent conflict in Northern Ireland. The so-called 'Troubles', which

Ruth McCollum of the Ulster Bank on College Green makes history in 1972 by becoming the first operator of the first electronic cheque-cashing machine to be installed in Ireland. The machine, known as the 'chequemaster', was considered the height of sophistication for its time, eliminating much of the physical handling of money by the bank clerk. McCollum is pictured here cashing the cheque of Ulster Bank Director Patrick Daly. *(IBOA Archive)*

erupted from the Northern Ireland Civil Rights campaigns of the late 1960s, gained a ferocious momentum in the early 1970s. Daily life in Northern Ireland was routinely disturbed by murder and mayhem, yet the attendant security concerns spread island-wide. In April 1970, for instance, a member of An Garda Síochána, Richard Fallon, was killed in an attempt to prevent an armed raid on the AIB Branch on Arran Quay in Dublin. As violence escalated, banks and their officials were placed literally in the firing line. In 1971, 55 branches of the Ulster Bank alone were damaged by bombs.[76] Such events set the dismal tone for much of what followed. Throughout the 1970s and beyond, the work of a bank official carried with it an ever-present threat of robbery, kidnap and attack. As if to underline just how real was that threat, one Northern Bank employee wrote of his experience of being 'buffeted about by machine guns, revolvers, bombs, stones, telephone calls and murdered civilians' in the course of his duties.[77] This may have been an extreme case, but it was not isolated. Indeed, so prevalent a problem was that of armed raids in the Republic that the banks agreed to pay a minimum of £50 to each member of the staff present on the premises during an armed raid, with the provision that such a staff member had to have been involved in or affected by the raid.[78] The IBOA, for their part, engaged with both the government and banks in an effort to reduce the risks to members, but there was an acceptance that there was 'no gilt-edged security against armed determined criminals'.[79] The advice was therefore towards vigilance and common sense with bank officials warned of the importance of secrecy and discretion lest 'loose talk' outside work might provide vital information to people with criminal intent.[80]

The slide into violence and civil conflict in Northern Ireland is neatly illustrated by this anti-terrorist billboard, erected beside the Belfast Savings Bank in April 1972. Two years later, in 1974, members of the Belfast Savings Banks were admitted as members of an IBOA. The so-called 'Troubles', however, would have a profound effect on the working lives of bank officials over the following quarter of a century. *(Getty Images)*

IV

BACK TO STRIKE: 1976

The fortitude of Irish bank officials, particularly those in Northern Ireland, in the face of violent threat was a source of justifiable pride to the IBOA and it was understood to be one of the few issues on which they could command public support. That was because the matter about which bank officials were most often in the public eye remained that of pay and here they evoked little sympathy – with either the general public or the government. In the wake of the 1970 bank strike and various other trade union disputes, the government took steps to overhaul the practice of Irish industrial relations. A system of centralised bargaining, designed to address concerns around productivity and inflation, was introduced as a means by which employers and trade unions at national level could agree rates of pay and reduce the risk of immediate, and damaging, strike action.[81] The process did not preclude the practice of local bargaining, however, so the actual effect was to create a two-tiered system of both centralised and local bargaining, which proved in the long run to raise inflation above what might have been expected under the older decentralised system.[82] According to the historian Joe Lee, the series of national wage agreements that resulted in the early 1970s did nothing to inculcate a culture of either restraint or responsibility. An agreement reached in 1972, for instance, delivered a 21 per cent pay increase over a period of eighteen months. It was an inflationary pact that would soon be compounded by an international oil crisis, which helped drive up prices further. Lee wrote: 'The deliberate refusal on the part of both government and trade unions to think in terms of long-term strategy, and to opt instead for a for a short-term fix, became an integral part of Irish policy-making in those years.'[83] What Lee saw as a 'flight from reality', the IBOA saw at the time as something altogether different. For the Association, centralised bargaining was nothing less than a mechanism imposed to thwart future pay ambitions.

The IBOA was aghast at the new direction of industrial relations. They opposed what they perceived to be the politicisation of wage bargaining and did their best to remain aloof from it. They did so for two primary reasons: firstly, they believed that trade unions that subscribed with their employers to national wage agreements were in danger of 'divorcing' themselves from their own membership; secondly, they stressed the 'exceptionality' of banking. 'This is not knocking the nation', John Titterington stated in April 1972. 'Banking is an intricate, complex organisation which must have its own rules. It must have its own type of increments. It must have its own type of promotion.'[84]

Proclaiming uniqueness at a time of gathering consensus – among government, employers and unions – put the IBOA outside the mainstream of opinion. And when a new coalition government came into office in the Republic in 1973, it moved to bring them into the fold. Legislation was introduced to refer to the Labour Court a salary agreement that had already been reached between the banks and their staff.[85] The IBOA judged the move to be 'punitive' and potentially unconstitutional', while voicing scepticism as to the Court's impartiality and understanding of the banking industry.[86] In the end, the Labour Court endorsed the banking salary agreement, but the right of banks and the IBOA to engage in wage bargaining independent of other considerations had been compromised.

In December 1975, however, the Minister for Labour, Michael O'Leary, introduced another piece of legislation to freeze pay levels in the bank sector temporarily, pending a review by the Labour Court of the pay deal agreed earlier that year, a move which fuelled a conviction among bank officials that they were being unfairly targeted by government.[87] When the Labour Court reported, it found that bank officials would have earned 7 per cent more than other workers under the terms of the national wage agreements.[88] The IBOA, which had opposed government efforts to cut their wages and launched a challenge to the legislation in the courts, made a move towards conciliation.[89] Following discussions with the banks, it agreed to a measure of voluntary restraint, reducing their demand to 3.5 per cent of the originally negotiated pay agreement, a figure that was still above what the Minister for Labour had requested. The proposal was put to a ballot of members and approved by a narrow majority.[90]

No sooner had that vote been taken than the IBOA entered talks on pay for the following year. The talks stalled, then broke down due to an unwillingness on the part of the banks to offer increases above what other workers were likely to receive. The approach adopted by the banks, however disappointing to the IBOA, was nevertheless consistent with government policy. So much so that in June 1976, before a new national wage agreement had even been reached, the Minister for Labour stated his intention to introduce further legislation to ensure that bank officials did not receive pay increases 'out of line with such movements in monies as may be afforded throughout the economy'.[91] Significantly, the legislation transferred the power to prohibit increases in renumeration from the Labour Court to the Minister himself. What all this meant in effect was that no salary increase could be agreed until the conclusion of a new national wage agreement. But it also meant that banks were neither incentivised nor completely at liberty to make improvements to their pay offer.[92] The slow drift towards a strike suddenly became a rush.[93] Bank officials stopped working on 26 June 1976, citing government interference as the primary cause. Their strike lasted for much of the summer, ending on 31 August, after a revised offer from the banks, acceptable by the Minister for Labour, was put to a ballot of bank officials. The agreement was reached only after the government appointed an independent adjudicator, Maurice Cosgrave, deputy chairman of the Labour Court. The agreement comprised two essential parts: one part related to productivity, the other part to pay. The Executive Committee recommended rejection; the members decided differently. IBOA members approved the pay terms, but rejected the productivity deal. It was enough to ensure the banks reopened.[94]

So why did members vote to return to work against the wishes of their Executive Committee? The reasons were many, but one major factor was undoubtedly their harsh experience of the strike. As in 1970, many sought alternative employment. Unlike 1970, only a minority found it. Jobs were scarce in the depressed economies of

Ireland and Britain and there was less goodwill than previously on offer. As if to underline the point, the influential Council of Irish Counties Associations in Britain appealed to all Irish clubs, societies and centres to withhold their services, social facilities and all forms of advice to striking bank officials. They did so in the belief that it was somehow immoral for striking officials to be seeking employment across the Irish Sea.[95] The strike experience of 1976 was therefore something of a rude awakening. A subsequent report into the conduct and outcomes of IBOA strikes during this period claimed that the dispute effectively destroyed 'the myth' that industrial action could be taken without financial cost to members.[96] For the IBOA, there could be no claim to victory. The strike had exposed divisions within its ranks, delivered a first major defeat in its history and raised questions as to how it would approach industrial action into the future.

The 1970s ended as it had begun with the issue of salaries at centre stage. This was, as the IBOA's own *Newssheet* acknowledged, inevitable. Although the Association continued to press the interests of members on a range of concerns – from pensions to staff loans to the plight of managers compelled to live above bank premises – the issue of salaries was the only one which might deliver benefits to all of its members all of the time.[97] Twice in the 1970s alone the pay question had embroiled the Association in bitter disputes, but the approach that emerged towards the latter part of the decade hinted at a new moderation. There was a deliberate retreat from confrontation. Not that this implied approval of the prevailing orthodoxy in industrial relations. It did not. The Association still railed against the principle of government interference and stuck to the position that it was not bound by national agreements, yet to all intents and purposes it acted in concert with it. Job Stott explained the new thinking in 1978: 'Obviously any agreement arrived at by the vast majority of workers in the country and by the vast majority of employers in the country and with the sanction and blessing of the government must have some relevance for us.'[98]

The IBOA was not unique in reflecting upon its methods of operation. The government did the same. In the second half of the

1970s, it began to develop a more integrated pay agreement which would take account of wider concerns such as social welfare, government finances, employment and unemployment. The concept took the form of a 'National Understanding for Economic and Social Development'.[99] And yet, although various sides were keen to avoid dispute, it was perhaps appropriate that the 1970s ended not in harmony but rancour. Even the threat of strike, which had receded after 1976, resurfaced. Bank officials who had been required to adjust to decimalisation at the beginning of the decade were required to see it out with yet another big change in currency management. The European Monetary System (EMS), a scheme for

Throughout a turbulent decade, there was still plenty of time for sport and recreation. This photograph of the AIB Women's Tug o' War team was taken at the IBOA Sports Day in College Park, Dublin, in July 1977. *(IBOA Archive)*

closer monetary cooperation and stability, was introduced in 1979.[100] What this meant in practice was a historic break in the link between the Irish punt and the pound sterling. The divergence of currencies would certainly benefit the banks, but the extra workload it imposed on staff gave rise to a claim by the IBOA for compensation.[101] The banks demurred. Before the impasse was finally broken with a one-off lump-sum payment to bank officials, industrial action closed the banks for a week and brought down upon the Association a torrent of criticism. The tenor of the commentary spoke volumes for how the public reputation of bank officials had been damaged by the events of a turbulent decade. The verdict of some was merciless. After condemning the decision to withdraw services as an 'act of unforgiveable selfishness', an editorial in *The Irish Times* stated:

> If bank officials were poorly-paid, underprivileged members of society, it might be possible to see some sense in their action, even without condoning it. But they are not. They are a well-paid elite, secure in their jobs, protected from the rigours of foreign competition, and cosseted by cheap loans from their employers. There is a clear sense, if ever there was one, of a protected group in society trying to protect its monopoly power, whatever the cost to the whole community as a whole. And the costs are considerable.[102]

8

The 1980s

On 9 January 1980, the Taoiseach, Charles Haughey, then less than a month in office, addressed the Irish people in a special television broadcast. It was a speech that would define a decade and a political career. His tone was grave and his message stark. Staring down the lens of the camera, he announced: 'As a community we are living away beyond our means . . . We have been living at a rate which is simply not justified by the amount of goods and services we are producing . . . We have got to cut down government spending. We will just have to reorganise government spending so that we undertake only the things that we can afford.'[1] It would be years before the excesses of Haughey's personal lifestyle, and the manner of its financing, would expose fully the crass hypocrisy that lay behind the speech, but the analysis it provided of the country's dire economic plight was, at that time, essentially correct. In the area of public spending, prudence rather than profligacy would need to become the new order of the day. In short, the Republic would need to become more frugal. As it turned out, Haughey was unwilling to administer the medicine to an illness he had so properly diagnosed and the country's economic woes became even more entrenched.[2] The 1980s was, for the most part, an era of grim austerity, a decade stained by high unemployment and soaring emigration. If the brunt of the hardship was most forcibly felt by those on the margins of society and those forced to leave for want of work, the cost of maintaining a functioning state was borne, perhaps inevitably, on the broad shoulders of Ireland's Pay-As-You-Earn (PAYE) workers.

By the beginning of the 1980s, however, this was a group in open revolt. Before Charles Haughey had even begun talk of cutbacks, PAYE workers had come to an understanding that they were being unfairly burdened by the Irish system of taxation. There was ample evidence to prove it. In the four-year period leading up to 1978, PAYE workers contributed £1.8 billion in income tax as against £320 million from self-employed people and a mere £20 million from farmers.[3] Outrage at these inequities eventually gave rise to a campaign of protest by Ireland's white-collar workers. They took to the streets in vast and unprecedented numbers. On 20 March 1979, 150,000 people marched through Dublin to demand reform. Thousands more attended similar rallies in other cities and towns across the country.[4] Among them were members of the IBOA, demonstrating under the umbrella of the Irish Conference of Professional and Service Associations (ICPSA). The decision to participate was an easy one. 'Personal taxation is now an even more serious influence on net income than the inflation rate', the Association's General Secretary, Job Stott, explained to delegates attending their annual general meeting in April 1980. 'We could not, in light of the membership's feelings . . . opt out of a national upsurge of resentment where our own members were so badly hit and we had to show IBOA support for change.'[5]

I

ICTU AND ICPSA

Joining the mass protest movement of PAYE workers showed how far the developments of the 1970s, within banking and without, had moved the IBOA. It indicated an acceptance that the interests of its members were more closely than ever aligned with those of other white-collar workers, many of them in the public service. This was a far cry from 1970. Back then, notwithstanding their historic alignment with the ICPSA, the estrangement of bank officials from the mainstream of Irish opinion was considered such that, in the aftermath of that year's infamously bitter and long-drawn out bank dispute, Professor Michael Fogarty likened them to 'men from Mars'.[6] In his extensive report on the dispute, Fogarty had criticised the Association's isolationist approach and suggested that they 'come in out of the cold' and throw in their lot with the Irish Congress of Trade Unions (ICTU).[7] The proposition met with a cool response. Although the matter surfaced occasionally at Association gatherings and a further recommendation to join Congress was made following a subsequent strike in 1976, there was little enthusiasm for the idea among either the rank or file of the Association, or its leadership.[8]

Why was this the case? There were, after all, obvious benefits to membership: an input into national wage agreements, the support of other unions in a dispute situation and the use of the facilities afforded by Congress to members.[9] Congress itself would have benefited from the sheer numerical strength that the bank officials would have brought to it. This was a point made by Michael O'Leary, the former Minister for Labour, who argued in 1978 that the effectiveness of the whole trade union movement would have been greatly improved by the affiliation of such groups as still remained out of Congress. Referring specifically to the IBOA, O'Leary contended that there was 'no good reason for [its] continued reluctance' to affiliate, especially given the involvement of other white-collar civil service unions.[10] Many of these civil servants, like the bank officials, had benefited from wage increases throughout the 1970s only for inflation and tax to erode their worth. And yet the IBOA saw little merit in joining forces. As Job Stott explained it, the reasons for remaining aloof from the Congress were both ideological and practical. Whereas many Congress members would have been in favour of bank nationalisation, this was anathema to the staff of the banks. This same staff was equally reluctant to surrender any independence when it came to wage negotiations. There was a clear sense that centralised bargaining would not deliver the best outcome for bank officials. 'Since 1970, the national wage agreements seem to have been aimed at the closing of differentials between higher and lower paid workers, rather than improving the lot of the underpaid workers', Job Stott stated. 'I really don't feel that it is in the interests of our members, nor of many other workers for that matter, to engage in centralised bargaining. There are many workers, including ourselves, who have lost out as a result.'[11]

As the PAYE protests of 1979 and beyond revealed, the retention of independence on wage bargaining did not preclude the IBOA from throwing its considerable weight behind causes of common concern. That it did so under the umbrella of the ICPSA rather than the ICTU is nevertheless significant. These two groupings were in competition for membership and relations between them were frequently strained. The ICPSA, for its part, was dismissive of the efforts of the ICTU to defend the interests of the middle-income PAYE worker. It regarded itself as the only authentic voice of the white-collar class, a group that had, by its own analysis, become the 'new poor', shouldering an unfair share of the national burden in the face of rampant tax evasion and a thriving black economy.[12] The ICPSA contrasted the quiet and effective leadership it provided for this cohort of middle-income workers with that of the ICTU, a body it chastised as being 'tainted with mediocrity and political opportunism.'[13]

To an extent, the hostility of the ICPSA towards the ICTU was born of insecurity. It had lost members to the ICTU and was determined to keep the IBOA within the fold. By the mid- to late 1980s, indeed, the IBOA had become its largest single affiliate and its members were increasingly represented in leadership positions. As if to illustrate this growing influence, IBOA Honorary Officer, Margaret Browne, was elected as the first female President of the ICPSA in 1984.[14] Previously, in 1981, Ken Doyle of the IBOA had served as Assistant Secretary of the ICPSA when it made a submission to the first Commission on Taxation, which had been established in response to the widespread public unrest.[15] The Conference submission emphasised the need for equity, as well as demanding action on such issues as the restoration of the real value of personal allowances, the clampdown on tax evasion, the introduction of realistic capital taxation programmes and the effective regulation for disclosure of benefit in kind.[16] The setting up of the Commission of Taxation did not dampen demand for reform and the IBOA,

through its involvement in the ICPSA, remained enthusiastic proponents of change, going so far as to lend its support to a small number of PAYE reform candidates who, standing on an independent platform, contested the February 1987 general election. None

A massive demonstration by PAYE workers brought 150,000 people, IBOA members among them, onto the streets of Dublin on 20 March 1979. Thousands more attended similar rallies in other cities and towns across the country. The following year, prior to the 1980 budget, the largest protest in the history of the state up to that point took place when 700,000 workers marched at 37 centres around the country. The PAYE demonstrations continued into the mid-1980s. *(RTÉ Stills Library)*

of them came close to claiming a seat in an election remembered most for the arrival on the national political scene of another tax reform party, the Progressive Democrats, yet the IBOA expressed satisfaction that valuable publicity had been earned on an issue of huge importance to their members.[17]

II

PAY AND TECHNOLOGY

The IBOA's support for the campaign on tax reform was driven ultimately by fears that the income of members was seriously threatened. Delegates to the Association's Annual Delegates Meeting in 1983 expressed increasing alarm at the combined impact of inequitable taxes on disposable income and rapid price inflation on living standards.[18] There was nothing imaginary about this sense of precipitous decline – Irish living standards at the time stood well below the European norm. The early 1980s saw the worst of it: between 1981 and 1983, with inflation spiking in the aftermath of a second global oil crisis, the take-home pay of those in employment fell in real terms by 20 per cent.[19] This worsening of national economic circumstances coincided with a period of unprecedented political instability and a breakdown in the then established procedures for industrial relations. Three general elections were held in the eighteen months from June 1981 to November 1982, which saw power swing from Fianna Fáil to a Fine Gael-led government and back again. For all the differences in the personality and personnel of the two leading political parties, there was, by 1982, a general consensus around the need to cut spending and to reduce to the national deficit.[20]

The effect of this was to diminish the power of the trade unions. The waning influence of a movement whose membership had peaked at 524,000 at the start of the decade was crystallised in the ending of centralised bargaining.[21] When the second 'National Understanding' came to an end in 1982, industrial relations retreated to the pre-1970 system of decentralised bargaining. Pay deals would once again have to be negotiated, sector by sector and firm by firm, though soaring rates of unemployment insured against a slide into chaos. Writing of this transition from centralised to decentralised bargaining, the economist Joe Durkan observed how the pay awards that resulted managed to better reflect the economic circumstances of the firms and sectors involved. More specifically, they led to 'a sharp deceleration in wage inflation'.[22]

So how did all this play out with the IBOA? Although the Association had not been bound by the national wage agreements, these invariably set the parameters of the deals it reached with the banks. One of the problems the IBOA's negotiators had to contend with in the early to mid-1980s was the management of members' expectations. When, for example, Job Stott addressed members in April 1983 and told them that the most 'outstanding feature' of the previous year was the salary increases achieved, he accepted that the award might still be open to criticism for falling short of the target which the Association itself had set. Stott nevertheless impressed upon members that the settlement reached, in delivering increases above the cost of living, was both 'unique in Irish terms and unique internationally'.[23] Indeed, against a grim economic backdrop, the IBOA's negotiators enjoyed not inconsiderable success during the 1980s. The gains achieved may have been more modest than spectacular but they were no less significant for that. Context was everything and at a time when pay increases across the board were being scaled down, the IBOA fared better than most employee groups.[24]

The pressure on the IBOA's negotiators during these years was substantial. On issues of salary and other matters, they were compelled to negotiate on three separate fronts. As well as working through the different industrial relations structures that existed in the Republic of Ireland and Northern Ireland, they also had to contend with representing members interests in Britain, a market in which the Bank of Ireland and the AIB had both developed a retail foothold in the 1970s.[25] If, for the IBOA, the issues in each jurisdiction were often the same, the specific demands of their members were not. In 1985, for instance, the staff in Allied Irish Banks in Britain rejected a 5.25 per cent salary increase, which had

"I don't know how it is, but everytime I come she's always dry".

Staff pay demands in the 1980s and 1990s were set against the backdrop of soaring bank profits. The IBOA had little difficulty with the scale of the profits achieved, but argued that it should be more equitably shared. *(IBOA Archive)*

resulted from a Northern Ireland Arbitration award and which carried the imprimatur of the ACAS, the British equivalent of the Labour Court. Low morale, brought on by inadequate staffing and excessive overtime, led to a week-long strike in Britain in support of an enhanced pay offer, which they achieved.[26] The dispute ended on favourable terms for the bank officials, but it also exposed divisions within their ranks. Over 20 per cent of all officials in the British-based Irish banks, under pressure from the managements of their banks, failed to carry out IBOA directives in the course of the dispute. Many of these were subsequently 'expelled or suspended' from the Association, which above all prized loyalty. As Stott declared shortly afterwards: 'We would be better off with a membership that is 100% loyal than a 100% membership which is disloyal.'[27]

This dispute was typical of those that occurred in the 1980s. While distrust of the banks still ran deep, there were no reruns of the epic confrontations of the previous decade. Instead, the few strikes that took place tended to be short-lived and localised.[28] One reason for this was the success of the Association in smoothing over such potentially contentious issues as new technology. The challenge of technological change was one the Association met head on. They eschewed any semblance of Luddism. Instead, in the pages of the *Irish Banking Magazine* and at gatherings of District Secretaries and annual conferences, the Association prepared its members for the impending banking revolution.[29] Addressing an IBOA conference in 1983, Ken Pooler, President of the Banking, Insurance & Finance Union (BIFU) – formerly known as NUBE – spoke of how the arrival of new technology would make the coming years the 'most difficult' that bank officials anywhere had ever known.[30] Rather than attempt a futile denial of the reality of change, the IBOA sought to shape it. They insisted that technology could only be effectively introduced with the cooperation of bank employees themselves. It could not be simply imposed from above.[31] The result was a far-reaching, five-year

Banking changed with the introduction of new computer technology. Rather than deny the reality of change, the IBOA sought to shape it. In 1982, they concluded a five-year Technology & Change Agreement with the banks. *(RTÉ Stills Library)*

Technology and Change Agreement, which the banks and the IBOA struck in 1982. Coming after exhaustive negotiations which took place at Joint Industrial Council level and the Labour Court and with the endorsement of its members, the deal, later extended to Northern Ireland and Britain, was a triumph for the IBOA, winning 'envy and admiration' from Bank Unions throughout Europe. 'No other union', an IBOA commemorative book later reflected, 'fought for and got such a definitive statement of bank plans, which imposed a firm obligation to further consultation if varied or exceeded. No other Union won the benefits and compensatory provisions which were included.'[32]

III

QUALITY OF LIFE

The achievements in salary negotiations and technology overshadowed other developments without ever eclipsing them. In 1981, Pat Coffey, the then President of the Association, remarked that the 'simplest way of improving the quality of life for members is for the members to have a say in where they live.'[33] What Coffey was referring to was a long-standing grievance among bank officials whereby they could be uprooted from their place of work, their home and their community at the whim of their employer. The issue had been a running sore since the 1970s. Towards the end of that decade, a predecessor of Pat Coffey as President of the Association, Tim Godfrey, had complained of certain banks, which had taken to moving people about 'like draughts'.[34] Godfrey criticised the 'lack of humanity and the lack of kindness' exercised by the banks and referred, by way of example, to one region of the country where 'three managers had been moved from one town to another. All three were married and two had families. Each of them was moved without promotion, yet at serious cost to them and their families, involving the uprooting from houses, schools and neighbours.'[35]

The treatment of staff by the banks was no less cavalier in the 1980s. In 1981, the *Irish Banking Magazine* told of one soon-to-be-married female employee who, having applied for a loan to build a house near her branch, found herself transferred within a week of making the application. Her loan application was subsequently rejected.[36] This case was unexceptional, yet the banks defended this system of transfers on the basis that officials benefited in terms of experience and promotional opportunities. Many officials viewed it differently and believed the issue was not being accorded the urgency it required. In July 1981, with the Association's gaze concentrated on discussions over technology and change, one bank official from Gorey professed himself sickened at the sight of transferability being 'pushed into the background once again'.[37] However, a major problem for the IBOA was the lack of agreement among its own members about what to do on the matter. Some bank officials were opposed to any transfers at all, while others, anxious to progress their careers, wished to avail of them once they could avoid a financial loss. The IBOA struggled to accommodate these competing interests in a coherent policy. The confusion that prevailed was summed up by Jim McCartney, an official at the Bank of Ireland in Kells, County Meath, who, when wondering what exactly the Association's stance should be, asked: 'Should it be that no one is transferred unless they asked for it? Should it be that they get a transfer if they ask? How exactly will the system work? Most transfers involve more than one person.'[38] In raising the essential questions, McCartney pointed to a clear way forward: 'What we have to try to do . . . is to find out what exactly is the difference between one person's right to obtain a transfer for reasons of marriage, promotion, family reasons or whatever and another person's right to refuse a transfer . . . Finally, there should be some protective rights for the person to refuse that transfer when there is justifiable cause.'[39]

The IBOA eventually settled on a position best described as one denying the banks the 'absolute right of transfer'.[40] They took their case to the Labour Court and when the banks failed to yield on the issue, the Executive Committee imposed first a blanket ban on all transfers that were against the wishes of officials and later a ban on overtime.[41] The upping of the ante helped speed a resolution. In 1986, the IBOA reached a landmark agreement with the banks on transferability. The accord provided for both consultation and notice where a transfer involved a change of residence (those in management position were afforded added safeguards), as well as an appeals procedure overseen by an independent third party.[42]

What bank officials gained in terms of their influence over their own transferability, it appeared that they were set to lose elsewhere. The 1980s witnessed a mounting of pressure to extend the opening hours of banks. The banks argued that such a move was necessary to halt a slide in market share to the building societies.[43] The IBOA countered that not only was there no 'proven demand' for longer opening hours, but that any such demand that might exist into the future could be met by new technology.[44] The debate around extended hours was emblematic of the broader changes in the banking sector and how these might impact on staff terms and conditions. Writing to the *Irish Banking Magazine* in October 1983, the Dublin Ladies' Committee claimed that were the banks 'to obtain a foothold on Saturdays, this would be extended further and the operation escalated to change the structure of opening hours. This is not on.'[45] Irish bank officials were not alone in resisting a change to the status quo. Fritz Johannsen, Vice-President of the International Federation of Employees, Technicians and Managers (FIET), a body to which the IBOA affiliated in 1983, impressed upon IBOA members the international dimension to the discussions they were having. 'If one country opens on Saturday, then we have a domino effect', he said in 1984. 'It is very important that every country fights back.'[46] As the decade wore on, however, the debate around opening hours appeared to have been significantly recast. The question was more and more about the how and when of longer opening hours than whether or not it would actually happen. The drift towards acceptance in principle appeared inexorable. In 1986, for instance, a tribunal in Northern Ireland rejected the banks' rationale for extended opening hours, but raised no objection to the idea of their introduction. In accepting that there might be practical difficulties involved in implementation, the tribunal simply advised that the banks and the IBOA discuss ways to ensure that they were overcome.[47] Bank officials were nevertheless united in the conviction that the concession of longer hours could not be agreed 'at any price' and they agitated for an ongoing salary increase instead of the lump sum that the banks were prepared to offer.[48] A survey of members showed that almost 96 per cent were opposed to change without compensation.[49] On the other hand, with appropriate compensation, some 56 per cent of members were willing to accept extended hours. By the end of the decade, the banks were under no illusion as to what their employees' position was. The IBOA mantra was clear: 'If there is not a penny onto salaries, then there will not be a minute onto Opening Hours.'[50]

IV

A SPORTING LIFE

When bank officials were not working, many were engaged in the bewildering range of social activities organised under the auspices of the IBOA. Dances, music nights, quizzes, fashion shows and other events were staples of IBOA social life and provided opportunities for socialisation across the various banks. So too did sport. Indeed, the Association fully realised that it was often through the medium of sport that many bank officials came to appreciate that for all the ferocity of the commercial competition that existed between rival banks, there was more that united officials than kept them apart. While members mostly participated out of a sense of fun and for the simple pleasure of participation, the role that sport was expected to play within the life of the Association was unambiguously defined. Rather than serve as simply a recreational distraction and a break from daily stresses of bank life, sport came loaded with a clear mission statement. In short, it was intended to strengthen the IBOA by building fraternalism among the staffs of different banks. The link between pastime and politics was most explicitly drawn in the pages of the IBOA's own *Newssheet*. In September 1980, a front-page editorial read: 'It has been said that the Battle of Waterloo was won on the playing fields of Eton and the same spirit of brotherhood has been forged in our members through the various IBOA sports competitions.'[51]

The sporting programme set out by the IBOA laid claim to be

one of the best of any trade union in Western Europe.[52] Whatever the truth of the boast, there is no denying its comprehensive nature. Year in, year out, the IBOA published a calendar of national sporting fixtures that was overseen by a sports secretary who sat on the Executive Committee.[53] This told only part of the story, however. Below national level, individual districts and individual sports made their own arrangements.[54] The overwhelming emphasis was on choice: the sheer diversity of sports meant that there was something for everyone. For the casual competitor as much as the serious sportsperson, the IBOA catered for all tastes and all abilities. To a large extent, the rhythm of the seasons dictated what sports were played and when. Where the dark and cold of winter ensured that priority was given over to such indoor activities as snooker, swimming and ten-pin bowling, the focus in summer shifted to the outdoors. Then the days were filled with inter-bank competitions in the popular field games of hurling, Gaelic football and soccer, as well as athletics, golf and a range of other individual pursuits.

Many bank officials combined work with a high sporting profile. Among them was Mary McKenna, who worked in the Bank of Ireland's College Green branch in the early 1980s and who, by then, was a regular on Irish international and Curtis Cup golf teams. *(Getty Images)*

In many districts around the country, large sporting jamborees were held on summer evenings, drawing large crowds. Over two evenings in July 1980, for instance, over 400 men and women participated in what was by then an annual evening sports festival (it began in 1974) in Castlepollard, County Westmeath, with competitions for everything from soccer to pool to the hula hoop.[55] A similar event organised for the Portlaoise area during the same summer included on its menu of activities soccer, golf and a treasure hunt.[56] There were, of course, sporting passions which defied the conventions of such programmes. Angling was one. It was, according to a reporter with *The Irish Times*, a pastime that appeared to come easily to bankers. The reporter, who was invited to join an outing of bank officials on the shores of Lough Conn in County Mayo for a fly-fishing competition in the early 1980s, wrote somewhat unflatteringly: 'The outwitting of an innocent fish apparently is a sort of game more easily learned by them because of the professional experience in the wide world of finance.' When it came to duping fish some officials were clearly better than others: of 66 entrants, only 34 succeeded in catching anything, though their haul of 54 fish came to an impressive weight of 60 lb 11.5 oz.[57]

The IBOA not only fostered competition amongst bankers, however; it also encouraged participation in the wider sporting scene. When the Dublin City Marathon was launched in 1980, the enthusiasm of the public response was such that the *Irish Bankers Magazine* heralded it as 'one of the most dramatic successes in modern Irish athletics'. The following year it duly published a training schedule for beginners brave enough to contemplate the gruelling trek through Dublin's streets.[58] Over 200 bank officials rose to the challenge and on the day of the 1981 race the Association's headquarters on St Stephen's Green was – as it would be in subsequent years – turned over to them so that they could properly prepare and recover before and after the race.[59] The participatory ethos of the marathon was very different from that at the elite levels of various sports. Yet bank officials were represented there too. There were many employees of banks who combined work with a high sporting profile. In January 1980, for instance, the *Irish Banking Magazine* ran a special feature on six women golfers, all of them bank employees and each of them an international player at either junior or senior level. The most celebrated of them was Mary McKenna, who worked with the Bank of Ireland in Dublin's College Green and who, since the late 1960s, had been ever-present on Irish international and Curtis Cup golf teams.[60]

The full spectrum of sporting life was reflected in the pages of publications like the *Irish Banking Magazine* and the *IBOA Newssheet*. But, as the latter readily acknowledged, the mere reportage of such events as took place and of who won what and when could 'scarcely touch the depth of their importance in IBOA life'.[61] Sport served as social oil, smoothing relations between employees of different banks. In many cases, it also provided a prelude to further social engagements involving dinner and dancing which brought business into pubs, restaurants and hotels in towns across the country. In the cities of Dublin and Belfast, however, the hub of such activity tended to be the bankers' clubs. The Belfast club, still situated on Donegall Place, had been destroyed by fire but when it reopened it boasted a lounge, a pool and darts room, a snooker room and a large hall to host functions of up 150 people. The Troubles continued to restrict its operation, however: for much of the early 1980s, for instance, its doors remained closed on Saturday nights for the very simple reason that violence, or the threat of it, had depressed the social life of Belfast city centre.[62]

The Dublin Bankers' Club had to contend with nothing like these challenges. This was the place where, in the words of bank-official-turned-broadcaster Terry Wogan, 'the real bankers of Ireland met . . . This was where they came for shelter and succour from the misery of their bedsits and boarding houses. The Bankers' Club was where they were sure of meeting people as badly off and as lonely as themselves.'[63] By the early 1980s, the lot of the bank official had – thanks mainly to the IBOA – improved greatly, yet more and more of them appeared disinclined to place the Dublin Bankers' Club at the centre of their social lives. Despite having almost 3,000 members – itself a small proportion of overall membership – the club had only a hard-core clientele of 300. The gap between the figures for membership and patronage did not simply reflect the fact that many members lived outside the capital, too far away to frequent the venue. It was also the case that bank officials in the Dublin area found little reason to cross its threshold, preferring to socialise elsewhere.[64]

In an effort to encourage more people to use the facilities, the club received a makeover. And not just once; the Dublin Bankers' Club was renovated twice in the 1980s.[65] By the end of the decade, it had been turned into what the Association believed was 'one of the most luxurious establishments in St Stephen's Green'.[66] The building was extended and a new bar included. This, however, was only one of many attractions. The club's facilities also included a squash court and rooms for reading, watching television and playing snooker. Open to members and pensioners six days a week, the club's newly restored premises were also available to rent for birthday functions, celebrations and parties.[67] Attending the official reopening of the premises in September 1987, the General Secretary of the IBOA, Job Stott, remarked that members could draw encouragement from the refurbishment: 'That people were interested enough to have their club adapted to the best in modern standards augured well for the future and was, in itself, a vote of confidence in the Association.' [68]

V

MEMBERSHIP

In many ways, the value of organised social activity to the integration of members had become more important with time. By the 1980s, the IBOA was on its way to becoming an increasingly diverse organisation. In recognition of the growing integration of financial services worldwide, the Association was intent on broadening its reach to include new financial institutions and the subsidiaries of existing affiliates. In 1985, Larry Broderick, previously a full-time official with the ITGWU, was appointed as Assistant Secretary to oversee recruitment from this sector.[69] And yet, for all that this reflected a need to adapt to changes in the delivery of financial services, one feature of the Irish banking system seemed impervious to any change. Banking was still a sector predominantly staffed by women and run by men. Despite being brought to the fore in the 1970s, the rights of Irish working women continued as a point of protest throughout the 1980s. There was good reason for this. Across the economy, the barriers to the progress of women in the workplace were proving fortress-like: in 1983, a report published by the ICPSA showed that despite the introduction of legislation guaranteeing equal entry into many occupations, women accounted for only 10 per cent of top management positions and 66 per cent of secretarial positions.[70] Worse still was a study by *Business and Finance* magazine of the top 200 companies in the country, which revealed not a single woman in an executive position.[71]

The story inside Irish banks was consistent with these findings: women were still concentrated in the lower ranks and were routinely passed over for promotion. In fact, the longer women stayed working in banks the longer they stood still. The figures bore this out: in 1985, 79 per cent of staff with 15 to 25 years' service represented at Senior Bank Official (SBO) level were women. Significantly, this figure collapsed the higher up the employment ladder you went. Women consituted 39 per cent of staff in the Officer grade, 15 per cent of the Assistant Manager grade, and a mere 1.36 per cent of the Manager positions.[72]

Despite the IBOA's lengthy record of agitation on issues of equality, there was a discernible body of opinion within the Association which held that female bank officials were somehow complicit in their own subordination. Editorials in the *IBOA Newssheet* directed criticism at the poor levels of female participation in IBOA affairs and suggested that change would only be meaningfully affected when women assumed more responsibility for its delivery.[73] Until that point was reached, there was at least one member, a Bank of Ireland employee in Mayo, who felt that the profile afforded to women's issues was unwarranted. In a letter to the *Irish Banking Magazine* in February 1983, he wrote: 'Your continued ballyhoo about the role of women in the Association makes me cringe. When women begin to pull their weight and by that I mean, take on some of the initiatives and worries of men, stay in town at weekends and many more things, then I will give them equal treatment. Until then would you please hold your fire.'[74]

The IBOA did not hold its fire. Nor did the Employment Equality Agency and nor did the government. When the Association continued to press both the problem of promotions for women and the difficulties of accessing fringe benefits like home loans, Sylvia Meehan, the Chairwoman of the Employment Equality Agency, voiced her support. Meehan agreed that the small proportion [of women] in management positions was 'so appalling that the age profile alone [of the women] could hardly explain it'. She added that any discrimination in the granting of loans was covered by the Employment Equality Act and she hoped that the union would take up the case of its women under the terms of this legislation.[75] The renewed focus on women in banking drew a response from the chamber of the Dáil where Nuala Fennell, the Minister of State for Women's Affairs, appealed to both the banks and the IBOA to consult on the development of a comprehensive equal opportunities programme.[76] What emerged was somewhat different. The Bank of Ireland took the historic step of appointing an Equal Opportunities Manager, the first major private sector organisation to create such a position.[77] The IBOA, meanwhile, embarked on a series of meetings and seminars where the issue of equality and women in banking was put under the microscope. These gatherings helped not only to crystallise what the key problems were, but where the possible solutions lay. The latter demanded action on numerous fronts by the banks, including the adoption of a fairer approach to staff training; the appointment of equality officers in all banks; the inclusion of women on interview panels for promotions; the elimination of loan discrimination; and the development of childcare facilities in the workplace for all staff.[78] This series of meetings and seminars was an impressive exercise in internal democracy, but what is showed above all was not how far the women's agenda had already progressed, but how far it had yet to travel.

The predicament of female bank officials stood in stark contrast to that of their mostly male manager colleagues. Where the primary frustration of women in banking was the glacial pace of change in respect of the roles they filled and responsibilities they carried, the complaint among managers was that their responsibilities had become far too onerous. The piling of work upon work led to accusations that bank managers were being both overburdened and excessively pressurised by their employers. The status of the manager had certainly increased with the expansion in the financial services offered by banks. So too, however, did the strain that came with the job. As the *IBOA Newssheet* put it: 'Specialist services and sophisticated management information systems were designed to place in the Managers' hands the ability to deal with the complexities of today's financial world, full of potential but also with the competitiveness honed to a razor edge.'[79]

The commitment demanded of branch managers had become total. It was said, for instance, that some managers had taken to referring to themselves as 'Bank Prostitutes'.[80] As well as attending to their jobs, they were expected to turn up to social and business functions in the evenings and at weekends. They were essentially on call 24 hours a day, 7 days a week. Furthermore, they were expected to do all this without extra pay or resources to support them. With gripes about inadequate staffing commonplace, stories were told of bank managers going into their offices at weekends to type up correspondence because their banks would not supply them with a typist.[81] The IBOA complained that managers were being set targets without the means of their achievement.[82] Wedded to these concerns, however, was a growing unease at how the role of the manager within the bank sat with involvement with the IBOA. As Job Stott told delegates attending the Association's annual conference in 1984, a situation had evolved where 'the manager is supposed to motivate and lead staff from porters up to bank officials to assistant manager ranks during industrial disputes or in all sorts of circumstances where he is expected to devote his total commitment to the bank'.[83] Stott here was touching on a raw nerve. There were certainly those among the rank-and-file membership who felt that managers were not only guilty of transferring unreasonable pressures from themselves onto their staffs but were equally culpable of trying to influence union ballots in the interests of the banks. One such member of the rank and file, in calling for less sectionalism and more solidarity among members, asked that managers examine their role and 'resolve that no action of theirs . . . should ever again be seen to imperil the IBOA'.[84]

VI

PARTNERSHIP?

The question of the role of the manager went to the heart of the changing culture of Irish banking. It offered a clear illustration of how the drive towards greater competitiveness was impinging on both the working lives of bank officials and the broader relationship between the banks and their employees. The pressures on managers to deliver results, the introduction of new technology and the push for extended opening hours were all part of a wider scheme to create a leaner, more competitive and profitable banking system. But at what cost? In his address to the 1984 annual

IBOA democracy: delegates attend a District Secretaries' Conference in 1987.
(IBOA Archive)

conference, Job Stott had pointed ominously to where all this might ultimately lead: 'Targets are being set, with the new dispensation by more subtle and sophisticated means than in the pre-1970 era. It was with those exercises in pre-1970 that the Banks laid the foundations for the 1970s closure. Between all of this, they may be working to generate the same pressures that led to that dispute. They could be doing the same thing at the present time.'[85]

There was, of course, a wider context to all this. The IBOA was acutely conscious that the old rules governing industrial relations were in state of flux. Indeed, throughout the 1980s, it appeared that trade unionism everywhere was on the retreat.[86] In December 1986, for example, the *Irish Banking Magazine* reprinted an article from the journal of the United Mineworkers of America, which offered a fascinating insight into the modern strategies used to undermine and defeat trade unions. Entitled 'The 10 Warning Signs of Union Busting', it observed how the traditional images of armed picket lines and assaults on union members had been replaced by more subtle and sophisticated methods of attack. 'In recent years', the article claimed, 'most union busting managers and their "consultants" have traded in their billy clubs and machine guns for briefcases and three-piece suits.'[87] From the Irish bank officials' perspective, perhaps the most interesting lessons to learn were the ways in which employers got around union opposition by dividing the workers. They did this, it was claimed, by a variety of means, including the provision of union benefits to non-union locations and attempts to take credit for any improvements in wages, benefits and working conditions.[88]

Nowhere was trade unionism under greater siege than in Britain. After the massive demonstrations of union omnipotence in the 1970s, the 1980s brought a backlash. It was led by the Conservative Prime Minister Margaret Thatcher, who introduced radical new legislation designed to limit their scope for industrial action.[89] The effect was felt by British bank officials: speaking to a gathering of IBOA members in 1984, Ken Pooler, President of Britain's Banking, Insurance & Finance Union (BIFU) summed up the difficulties faced by all British trade unions when he remarked on the 'climate of opinion' that had been aligned against them.[90]

In Britain, the electoral appeal of Margaret Thatcher lay in part in her boast to have brought the trade unions to heel and while her totemic victory was that over the mineworkers in 1984, the entire trade union movement emerged from her period in office a more cowed presence in British life.[91] In Ireland, however, there was little stomach or interest in Thatcher-style attacks on the trade unions. Quite the opposite: the Irish government shunned the politics of confrontation for that of cooperation. The result was the rebirth of centralised bargaining. Against the backdrop of national economic crisis, the impetus came from a report by the National Economic and Social Council (NESC), an advisory group comprising employers, trade unions, farmers and senior civil servants, published the year before. The NESC's *Strategy for Development* formed the basis a *Programme for National Recovery* (PNR) which ran from 1987 until 1990.[92] The central feature of this partnership plan was employee acceptance of modest pay rises in exchange for a government commitment to protect social benefits and reform income taxation.[93]

The PNR established a model of social partnership that would underpin Irish economic development for the following 20 years. Like the national wage agreements before it, the PNR would of course provide a steer for future salary negotiations in Irish banking, but what is most striking about industrial relations in the sector at this time was how far removed they were from the prevailing mood of national consensus. Put simply, the principle of partnership that lay at the core of the new Irish economic model was less than conspicuous in Irish banking. By the late 1980s, the major banks appeared increasingly disinclined to engage with the IBOA on issues of vital importance to their members. When, for instance, the five-year Technology and Change Agreement came to an end in 1987, the banks initially dismissed IBOA calls for fresh negotiations by insisting that the original deal was, in fact, open-ended.[94]

This was only part of it. A new deal was eventually reached on technology and change, but, at every turn, it appeared that the IBOA was confronted with new bank policies which threatened to undermine the terms and conditions of the vast majority of their members. By way of example, the Bank of Ireland, in the name of reorganisation, began to press for the introduction of a new grade of lower-paid staff. In 1987, the very year that social partnership

Throughout the 1980s, trade unionism appeared everywhere to be on the retreat. In Britain, the defeat of mineworkers in 1984, seen here clashing with police in Doncaster in March that year, symbolised the diminished influence of the labour movement in British life. While the Irish approach to industrial relations favoured consensus over conflict, the IBOA warned its members of the more subtle and sophisticated techniques that employers used to undermine trade unions. In 1986, quoting from an American journal, they observed how 'union busting managers and their "consultants" have traded in their billy clubs and machine guns for briefcases and three-piece suits'. *(Getty Images)*

was launched, the bank announced plans to replace 2,000 of its officials with a cohort of school leavers whose maximum salary would reach only half that of existing bank officials.[95] Soon after, the bank heightened tensions with the IBOA further by secretly negotiating individual pay deals with 600 of its managers. *The Irish Times* reported at the time that the deal guaranteed increases of between 5 and 10 per cent in return for a stipulation that 'they would continue to work during disputes'.[96]

The Bank of Ireland was not the only institution to embark on a programme of reorganisation and restructuring. The 1980s ended with all the leading Irish banks setting out their visions for the decade to come. Alongside the Bank of Ireland's 'Plan for Improved Competitiveness' sat the AIB's 'Competitive Strategy for the Nineties', the Northern Bank's 'Fast' plan and the Ulster Bank's 'Competitive Edge' plan. Each of these strategies was essentially concerned with cutting costs, and bank officials in the various institutions spent the dying days of the decade trying to soften their impact on the terms and conditions of their working lives. They did this by way of ballots, negotiation and protest. Irish banking was heading towards an uncertain future.

9

The 1990s

In December 1999 the writer Fintan O'Toole reflected on the decade then drawing to a close. He observed how, over the course of a few short years, the 'flow of history' had effectively been reversed. 'For 150 years', he wrote, 'the Irish had gone as economic migrants to the world economy. Now, the world economy had come to Ireland. Abroad had become home.'[1] The change in Ireland's economic fortunes was indeed remarkable. An economy and society that had been blighted by unemployment and emigration in the 1980s was turned on its head. Ireland, so long the laggard of Europe, suddenly stole international headlines for the speed and scale of its economic growth. The statistics alone were staggering: by the mid-1990s, Ireland was creating 50,000 new jobs a year and growth rates of 7.5 per cent were the highest in the world, while inflation and nominal interest rates were kept low.[2] As unemployment plummeted from 19 per cent to 4 per cent and emigration was replaced by net immigration, Irish living standards belatedly rose to match those of the wealthiest of the country's European neighbours.[3]

What brought about this transformation? The short answer is a mixture of good decision-making and good luck. The stability delivered by social partnership certainly played a part, as did the attraction of massive levels of foreign direct investment, especially from US multinationals. But Ireland also benefited hugely from the transfer of structural funds from the European Community, as well as from a favourable demographic profile, with a large young working population supporting fewer and fewer dependants. A combination of these factors underpinned the new era of Irish prosperity, perhaps the most striking and obvious symbol of which was the Irish Financial Services Centre (IFSC). A mountain of shining steel and glass planted on 27 acres of Dublin's docklands, the IFSC was the brainchild of financier Dermot Desmond and the pet project of Charles Haughey, who began the 1990s as Taoiseach. The idea was to turn Dublin into a hub of international financial services and in the process create 7,500 jobs in five years.[4] That target and timeline may not have been met, but the IFSC, where trade unions had no presence, was still considered a major success: a large number of jobs were created and significant tax revenues earned.[5] To a large extent, the very forces that made possible the IFSC – developments in technology and the deregulation and inter-dependency of global financial markets – were those which drove changes in Irish banking into the 1990s. Irish banks provided an increasingly diverse range of services, but competitive pressures and new technology endowed them with both the cause and means to embark on large-scale cost-cutting plans. For the IBOA, therefore, the 1990s presented an appalling paradox: extraordinary economic growth had ensured that the conditions for banking in Ireland had never been better, yet bank officials were faced with unprecedented threats to job security and to the terms and conditions of their work.

I

TOWARDS STRIKE

As the IBOA moved into the last decade of the twentieth century, the job of leadership passed to a new General Secretary. In 1989, Ciaran Ryan, previously a divisional director of the Federated Union of Employers and an official of the Irish Union of

Distributive Workers and Clerks (now MANDATE), was appointed as a replacement for the long-serving Job Stott, who was retiring after 16 years' service.[6] Ryan's arrival coincided with a revamp of the Association's organisational structure. In recognition of the massive burden on the Association's professional negotiators, and in order to address the increasing complexity of industrial relations, two new full-time posts, covering 'Industrial Relations' and 'Training and Development', were created.[7] At the same time, the Association discarded the practice of holding an annual delegates meeting, opting instead to stage biennial conferences, with three District Secretaries' conferences to be held in the intervening periods.[8] The first biennial conference was held in April 1991 and, in a new departure, it was opened up to the media in the hope that it might win favourable publicity for the aims and objectives of the Association. These at least were unchanged: the priorities of the IBOA under Ciaran Ryan were no different from those under any of his predecessors.

The primary focus remained on pay and the IBOA began the 1990s by claiming a salary increase of 6 per cent in excess of the Programme for Economic and Social Progress (PESP), a successor to the Programme for National Recovery (PNR) in the Republic of Ireland. The question that most outside observers wanted answered was how this could be justified. Although not bound by the terms of the PESP, the IBOA was once again in a position of having to explain why their members should be considered distinct from everybody else. According to Ciaran Ryan, bank officials were different because the experience in banking itself was different. The social partnership model was built on the provision of small pay increases in return for tax benefits for workers and job creation within the economy. In banking, however, over 2,000 jobs had been seriously reduced in economic value with the replacement of senior staff on salaries in the region of £20,000 and upwards with staff on an entry salary of just £7,000 per annum. 'Nobody could call that job creation. It was exploitation,' Ryan told delegates attending the first ever biennial conference in April 1991.[9] The new General Secretary added that the IBOA's willingness to facilitate cost reductions within the banks had not been matched by other internal groups. Quoting an Irish Management Institute survey on bank management salaries in the period from 1985 to 1989, he observed that they had risen by 65 per cent.[10]

The prosecution of the IBOA's pay claim put it on a collision course with the managements of the various banks. The prospect of conflict was brought even closer when a ballot of members returned a 'significant majority' in favour of industrial action.[11] In early January 1992, prior to any action being taken, the IBOA agreed to a meeting with the Banks Staff Relations Committee (BSRC). When no agreement emerged, the Executive Committee met to consider its options. What it decided upon was a limited form of industrial action. There would be no full-scale strike: instead members would adhere to strict working hours and refuse to collect fees for assurance- and insurance-related products.[12] The date of its commencement was set for 20 January 1992, but in the days before, the IBOA held further discussions with the BSRC. Whereas the latter held fast to its position that the national wage agreement threshold was sacrosanct and that there could be no deviation from it, the IBOA advocated more flexibility and pointed to recent settlements that had been achieved in the ESB and the Central Bank, where both parties were involved in the national pay deal. The irreconcilability of the two positions led to a breakdown of talks and the industrial action, limited as it was, began as planned.

Even at this early stage, it was apparent that this dispute would be different from anything that had gone before. One reason for this was the tactics deployed by the IBOA; another was the response by the banks. In the case of the IBOA, the strategy adopted was more akin to guerrilla fighting than trench warfare. Measures taken were deliberately intended to hurt their employers, and not their customers. What was denounced as 'immoral' by one bank spokesman was described as 'novel' by one outside observer.[13] These new-style tactics, surgical in design, were dictated by pragmatism. As well as being more 'customer friendly', they were, as one contemporary commentator noted, 'considerably less punitive to the members in cash terms and more astute in hitting the banks. Unlike in former years an all-out strike would be much less effective, as the banks would be able to keep much of their business running. The so-called "hole in the wall" machines alone have transformed the situation.'[14]

The ongoing development of technology undoubtedly shaped the approach taken by the IBOA, but it was equally a factor in shaping the attitude of the banks. In effect, it meant that they could maintain reduced levels of service and avoid a complete shutdown of the system. Writing at the time, UCD economist Moore McDowell observed that the microchip revolution had dovetailed neatly with the cost-cutting plans of the banks. The advance of new technology had, McDowell pointed out, 'drastically reduced the dependence of the banks on labour, both in terms of quantity and quality'.[15] The journalist Matt Cooper, writing in the *Sunday Business Post*, was another to imply a wider motive to the banks' resistance. Were they to succeed in breaking the unions on this issue, he suggested, they might 'find it easier to close uneconomic units throughout the country . . . and by implication, [reduce] their staffing levels.'[16]

No sooner had the IBOA action commenced than complaints began to be heard of widespread intimidation of staff in both Bank of Ireland and AIB. Under pressure from management, it was claimed that a 'small number of members' had given commitments to their banks. The Association argued that any such commitments, given under duress, were lacking in moral or legal value.[17] It was against this fractious industrial relations background that the Association and the banks came together for discussions throughout the month of February. They ended up at the Labour Relations Commission, where conciliation talks continued until early March when they eventually collapsed. This signalled a serious escalation in the dispute. On 3 March 1992, the IBOA issued a directive to members extending the industrial action to include the non-collection or processing of charges and commissions on a range of products and services, including bank drafts, management charges and gift cheques.[18]

A number of banks reacted swiftly and in a manner which worsened relations further. Ulster Bank, National Irish Bank and Bank of Ireland threatened staff with a pay reduction of 20 per cent if they adhered to the IBOA directive. The pressure mounting on employees was severe; they were asked to sign forms agreeing not to participate in the industrial action during the current dispute. Failure to do so would result in the automatic loss of one-fifth of their salary. AIB took a different approach from the other Associated Banks. Initially, they circulated a memorandum to staff which stated that any member who refused to collect charges and fees was liable for prosecution under the provision of the Falsification of Accounts Act, 1875. As it turned out, the memorandum was a mere prelude to more punitive measures. On 12 March, AIB started to suspend staff. The IBOA rushed immediately to their defence, promising to picket AIB branches unless their members were reinstated the following day.

Positions remained entrenched for the rest of February. Even when the Labour Court intervened to hear both sides of the dispute, the hostilities continued, with AIB suspending more and more staff.[19] The report that eventually emerged from the Labour Court would prove a major body blow to the IBOA. Their salary claim was rejected and 'an alternative approach' to the pursuit of their claims was advised. This alternative approach promised to deliver a 6 per cent salary increase, as well as a lump sum of £750 and an extra day's annual leave in return for increased opening hours.[20] The IBOA had always opposed any linking of salary with opening hours and planned only to ballot its members on the Labour Court's recommendation on the substantive issue of the salary claim. Before it could do so, the banks intensified the pressure further. In a move that was tantamount to pouring petrol on smoking embers, the bank managements announced plans to extend opening hours from early May.[21] Bill Brown, Secretary of the Banks' Staff Relations Committee, was bullish in his defence of the move. 'The time for filibuster and veto is over', he declared. 'We are trying to run a business. Enough is enough.'[22] The IBOA responded in kind. This unilateral imposition of new terms and conditions led the Association to call for full-scale industrial action in all banks. The date set was 6 April 1992.

The dispute was now, in the words of one Dáil member, in 'a state of freefall'.[23] On the morning of 6 April, after yet another failed intervention by the Labour Relations Commission, the IBOA placed official pickets on all branches of the AIB, Bank of Ireland, Ulster Bank and the National Irish Bank. With the IBOA and the

IBOA members on the picket line on Dublin's Grafton Street during the 1992 bank strike. The strike exposed many of the divisions among bank employees, with the vast majority of managers opting to work through the dispute. *(RTÉ Stills Library)*

banks locked in stalemate and the state's industrial relations machinery unable to shift them, it took the intervention of the ICTU to break the impasse. On the very first evening of the strike, the ICTU issued a statement to the effect that it was not prepared to stand by while efforts were being made to 'undermine the rights of a trade union to function in the legitimate interests of its members'.[24]

Congress met both the Minister for Labour and the employers' representative body, the Federation of Irish Employers, to hammer out a compromise to bring an end to the bitter dispute. What emerged was a revised settlement, rubber-stamped by the Labour Court. The new terms retained a provision for lunchtime opening, but deferred the introduction of late opening to 4 p.m. until the following January. They also provided for increased lump-sum payments to staff from £750 to £1,000. In addition, it was agreed that the IBOA would be free to raise concerns about change in the context of a review of the 1987 Technology and Change Agreement. Crucially, the Association also secured a 'no victimisation' clause, which was backed by the Minister for Labour, Brian Cowen.[25] This was important. While the new terms bore little resemblance to the IBOA's original demand, the no-victimisation clause at least allowed for a return to work with dignity. This is exactly what it did. On 25 April 1992, IBOA members around the country voted by a narrow majority to end the strike.[26]

In a lengthy analysis of the 1992 bank strike for *Irish Industrial Relations Review*, published shortly after agreement had been reached on a return to work, the journal's editor, Tom Hayes, described it as a 'watershed' moment. This was because the dispute saw the 'working out of a new power balance in industrial relations between the IBOA and the bank managements'.[27] Hayes was critical of the 'macho-ness' of the various bank managements, which had been manifest in the use of threats and intimidation and the deployment of strike-breaking temporary staff, but he also had harsh words for the IBOA. In resorting once again to the threat of strike, Hayes argued that the Association was still wedded to outmoded methods of protest. In the past, IBOA militancy had worked because the banks exercised a monopoly over the provision of banking services and because the Association exercised a monopoly over the employees who delivered those services. Hayes maintained that this was a 'false militancy' as it was adopted 'in the knowledge that it was without cost'.[28] The 1992 strike changed all that. What developments in technology had done was to give the banks the means to maintain a functioning service and this, in turn, enabled them to test the true character of the IBOA's militancy.

Ciaran Ryan addresses a mass meeting of IBOA members in The Point Theatre, 29 March 1992. In the words of one observer, the 1992 bank dispute essentially involved the 'working out of a new power balance in industrial relations between the IBOA and the bank managements'. *(IBOA Archive)*

Amidst allegations of widespread intimidation of staff by bank managements, it soon became clear that the IBOA did not command the support of all its members. In fact, the strike exposed serious fissures in the Association's ranks. To the consternation of the Association and the anger of those on strike, a significant minority passed the picket lines and went to work. Among them was a former IBOA President, Dermot Twomey, who 'led a group of managers' past a picket in Castlebar.[29] The sense of betrayal cut deep. In a letter to a national newspaper, written in the immediate aftermath of the dispute, one IBOA member assessed the fallout from the tactics of the banks and the willingness of so many staff members to defy the pickets. G. F. Dalton from Dun Laoghaire wrote: 'This dispute has left a legacy of bitterness between banking colleagues and the team spirit that has been built and nurtured over years of hard work has been seriously shattered. Staff are now demoralised, questioning their loyalty to an employer who uses such ham-fisted and bootboy tactics in response to their Association's legitimate request for a salary increase.'[30]

The IBOA emerged profoundly changed from the 1992 strike. For a start, it was a seriously shrunken organisation, its numbers greatly reduced. Four thousand members, 1,000 of them managers, were expelled when the Association took the decision to purge itself of those whose loyalty it could no longer rely upon.[31] It left the Association representing only 50 branch managers in all 4 Associated Banks.[32] The expulsions were the harshest of sanctions and one that would damage the income stream of the Association. It would also have a significant impact on recruitment, since bank managers had been influential in persuading new entrants to join the Association. Nonetheless, the expulsions met with popular internal support. Indeed, the anger directed at those who opted to work through the strike would prove slow to cool. Five years on, in 1997, the issue of the readmission of expelled members gave rise to lengthy and contentious debate at meetings across the country. It continued through to the biennial conference in Dublin where one delegate, an AIB official from Nenagh, expressed a concern that the Association might be 'infected' by the return of 'rats' that had deserted the ship in 1992.[33]

By then, however, the strength of the IBOA was not solely dependent on the size of its own membership. In a historic move, the Association had jettisoned a tradition of defiant independence and allied itself with the ICTU. The decision to affiliate to Congress, taken in December 1992, signalled an end to the idea of IBOA exceptionalism. By stepping into the mainstream of the Irish trade union movement, Peter Cassells, the General Secretary of the ICTU, stated that bank officials (and airline pilots, whose representative body joined at the same time) were no longer holding themselves up as something separate or apart. 'We've come a long way', he said, 'from the blinkered stereotypes of bank clerks as well-bred gentlemen with starch collars, condescending looks and *The Irish Times* on order.'[34] This was undoubtedly the case, but the decision taken by the IBOA was born of a hard-headed pragmatism and self-interest. It was to do with what was best for bank officials. The Association had begun to look afresh at its relationship with the ICTU in late 1990 when a special group was appointed to conduct a detailed examination of the affiliation question, which would involve discussions with various neutral bodies and experts in the industrial relations field.[35] But it was the positive role played by the ICTU in bringing closure to the 1992 dispute that acted as the real catalyst to membership. That dispute brought into sharp focus the vulnerability of bank officials, the inefficacy of established responses to challenges from management and the dangers of isolationism. Ciaran Ryan, a firm advocate of affiliation, was clear on the need for the Association to adapt to the new circumstances that prevailed. In any case, the old concerns about Congress being dominated by industrial-based unions no longer held. The growth of the ICTU, an all-island body, was largely explained by an influx from the professional and public sectors. These groups overwhelmed the industrial-based membership, which, by the early 1990s, accounted for only 36 per cent of the total.[36] As Ryan explained it, the advantages of membership outweighed all other considerations.[37] The membership, north and south, agreed, voting by a large majority in support of a motion which came with a recommendation from the Executive Committee.[38]

In April 1993, Peter Cassells addressed the biennial delegate conference of the IBOA and spoke of how the 1992 dispute had forged a 'special bond' between the IBOA and the ICTU, and how their decision to join Congress meant that they were now linked up with half a million other workers and their families, among them 'teachers in classrooms, nurses in hospital wards, workers on the factory floor, people on building sites and workers in the hotels where they [the bank officials] held their conferences'.[39] The simple truth was that these were occupational groups that Irish bank officials would have been at pains to distance themselves from in previous decades and the fact they were now gathered under the one organisational umbrella spoke volumes for how far the industrial relations landscape had shifted.

Unquestionably, affiliation to Congress had the effect of making the IBOA more outward-looking. For a start, it provided a wider frame of reference by involving IBOA officials and members in the various activities and campaigns organised under the ICTU banner. In promoting the case for Congress in 1992, Ciaran Ryan had made the point that the IBOA would get out of the relationship effectively what they put into it. Influence, he insisted, would flow from 'positive active participation'.[40] Ryan himself would marry his responsibilities at the IBOA with membership of the Executive Council of the ICTU, but engagement occurred at many levels. In March 1994, for instance, the IBOA participated in its first ICTU Women's Conference and its representatives secured the passage of two resolutions dealing with issues of sexual harassment and the transferability of employees.[41] All of this was reported in the pages of the *IBOA Newssheet* which did much to inform its readers of developments in the wider trade union movement; information was routinely carried on ICTU initiatives and events and coverage was also afforded to disputes involving workers in other sectors of the economy. Whether it was the plight of workers at the 'Pat the Baker' factory in Dublin, at Dunnes Stores, or baggage handlers at Ryanair, the *Newssheet* rallied to the cause of trade union solidarity.[42]

If there was one issue on which the members of the IBOA and ICTU had always found common purpose it was opposition to conflict in Northern Ireland. Both organisations had a cross-border membership who had for many years found themselves as innocents caught up in the storm of political violence. Since the early days of the Troubles, Irish bank officials had been the victims of repeated bank raids by paramilitary groups. The frequency of attacks had tended to rise and fall, but in the early 1990s there were worrying signs of yet another escalation, with criminal gangs adding to the threat already posed by paramilitaries.[43] The decade began ominously: in January 1990, staff and customers of the Bank of Ireland in Athy, County Kildare, were held hostage as their building was surrounded by armed detectives, the siege ending with the Gardaí opening fire and one of the armed gang receiving a fatal bullet to the head.[44] Two years later, in November 1992, an armed robbery on a TSB branch in New Ross, County Wexford, ended with the murder of a bank employee, Carol Walsh.[45] Then, in the very month that two men were put on trial for Walsh's murder, the chief executive of the National Irish Bank, Jim Lacey, was kidnapped and held captive in his home. The Association's response to these events and to the growing phenomenon of kidnapping and armed raids was two-sided: on the one hand, it advised members on the importance of vigilance and consulted with the Gardaí and the RUC in drawing up a security document for staff; on the other hand, it publicly denounced the leniency of the law in dealing with those found guilty of serious crimes like kidnapping and robbery. In the Irish Republic, the IBOA was part of a vocal lobby which called for an amendment to the bail laws, making direct representations to the Minister for Justice.[46] Even so, it took the murder of journalist Veronica Guerin and an ensuing public outcry to force political action. The government introduced a raft of anti-crime measures, among them a proposal to give the courts more power to restrict access to bail. This required a constitutional change and a referendum was held in November 1996. Despite a very low turnout, the result of the referendum was clear cut: the amendment was passed by a large majority, with almost 75 per cent of those who voted approving of the change.[47]

The impetus behind the introduction of tougher bail laws came from the growth in the activities of criminal gangs rather than those of paramilitaries. Yet the 1990s witnessed some of the bloodiest scenes of the Northern Ireland conflict. Paradoxically, it also saw significant political development. A peace process emerged in the

Armed detectives surround the Bank of Ireland in Athy in January 1990 as staff and customers are held hostage inside. The siege ended with gunfire and the death of one of the armed gang. The early 1990s saw an increase in the frequency of armed attacks on bank premises. *(Robert Redmond Photography)*

early 1990s but its course ran anything but smoothly. Momentum was stop-start as political progress competed with violent setback. A major breakthrough was undoubtedly the declaration of an IRA ceasefire in 1994, but this ended when the same organisation planted a huge bomb in London's Docklands in February 1996. The following month, more than 100,000 people participated in massive peace demonstrations on the streets of towns and cities in both the Republic and Northern Ireland. Among them were IBOA members who responded to a call from the ICTU for workers 'to express their abhorrence at the return to violence' and to demand that political and community leaders dedicate themselves to the achievement of a permanent peace.[48] This, indeed, is what most of them did. After painstaking negotiations, the signing of the Good Friday Agreement in April 1998 was a historic landmark. The peace it delivered may have been imperfect, but the agreement provided a political road-map out of Northern Ireland's 30-year cycle of violence and blood-letting. The *IBOA Newssheet* was quick to acknowledge the historic nature of the settlement, which was heralded in a series of editorials in the summer of 1998.

An association for all the family: bank officials and their children enjoy a day out at Dublin Zoo in 1997. *(IBOA Archive)*

II

REBUILDING INDUSTRIAL RELATIONS

If the forging of closer links between the IBOA and ICTU was one of the most obvious by-products of the 1992 dispute, what about relations within banking itself? To what extent, if at all, did they repair or improve? In adjudicating on that bitter dispute, the

Labour Court had recommended that a special review of the industrial relations climate be conducted by a senior official of the Labour Court in conjunction with the two parties involved, the representatives of management and staff. It was badly needed. An alarming feature of the 1992 strike was that it exposed the same deep-rooted weakness in banking relations as Professor Michael Fogarty had discussed in his report on the lengthy dispute of 1970. For all that the job of banking had changed in the intervening years, relations between management and officials were still characterised by distrust on either side. The purpose of the climate review was to create conditions to foster an improvement in this situation. It never fulfilled that ambition. Two years after the conclusion of the dispute, Ciaran Ryan lamented the failure of the review body to deliver any substantial progress.[49]

The reasons for this were cultural and practical. In truth, the atmosphere of suspicion, built up over many years and reinforced during the 1992 strike, was always going to be difficult to dispel. But this difficulty was compounded by the collapse of the traditional channels of communication. In January 1994, before the review of the industrial relations climate had even been concluded, the BSRC was wound up. It had been in existence for 75 years, its forerunner having been established to coordinate the response of the banks when the IBOA had been founded in 1918. Such longevity notwithstanding, its demise came as no great shock to the Association. From the mid-1980s, the various banks had become increasingly inclined to negotiate separately with their staff. Nevertheless, the elimination of industry-wide bargaining presented the IBOA with major problems. The immediate priority was to confirm that existing agreements on the terms and conditions of employment for bank officials would be honoured. As for the longer term, the Association would be forced to conduct all future negotiations on a bank-by-bank basis. This added hugely to the burden of the Association's workload, raising concerns about its ability to press its members' claims properly. Writing in the *IBOA Newssheet*, Ciaran Ryan stated that the change in the arrangement with the banks 'constituted the greatest challenge that has been faced in the history of the Association'.[50] This was little exaggeration. The demands placed on

IBOA negotiators grew exponentially. Between 1993 and 1995, the Executive Committee was required to deal with almost 250 collective industrial relations issues, a figure that did not take account of the work done on behalf of individual members.[51]

While most banks were content to deal with the IBOA on an individual basis, there was one notable exception. Even before the dismantling of the Banks' Staff Relations Committee, Northern Ireland's largest bank, Northern Bank, was attempting to bypass the IBOA in the implementation of a programme of change. The decade had begun with IBOA members in the bank rejecting a cost-cutting plan, known as F.A.S.T., on the grounds that it would undermine the terms and conditions of all existing and future employees.[52] When bank officials in AIB in the Republic rejected a similar plan from their bosses, the two sides entered into negotiations and reached a resolution. There was no engagement of this sort in Northern Bank.[53] Instead, the bank decided on the unilateral introduction of its cost-cutting strategy. What it involved was a complete undermining of existing terms of employment. A bank profit share system, enjoyed by most employees, was replaced by a performance bonus scheme that was available to a much more limited number; a new appraisal system was introduced with implications for the future career prospects of all employees; and Saturday opening in the bank's Bloomfield branch was introduced without any consultation with the IBOA. Not only did the bank offer staff nothing in return for these changes, it refused to provide any reassurances on the integrity of existing agreements, on job security or on the placing of consultation and agreement at the heart of any future change.[54]

The IBOA responded with industrial action, endorsed by a ballot of demoralised Northern Bank officials. A one-day stoppage, held on 16 September 1994, had the desired effect. It forced the bank into negotiations with the IBOA under the auspices of Northern Ireland's Labour Relations Agency, arising from which an agreement was signed by both parties. Within weeks, however, the IBOA was accusing the bank of having breached its terms. An essential part of the agreement had been a Northern Bank guarantee that there would be no victimisation of any staff members arising out of the dispute.[55] The IBOA claimed that this had not been honoured and pointed to the fact that a payment of £150 had been made to those who had worked on the day of the stoppage. The IBOA claimed that this was a deliberate act of discrimination.[56] The upshot was that a dispute that had appeared settled flared up with even greater intensity. It ran until the summer of 1995, with the emphasis shifting to the terms of a new salary restructuring programme, as part of which several hundred staff would have had their pay reduced by £5,000 in return for a once-off lump payment. Under the new salary scales, the IBOA estimated that, in simple terms, a Senior Bank Official with 20 years to go to retirement would lose £100,000.[57] As Peter Cassells, the General Secretary of the ICTU put it: 'No worker in Ireland or anywhere else in the world had ever been asked to accept either a £5,000 pay cut or never get another pay increase for the rest of their life.'[58] The sense of outrage was not confined to trade unionists. In an extraordinary demonstration of cross-community consensus for the time, the leaders of three of Northern Ireland's main political parties – Rev. Ian Paisley of the Democratic Unionist Party (DUP), John Hume of the Social Democratic and Labour Party (SDLP) and John Alderdice of the Alliance Party – wrote to the managing director of the National Australia Bank, which owned Northern Bank, requesting a reconsideration of the pay proposals put to staff.[59]

In the face of political and trade union pressure and intense media attention, Northern Bank refused to yield. In the end, the staff at the bank, assured by the guarantees they were given on job security and promotional prospects, voted to accept the new terms and conditions. It was a decision that ran contrary to the advice of their union. The President of the IBOA, Leonard Coote, made no effort to conceal his disappointment at the outcome. Coote remarked that the very essence of the Association was that employees had come together to ensure that their aspirations, in terms of salaries and conditions, could be put to the banks more effectively than as individuals. 'It would appear that a majority of members in the Northern Bank do not believe this to be the case', he said.[60] While the IBOA staff at headquarters and their Northern Bank Executive colleagues had 'left no stone unturned in their efforts to encourage staff to hold firm to their principles', Coote maintained that the 'fear factor' had taken hold and 'the lemmings rushed headlong to jump over the cliff into totally uncharted territory'.[61]

The Northern Bank dispute was yet another setback for the IBOA. As with the national strike three years before, when a significant minority of the workforce passed picket lines, it struck at the very idea of trade union solidarity, underlining the effectiveness of the banks in dividing workers and weakening the influence of the Association. Almost as important as the outcome of the Northern Bank dispute, however, were the issues that it brought to the fore. In its embrace of performance-related pay and cost-reduction packages, there was nothing unique about Northern Bank.[62] This would become an industry standard. Indeed, the same consultancy firm that advised Northern Bank on the introduction of performance-related pay in the mid-1990s provided similar advice to Ulster Bank (north and south) and to Bank of Ireland in Great Britain.[63] The Chief Executive of Northern Bank, John Wright, defended the incentivised system as 'a fair and equitable way of rewarding the individual . . . It allows staff to earn more based on their own personal performance and this clearly focuses everyone on the business of providing the best service possible to our customers.'[64]

The IBOA, for its part, was not opposed in principle to performance-related pay. Rather, they held serious reservations about the criteria used to assess it and the fact that it invariably came enmeshed with wider issues of pay reform. Across the banking sector, the drive to reduce costs had involved a diminution in staff numbers as a result of non-recruitment and voluntary severance packages. By the mid-1990s, however, the focus of the banks' cost reduction strategies moved from staff numbers to staff terms and conditions. The restructuring of salary packages was a way of continuing the cost reduction policy without further lowering the numbers employed by the banks. 'If you want to reduce costs and you can't reduce staff numbers, what do you do?' Ciaran Ryan rhetorically asked in an address to the Association's 1995 annual conference: 'You replace experienced officials earning for example, £22,000 a year and replace them with somebody on the lower salary levels of say £8,000 or £9,000, 40% of the original value of the job.'[65]

213

The IBOA struggled to reconcile the apparent necessity of wage cuts with the reality of rising bank profits. At every opportunity, the Association highlighted the fact that the terms and conditions of its members were being progressively eroded at a time when the banks were achieving record profits, when stock market valuations were climbing and when dividends were running far in excess of the cost-of-living increases or the pay awards the banks were willing to concede. The growth in bank profits was certainly remarkable, rising from IR£175 million to over IR£1 billion over the first six years of the 1990s.[66] However, it was not the scale of these increases which upset the IBOA. The Association fully accepted the importance of profit-making, but argued that the rewards should be more equitably shared and used as the basis to provide for greater job security.[67] As the 1990s wore on, however, the gap between IBOA aspiration and banking practice showed little sign of closing. Again and again, the Association felt compelled to stress that the beneficiaries of soaring profits in the sector were not those who helped produce it; rather it was the banks' shareholders and banks' directors who, it was pointed out, were increasingly in receipt of 'outrageously high' bonus payments.[68] While various banks moved to introduce profit-sharing schemes, these came nowhere close to meeting the expectations of staff, the IBOA's Larry Broderick deriding them as essentially 'meaningless'.[69] The strength of the Association's claim for a better return for their members was underlined by figures indicating the levels of profit that bank officials were generating for their employers. A point repeatedly made was that profits per employee in banking were higher than anywhere else: in 1996, for example, the level of profit per employee stood at IR£25,000 in Bank of Ireland and just under IR£28,000 in Ulster Bank. This compared with an average profit per employee of IR£9,235 in the top six industrial companies in Ireland, which included such household names as the Smurfit Group, Cement Roadstone, Avonmore, Kerry Co-op and Fyffes.[70]

Despite the mounting frustrations of bank officials at the unequal distribution of growing bank wealth, the late 1990s remained a period of relative industrial calm. There were two principal reasons for this: firstly, the IBOA, for all its opposition to the direction of banks' policy, was still actively engaged in the various banks and was intent on ensuring that the introduction of change would at least result from of a process of negotiation rather than imposition from above;[71] secondly, by joining Congress in 1992, the IBOA finally fell within the terms of national wage agreements in the Republic of Ireland. The social partnership model, begun in 1987, continued to shape the industrial relations landscape in the Republic through the 1990s. When the time frame of the PESP elapsed, it was simply succeeded by the Programme for Competitiveness and Work (PCW) which ran from 1994 to 1996 and then by Partnership 2000 which carried the arrangement into the new millennium. The essential elements of these agreements were broadly similar: each covered a three-year term and each involved commitments in relation to tax reform and pay, while allowing for a limited measure of local bargaining. Among IBOA members there was a general consensus that involvement in social partnership had been a positive experience and enabled them an input into strategic decision-making, yet there persisted a frustration at the inflexibility of local bargaining. This led to a shift in emphasis towards the end of the decade. As Partnership 2000 approached its conclusion, the IBOA began to examine ways of improving the co-operative model within the banking sector. In order for it to be developed into the future, they insisted that partnership in banking would need be underpinned by certain basic principles, which would address bank officials' wider concerns around proper profit sharing, job security, quality of life, family-friendly workplaces and union recognition.[72] In pressing these issues, the IBOA was laying down a firm marker for the future. What they were saying was that the partnership model should not be taken for granted; that it needed it to be developed and deepened. For this to happen, however, the banking industry needed to create a genuine 'partnership of equals', not a partnership where the Association was simply used to 'facilitate change'. [73]

Bank officials cheer on the Republic of Ireland soccer team during the
World Cup of 1994. *(IBOA Archive)*

III

TOWARDS THE NEW MILLENNIUM

While issues of pay remained paramount, the enlarging of the
IBOA's agenda to encompass 'environmental' concerns was
significant, if unsurprising. In many ways, the drift in IBOA
thinking was simply a mirror of developments in the wider trade
union movement and the social partnership model. But the new
emphasis was also a measure of the huge time and effort that the
Association had dedicated to the raising of members' awareness of
general welfare issues in the workplace. The impetus for much of
this work came from a decision to expand the core objectives of the

216

Association to include the establishment of 'equality of opportunity' for all members within the Association and within the workplace.[74] Arising from this constitutional change, agreed at the 1993 biennial conference, an equality subcommittee was established which became one of the most active in the Association. As well as highlighting the under-representation of women in senior management positions and the vulnerability of temporary and part-time workers, the sub-committee was instrumental in developing IBOA policy around issues of bullying, harassment and sexual harassment in the work-place. These policies were backed by the provision of practical assistance: IBOA members who made complaints of sexual harassment, for instance, were able to avail of the services of a team of trained advisers.[75]

All of this was important work and signalled the Association's willingness to adapt to concerns that arose from the changing working lives of its members. However, the provision of an enhanced range of services and supports was also a selling point for an Association intent on rebuilding its membership following the expulsions of 1992. Where they looked for them said much about the shifting landscape of Irish banking and financial services generally. The Association chased recruits among those on temporary and part-time contracts as well as those working in the emergent areas of internet-based 24-hour banking and telebanking call centres, a system that allowed customers to do routine banking business over the telephone. These were fertile areas for recruitment and they were aggressively targeted. To help with the job, a Membership Recruitment Officer was appointed in 1998 and in the last six months of that year, 1,000 new members had joined the Association.[76] Many of these were attracted not simply by the promise of representation in relation to the terms and conditions of their employment; they were also seduced by the value-added benefits that came from membership as the IBOA won favourable rates on everything from short-break holidays and mobile phones to health and car insurance.[77]

The rebuilding of IBOA membership – it stood at approximately 16,000 at the end the decade – occurred at a time of declining public confidence in the traditional Irish banking system. Towards the end of the decade, the sector was shaken by a series of scandalous disclosures. It began in January 1998 when RTÉ reporters Charlie Bird and George Lee broke a story which claimed that National Irish Bank (NIB) had been guilty of encouraging tax evasion. It was alleged that the bank had helped move customers' money into accounts held offshore by an Isle of Man investment company called Clerical Medical International (CMI). The CMI product had been pushed throughout the NIB branch network and sold to customers – farmers, publicans, shopkeepers and the like – as a way of earning interest on income that had not been declared to the Revenue Commissioners.[78] This was not the only malpractice that RTÉ disclosed. In March 1998, more wrongdoing came to light. The broadcaster produced evidence from insiders in NIB that interest and fees were being loaded onto customers' accounts as means of boosting profits.[79] Overcharging was done on a random and unscientific basis. Often, personal whim determined who would be targeted and by how much. 'It was a guesstimate', one bank official later confessed. 'I would have sort of thought what sort of a nuisance has he [the customer] been over the previous period and come up with a figure. Truthfully, I would say there was a lot of guesswork done on troublesome accounts, put on a bit here and there.'[80]

The revelations of wrongdoing in NIB caused a sensation. The political reaction was led by the Minister for Enterprise, Trade and Employment, Mary Harney, who appointed inspectors of the high court to undertake an independent investigation of the allegations made in the RTÉ reports. The IBOA, meanwhile, sought to ensure that senior management in the bank did not attempt to transfer the responsibility for the malpractices onto junior bank officials. 'What we are looking at is the implementation of management policy – not the individual initiative of employees', Ciaran Ryan emphasised in the *IBOA Newssheet*.[81] Ultimately, this was the conclusion reached by the high court inspectors appointed to investigate the scandal. Their report, published six years after the stories broke in the national media, exonerated the NIB's rank-and-file staff, the focus of its criticisms falling instead on the behaviour of senior management. Touching on the role of junior officials, the report simply stated that though they 'may have been aware of practices which were improper, they were not in a position to effect change, and so could not be held to be in any way responsible for their existence.'[82]

The scandals exposed at NIB were not isolated. Indeed, one of the most striking features of the inspectors' report into the bank was the acknowledgement of tax evasion as an 'industry-wide' phenomenon.[83] This was a clear reference to evidence that had emerged in a report from a parliamentary inquiry in the Republic into Deposit Interest Retention Tax (DIRT), published in December 1999. DIRT was essentially a collection tax introduced in 1986: deposit takers were obliged to deduct it at source from the interest they paid to borrowers and to pass it on to the Revenue Commissioners. The fact that it was not applied to non-resident accounts had led, however, to an astonishing increase in the number of non-residents opening accounts in Irish banks. By 1998 17 per cent of all Irish deposits were held by non-residents.[84] The extent of DIRT evasion was epic in scale: it was, as the inquiry report stated, 'large-scale, systematic and carried out over many years'.[85]

That this practice had persisted for so long raised serious questions for the agencies of the state. However, the DIRT Inquiry report was, first and foremost, a damning commentary on the ethical conduct of Irish banking. The inquiry found, for instance, that bank officials had both facilitated and partaken in DIRT evasion. They had done this by 'organising the opening and operation of bogus non-resident accounts for customers', as well as by establishing similar accounts for their own use.[86] In the midst of all the critical coverage that focused on the DIRT inquiries, which were held in full public view, the IBOA was quick to defend its members from public opprobrium. As with their response to the breaking NIB scandal the year before, there was no acknowledgement that any member might have in any way facilitated tax evasion or have been complicit in wrongdoing, yet this was certainly the case. As one NIB employee later conceded, these scandals were 'perpetrated by the staff at the insistence of the Senior Executives'.[87] In the face of this obvious truth, the IBOA chose to deflect attention from the involvement of its own members, its approach characterised by an insistence that ordinary bank officials should not be left to shoulder blame which they felt properly belonged elsewhere. The Association vowed to protect its members 'from being left carrying the can in a situation that was created by the greed and acquisitiveness of those in senior positions in the industry'.[88]

If the IBOA's response to the NIB and DIRT scandals was instinctively defensive, this was not to say they were equivocal about the wrongdoing or blind to the need to address the wider reputational damage of the banking sector. They were neither. The Association was at once emphatic in declaring practices like the loading of interest charges and fees as 'theft' and conscious that the best way to defend IBOA members was to protect the industry itself. It was, after all, rank-and-file bank officials who bore the brunt of growing customer cynicism and anger about how banks were going about their business.[89] To this end, the Association proposed that management and employee representatives combine to produce a joint code of ethics for the banking industry, to which everyone would subscribe. Were such a code to be introduced, the IBOA believed that the prospects of a repetition of the NIB and DIRT 'shambles' would be greatly reduced.[90]

The IBOA proposal was verdict enough on the banking system that had been created in the 1990s. In many ways, indeed, the working culture that had given rise to the abuse and corruption that had been exposed in the NIB and DIRT cases was one which the IBOA had done more than most to highlight. When the inspectors' report on events in the NIB referred to a 'target driven' operational environment where managers felt under pressure to achieve 'unreasonable' targets, they might have been quoting from any number of IBOA conference speeches or publications throughout the decade.[91] In April 1991, for instance, Margaret Browne, speaking on behalf of Dublin Branch Representatives, observed: 'New products and marketing ploys were presented on their [bank officials] desks every day of the week. They were expected to operate like robots. With diminishing Branch structures and the reduction of staffing, the matter was extremely serious . . . Management's only interest was the Balance Sheet, and their own performance, and what profits were being generated in each branch.'[92] The IBOA lamented that the pursuit of profit at all costs had become the guiding principle of Irish banking policy – and all to its ultimate disgrace.

10

The 2000s

A decade that ended in banking crisis gave way to one that would be remembered for banking collapse. The first decade of the twenty-first century saw the Irish boom turn to bust as high unemployment and emigration, the familiar markers of Irish economic failure, returned. The wrecking ball that destroyed the Irish economy was the country's banks. The scale of their folly was colossal in cause and consequence. Put simply, the banks took massive foreign borrowing and got 'caught up in the mass psychology of an unprecedented property bubble'.[1] When the bubble burst, the banks were exposed to crippling losses, which in turn raised concerns about their liquidity and solvency. The extent to which these losses imperilled the banks became apparent in September 2008 when, to the astonishment of the outside world, the Irish government felt compelled to introduce a blanket guarantee of all liabilities held by Irish-controlled banks. Radical as it was, this intervention was not successful. As the economy contracted and the Irish government injected large sums into bank recapitalisation, international confidence, both financial and political, in Ireland's ability to secure its financial system gradually ebbed away.[2]

By November 2010, it became clear that the Irish solution to the Irish banking crisis had failed. When the country and its banks were no longer able to borrow money on the international markets at affordable rates and the problems of Ireland threatened to engulf other euro-zone states, the International Monetary Fund (IMF) and the European Union (EU) stepped in. A massive, and controversial, rescue package worth €85 billion was agreed between the IMF, the EU and the Irish government aimed at stabilising Ireland's banks and public finances. A cornerstone of the deal was a promise to restructure completely the Irish banking system. The plan was for Ireland to have smaller banks and fewer of them. For the IBOA, the implications of this were profound. The Union was already in retreat as a result of the banking crisis: between September 2008 and November 2010, it had lost members as cuts were imposed across a drastically revamped banking sector. Six thousand jobs in the financial services sector were lost as five of the six domestic banking institutions were effectively nationalised and the State acquired a significant minority shareholding in the sixth. It turned out that these changes, seismic as they were, marked only the beginning of a much longer process of reform. Under the terms of the rescue package agreed with the IMF and the EU, a more fundamental restructuring of the banks was pledged and the loss of thousands of more jobs threatened.

The reverberations from the banking crisis were felt everywhere. Not only did it impinge upon all sectors of the economy and society, it also shook the political establishment. As the economy went into freefall and fiscal sovereignty was effectively relinquished, the credibility of the Irish government quickly crumbled. Within months of the conclusion of the international rescue deal, the Fianna Fáil-led coalition government had disintegrated and a general election had been called. The result was at once astonishing and entirely understandable. Fianna Fáil, the dominant party in the southern state since the 1930s, saw its share of the vote collapse (it fell from 41.5 per cent in 2007 to 17.4 per cent in 2011) as the electorate unleashed its anger on the party that had been at the heart of government for the previous fourteen years.[3] Ultimately, the election replaced one coalition with another. With Fianna Fáil and the Green Party obliterated at the polls, the Fine Gael and Labour parties were swept to power with a huge majority and a daunting in-tray of problems awaiting them. Perhaps the biggest – and most politically sensitive – of these problems was the derelict state of the banks. How they planned to deal with this mess soon became apparent. In March 2011, a matter of weeks after the election, the new Minister for Finance, Michael Noonan, unveiled a blueprint for the future of Irish banking. As expected, it envisaged a major redrawing of the Irish banking landscape. Of the six domestic banks, it was considered that only two – Bank of Ireland and AIB – had a long-term role as so-called 'pillar banks', with the latter set to acquire EBS as a subsidiary.[4] Meanwhile, the two worst performing institutions, Anglo Irish Bank and Irish Nationwide Building Society (which coincidentally had been the two most resistant to trade union organisation), were to be merged with a view to being wound down within ten years. While the immediate prospects for Irish Life and Permanent involved the disposal of its profitable life business in order to raise capital for its Permanent TSB banking arm, the long-term future of the latter remained in question.

This shake-up of the system was not restricted to Irish-owned banks, however. The Republic's two most prominent foreign-owned banking institutions, Ulster Bank (owned by Royal Bank of Scotland) and National Irish Bank (owned by Danske Bank in Denmark), had been engaged in major restructuring of their own since the onset of the crisis, with Ulster Bank shedding almost 1,000 staff in 2009 and National Irish Bank completing a programme of around 150 job cuts with the closure of half of its branch network in 2010. By way of contrast, Danske Bank's Northern Ireland subsidiary, Northern Bank, had come through the crisis relatively unscathed, its traditionally conservative approach to lending appearing to have prevented it from following the other major institutions on the island into recklessness. As for Halifax-Bank of Scotland, the most prominent of the other foreign-owned banks operating in Ireland, it opted to exit the market altogether, hastily winding down its business banking entity, Bank of Scotland Ireland, and closing its Halifax retail network, again with the loss of a substantial number of jobs.[5] The pace of all this change was bewildering. In less than three years, the Irish banking scene had been transformed in an extraordinary fashion and to a degree that it was virtually unrecognisable from that which existed at the turn of the millennium.

I

PAY AND PARTNERSHIP

The extent to which the banking crisis and the sharp economic downturn that ensued came as a shock to the Irish system was apparent from a report published in June 2008, a mere three months before the bank guarantee was introduced. An analysis of the Irish economy in the early twenty-first century, prepared by the National Economic and Social Council (NESC), the body which had inspired the social partnership model in the late 1980s, provided a broadly positive outlook. The NESC prediction was for Irish economic growth to slow, not to stop or reverse.[6] The report was in no way blind to the vulnerabilities of the Irish economy, however. In acknowledging immediate domestic and international difficulties, it told also of how the dynamics of Irish growth had changed for the worse in the early years of the new century. Between 2000 and 2007, growth in GNP averaged 4.6 per cent, the highest of any of the EU's fifteen member states.[7] However, unlike the mid-1990s, when Ireland's rapid economic growth was driven by exports, the growth levels achieved in the early 2000s resulted from an extraordinary period of house building.

It is a measure of how dangerously reliant the Irish economy became on construction that, by 2006, the industry accounted for 20 per cent of GNP.[8] Property prices ballooned and nowhere more than in Dublin: in the ten years from 1996, the cost of a house in Dublin increased by 360 per cent (235 per cent in real terms) and it was in recognition of this that the IBOA fought for, and won, a special Dublin living allowance for members in Ulster Bank.[9] In what the Association and many public sector unions hoped would be a precedent-setting concession, 1,500 Ulster Bank staff living within a fifteen-mile radius of O'Connell Street received an additional IR£2,000 a year.[10] The IBOA itself was a beneficiary of rising property values: in 1998 it had purchased 94 St Stephen's Green as an investment and derived substantial rental income from the building; later, in the mid-2000s, at the height of the boom, it opted to sell all of its property on St Stephen's Green. The buildings, which had provided a focal point of IBOA activity since 1918, were no longer considered fit for purpose and, protected as they were by a conservation order, would have been too costly to reconfigure.[11] In the search for a new headquarters, however, the Association did not travel far. A newly built office block was acquired on Stephen's Street, off Aungier Street, where staff were resettled during the summer of 2006. The wrench with St Stephen's Green, with all its historical associations, was great, but the sale of the three buildings proved necessary and rewarding: it left the IBOA 'financially sound' and with a wholly owned state-of-the-art facility from which to deliver an enhanced range of services to its members.[12]

In 2006, the IBOA relocated to a purpose-built office block on Stephen's Street, off Aungier Street, in Dublin. *(Tommy Clancy)*

The decision to move headquarters was taken in the wake of a strategic review of IBOA operations, an initiative of the new General Secretary, Larry Broderick. When his predecessor Ciaran Ryan retired in 2001, Broderick, then Assistant General Secretary, had been the obvious choice as his replacement. Described by ICTU's Peter Cassells as the 'boy wonder' of the Irish trade movement, Broderick brought to the role a deep understanding of the banking industry and industrial relations across the three jurisdictions in which the IBOA operated.[13] He also brought a sobering analysis of the state of Irish banking at the beginning of the twenty-first century. Despite the high profits in the sector, Irish banking was, Broderick believed, in a state of crisis. Against a background of hostile mergers, radical change programmes, branch closures and well-publicised scandals, Broderick called for a public debate on the future of banking in Ireland.[14] It was a future that must, he insisted, have customers and staff at its heart. As matters stood in 2001, the belief was that the demands being placed on staff were excessive. As Broderick explained it: 'Staff are expected to embrace major change without adequate training and support. Staff turnover has never been higher and new staff are not willing to stay in the Bank due to low pay, high stress levels and no progression. All anecdotal evidence also suggests stress levels are at an all-time high with staff morale at all-time low.'[15]

This was a brutal assessment and it contained within it a message that the IBOA was never more relevant or needed. The power of Broderick's IBOA to effect change on behalf of its members was immediately put to the test with the arrival of the euro. The introduction of the new euro currency was, the IBOA claimed, the 'biggest logistical exercise in Peacetime Europe'.[16] With the United Kingdom opting to retain sterling, the changeover impacted more upon bank officials in the Republic of Ireland. With members expected to facilitate the movement of more than 1 billion coins and half a billion notes, the period of transfer from the punt to the euro promised to have a bearing on even the simplest of transactions.[17] In essence, it meant that what bank officials were being asked to engage in was anything but business as usual. For this reason, the IBOA – alone among European trade unions – made a request for compensation in the form of a once-off recognition payment. The idea met with widespread, predictable resistance. Among those who lined up in opposition were the government and the Irish Business and Employers' Confederation (IBEC). The latter accused the IBOA of opportunism, while the banks insisted that the only concession would be an improved overtime payment for a limited number of staff.[18] Opposition served only to galvanise the IBOA. Faced with an attempt by the banks to delay discussions until such time as the work had been done, the IBOA took its case in respect of AIB to an independent tribunal, which upheld the Association's argument and recommended, amongst other things, a lump-sum payment to an agreed list of staff.[19] This precedent, and its extension to all banks, was a triumph for the IBOA and a source of envy for trade unions in other European countries, especially those in the financial services sector.[20] Indeed, no sooner was the euro introduced than the truth of IBOA predictions about additional workload became apparent – in Spain, for instance, it proved enough to ignite a series of demonstrations when trade unions in the banking sector protested against high levels of unpaid overtime linked to the introduction of the euro.[21]

For the IBOA, however, success on the euro changeover was not replicated on broader issues of pay in the Republic. Reservations raised about the general thrust of national pay policy in the late 1990s hardened into opposition in the early 2000s. Support for the national wage agreements did not so much ebb away as evaporate. Twice, IBOA members voted to reject the terms of pay deals negotiated between the government, employers and the trade unions. They did so in spectacular style. When *Sustaining Progress*, the sixth such agreement, which was planned to run from 2003 to 2005, was put to IBOA members, 98 per cent of them opposed it.[22] Apart from the inadequacy of the pay award – 5.5 per cent over eighteen months – the Association took particular umbrage at the inclusion of a 'binding arbitration' clause. It was claimed that this clause gave the 'upper hand' to employers in negotiations by restricting the ability of the IBOA to achieve meaningful improve-ments for its members.[23] Such was the vehemence of the IBOA leadership on this issue that members were informed that there was not a 'chance in hell' that the binding arbitration element would be carried forward into future agreements.

IBOA NEWS

Larry's €UROnly man for the IBOA

Staff at two more banks clinch euro changeover bonanza

Irish Independent
12/12/01

€-phoria as bank staff get windfall

Irish Independent
7/12/01

Ulster Bank staff win euro payment

Banks sort out euro agreements

Irish Times
12/12/01

Irish Times
5/12/01

NIB agree euro deal with staff

Irish Times
7/12/01

Irish Independent
18/10/01

Bank workers in strike threat over euro changeover

Irish Examiner
2/6/01

IBEC Says Unions "Undermine" Euro Changeover by Lodging Claims

IRN News
2/8/01

Banks' Cool Response to Euro-Changeover Pay Claim

IRN News
21/6/01

AIB Backs Special Euro Deal, Final Cost Could reach £5m

IRN News
6/12/01

Bank staff seek talks on euro compensation

Irish Times
1/6/01

Bank employees to be compensated for euro changeover

Sunday Business Post
1/7/01

Sunday Business Post
14/10/01

New IBOA chief eyes euro payment

The 'biggest logistical exercise in Peacetime Europe' was how the IBOA described the introduction of the euro currency in 2002. In the face of opposition from the banks and employers groups, the IBOA conducted a successful campaign to secure a lump-sum payment for some its members for the additional workload involved. A selection of the newspaper headlines generated by the campaign was reproduced in *IBOA News. (IBOA Archive)*

Yet *Towards 2016*, the successor to *Sustaining Progress*, offered little of the flexibility that the IBOA demanded. Binding arbitration remained and no provision was made for local bargaining. This was crucial in framing the IBOA's response. For while *Towards 2016* promised a 10 per cent pay increase over 27 months, an annual increase of 4.4 per cent and a figure broadly in keeping with the IBOA's pre-agreement target, cost-of-living increases would undercut much of the benefit to employees.[24] The IBOA's unease at the corrosive impact of inflation on earnings was matched by concerns at the weakness of the agreement's provisions on pensions.[25] The result of all this was that the IBOA rejected *Towards 2016* in much the same way as they had *Sustaining Progress* – by an overwhelming majority. In a high turnout of members, 95 per cent voted to oppose the new wage agreement.[26]

Rejection did not mean non-implementation, however. In its opposition to the two national wage agreements, the IBOA was clearly in a minority. The fact that the broad mass of ICTU members in the Republic approved of the agreements meant that the IBOA and its members became, ultimately, bound by its terms. What the debates over the national pay deals had done, however, was bring into sharp focus the divisions that existed within the Irish trade union movement. The fault line lay between the public and private sectors. The growing tensions between the two reflected the growing disparity in terms of trade union membership. Although the numbers involved in trade unions had increased with the growth of the Irish economy in the 1990s and 2000s, membership as a proportion of the total workforce showed a sharp decline. In 1980, for instance, unions organised 62 per cent of all employees at work; this had fallen to 39 per cent by 2006.[27] Of those remaining within the trade union fold, the vast majority belonged to the public sector. By 2004, 62 per cent of public sector employees were members of trade unions; the figure for the private sector stood at a mere 28 per cent.[28] These trends and the ICTU's willing embrace of the national wage agreements gave rise to discussions within the IBOA about the merits of Congress membership. 'The leadership of ICTU cannot see the wood from the trees', Mary Sexton, a delegate to a Special Conference in October 2005 declared. 'As long they keep the public sector unions happy', she added, 'ICTU are happy.'[29] Sexton's sentiments were echoed by the IBOA's General Secretary. 'The point we have to make', Larry Broderick told the same Conference, 'is if the trade union movement is going to be dominated by public sector colleagues who have done well out of benchmarking, they will have to realise that unless the needs of the private sector are addressed, there will be nothing to benchmark against.'[30]

Benchmarking lay at the core of the public-private sector tensions in the Republic of Ireland. The Public Service Benchmarking body had been established under the *Programme for Prosperity and Fairness* with a mandate to measure the pay of public service employees against those at similar grades in the private sector. Working on the presumption that private sector workers had fared better than those in the public sector from economic growth, the benchmarking process delivered a significant increase in the pay of the public service above and beyond the terms of national wage agreements. Any public-private wage imbalance was more than corrected by benchmarking. In fact, studies undertaken in the mid 2000s showed that Irish public sector workers on average earned substantially more than their private sector counterparts. One such study indicated that between 2003 and 2006, public sector weekly earnings had grown by 27 per cent, while those of private sector workers had increased by 17 per cent.[31] Similar findings emerged from a study commissioned by the IBOA itself. Economist Colm Rapple conducted a comparative analysis of the pay rates of bank officials and civil service grades. He also compared bank and public sector pay trends over the previous decade and the rise in average bank pay against the increase in bank profits. On both measures, bank officials, despite availing of modest profit-sharing payments, fared poorly: the gap in pay had widened with the Civil Service as a result of benchmarking; but it also widened at a time when there was a 'sharp increase . . . in the profitability of the main Irish banking groups and in the profits generated per employee'.[32]

These disparities fed the IBOA's sense of grievance. They fuelled a belief that national wage agreements had become one-sided and ill-fitted to meeting the interests of private sector workers. In 2007, an exasperated Mairéad Kelleher, a Bank of Ireland employee and

Executive Committee member, stated plainly that recent national wage agreements had been 'an absolute nonsense'. Explaining why, she added:

> They give highly profitable employers everything they want and the flexibility to introduce changes. And what do our members get? A miserable increase of a few euro that is swallowed up by inflation . . . The 'one size fits all' approach to national agreements no longer worked as the differences and priorities of workers in the private and public sectors are so significant that a single agreement just cannot meet the expectations of both sectors. There was a need to ask ourselves 'what value' ICTU membership provided to members and consider whether more could be achieved for members in direct negotiation with the banks than under the ICTU umbrella.[33]

Any pull away from the ICTU was more than counteracted by the draw towards it. Despite serious misgivings at the model of social partnership that had evolved, the principle of partnership was one to which the Association, like the ICTU, stressed its firm commitment. Events in other sectors of the economy also provided a stark reminder of the great damage that confrontational approaches to industrial relations could bring. In late 2005, a bitter dispute arose at Irish Ferries when management attempted to unilaterally replace over 500 workers with cheaper eastern European agency crew and to reflag its vessels to Cyprus to avail of lower standards of employment protection for seafarers. Such was the zeal of Irish Ferries management that they deployed a private security firm to bring agency staff on board the ships.[34] The stand-off that ensued was ended using the office of the Labour Relations Commission, but not before the trade union movement was mobilised in an impressive display of support. In December 2005, an estimated 100,000 trade unionists, IBOA members among them, protested in marches held in Dublin, Cork, Waterford, Limerick, Sligo, Athlone and Rosslare.[35] On the day of the demonstrations, Larry Broderick denounced the Irish Ferries strategy, and the aggressive tactics used to prosecute it, as 'a race to the bottom' approach to raising profits and lowering employment conditions.[36]

These were charges the IBOA more typically levelled at banks' managements, yet the early twenty-first century was, for the most

Trade union solidarity: IBOA members joined a march in support of Irish Ferries workers in 2005 when management at the company attempted, amongst other things, to replace over 500 workers with cheaper agency crew from eastern Europe. *(Graham Hughes/Photocall Ireland)*

part, a period of relative industrial peace in the banking sector. Agreements struck between the Association and AIB management in the early part of the decade, for example, were triumphs of consensus over conflict. In 2003, the two sides agreed a three-year plan which provided for significant guarantees and concessions to AIB employees. These included promises that there would be no compulsory redundancies and no closures of rural branches for the duration of the agreement. Most significantly, perhaps, it provided for the reduction of the working week from 36¼ to 35 hours a week.[37] This agreement built on a previous pact on 'Partnership Principles', which itself was a development of the Partnership 2000 deal, a provision of which required that trade unions and employers adopt a partnership approach at individual enterprise level.[38] This, in essence, is what the 2003 agreement was. According to Larrry Broderick, it was an attempt to 'live the principles of partnership in a very real way.'[39] The Minister of State at the Department of Enterprise, Trade and Employment, Frank Fahey, concurred, describing the IBOA and AIB agreement as 'trail-blazing' and a 'strong endorsement of the Enterprise Level Partnership model'.[40]

The IBOA–AIB agreement was not the norm in all banks. A similarly styled 'co-operation deal' with Ulster Bank was achieved, but in Bank of Ireland – AIB's biggest rival – the story was somewhat different. For employees in that bank's computer department, there was a conspicuous absence of partnership or co-operation.[41] In late 2002 and early 2003, the bank took a unilateral decision to outsource its Information Technology operations (mainframes, networks, services, output and printing) to the US computer giant Hewlett-Packard in a contract valued at €556 million over seven years.[42] The outsourcing plan affected upon 526 employees of the Bank of Ireland then employed in various IT roles in the Republic of Ireland, Northern Ireland and Britain.[43] Specifically, it involved the redeployment to Hewlett Packard of more than 350 computer staff, then employed in a wholly owned subsidiary of the bank known as ITSIS (IT Systems and Infrastructure Services).[44] Despite the Association's small presence among those employed at the bank's main computer centre in Cabinteely, Dublin, the IBOA led the campaign of staff opposition to the plan. In negotiations with the Bank of Ireland, the Association emphasised the importance of due process, collective bargaining and future job security, but without success.[45] A failure to secure assurances on these issues led affected IBOA members to serve notice of industrial action in April 2003.

The wider ramifications of the outsourcing debate in the Bank of Ireland were clearly understood by IBOA members across the banking sector. Addressing the IBOA's biennial delegate conference shortly after the vote to serve strike notice was taken, Kerry Christie of Ulster Bank in Belfast observed how the trend towards outsourcing affected 'all members, in all banks, in all jurisdictions, on their terms and conditions and on their job security. Outsourcing has a detrimental effect on our economy and diminishes the prospects for the next generation', she said. 'It has the potential to have a knock on effect on the IBOA, on its membership levels and therefore its strength, unless we ensure that we are recognised and that we can have an influence in any company which fulfils any bank function.'[46] Christie's contribution was reflective of the broad mood of the conference and its understanding of the need for the Association to take a firm stance on an issue of potentially far-reaching importance. This they did, but a preference remained for negotiation over industrial action.

Throughout the early summer of 2003, the IBOA and the Bank of Ireland stayed locked in discussions on ways to break the impasse. Only when these ended with the IBOA's rejection of the bank's proposals was strike action finally triggered. On 1 August 2003, IBOA members in Bank of Ireland ITSIS began a one-day strike and a ban on overtime, placing pickets on the bank's computer service centre at Cabinteely in Dublin.[47] The stoppage, the first by bank staff since 1992, was staged on the same day as both parties agreed to an independent chairman. There was, however, no agreement on who it should be. The IBOA's nomination as mediator for conciliatory talks, Phil Flynn, was unsurprisingly rejected by the bank. Flynn, an experienced negotiator, was nevertheless a veteran trade unionist and Chairman of Bank of Scotland (Ireland), a new and aggressive competitor of the Bank of Ireland in the Irish market.[48] The

August 2003: IBOA General Secretary, Larry Broderick, addresses a gathering of striking employees outside the offices of the Bank of Ireland/IT Systems and Infrastructure Services in Cabinteely, County Dublin. The dispute, the first to affect an Irish bank since 1992, arose over Bank of Ireland's plans to outsource its information technology operations to US computer giant Hewlett-Packard. *(IBOA Archive)*

preference of bank management was for the issue to be decided by the Labour Court on the basis that the outsourcing of IT services had wider implications for the economy.[49] In the end, Kieran Mulvey, Chief Executive of the Labour Relations Commission, was appointed as the third-party arbitrator. Mulvey considered detailed submissions from both sides and issued recommendations on 20 August 2003.[50] What he proposed was a compromise: the IBOA members voted to accept a deal that would still see them transferred to Hewlett Packard, but with a guarantee of future job security for up to five years and individual loyalty payments of between €5,500 and €10,000.[5]

II

MEMBERSHIP

The dispute at Bank of Ireland ITSIS was significant for several reasons – for the focus it brought to issues around outsourcing and for the fact that it was the first IBOA strike action in eleven years and the only strike action of the decade. In delivering major benefits in terms of job protection and enhanced terms and conditions, however, it also raised awareness of the enduring benefits of union membership. In an area where the IBOA previously experienced difficulty recruiting, membership surged to 95 per cent of the workforce.[52] It increased elsewhere too. Indeed, a feature of the Association's performance in the early to mid-2000s was the growth in membership across the booming financial services sector. Between 1999 and 2005, a prolonged recruitment campaign brought over 12,500 new members into the IBOA.[53] One of the few private sector unions to record such a rise, the success of the IBOA's recruitment efforts was more a product of design than accident. The IBOA planned for it. For a start, it rebranded itself as 'IBOA – The Finance Union' (and adopted the name officially in April 2009) the better to entice those working outside the traditional strongholds of Bank of Ireland, AIB, Ulster Bank, Northern Bank and NIB. But it also targeted workers for recruitment, using members as advocates within bank branches and the offices of burgeoning subsidiaries. Active local representatives were regarded as essential to successful recruitment. Without them the IBOA acknowledged that it could 'never hope to capitalise on recruitment opportunities that present themselves as a result of the employers' activities.'[54] One area where the IBOA did capitalise on an opportunity for recruitment was in the call centres, which were increasingly being used by banks to deliver products and services to customers. Over a three-year period, the Association built from nothing a membership of 700 in ten call centres in different locations across the Republic and Northern Ireland. To coordinate the activities of these members and act as a 'cross-jurisdictional pressure group on employers', a Call Centre Network was established in 2001.[55] Through this network it became apparent that there were significant discrepancies between practices in the different call centres, and a Call Centre Charter was published setting out minimum levels below which no call centre employer should fall in respect of such concerns as pay and reward and health and safety.[56]

The benefits of membership to call centre workers extended beyond advocacy. Membership brought with it access to a broad menu of entitlements and services. As well as a commitment to negotiate on pay and conditions and provide individual representation on various concerns – disciplinary procedures, complaints of bullying and harassment and general health and safety – the IBOA made much of the financial savings available to members as a result of special deals it had secured on insurance policies, holidays, flights, mobile phones and more.[57] Beyond that, of course, membership allowed entry into a thriving sporting and social scene, which provided opportunities for bank workers to meet and develop friendships away from the pressures of work. These activities were organised at local and national levels and catered not only for members, but also their families. The Association had always prided itself on its social role and the extent to which it was still valued by members was evident from the interest shown in such specially organised events as zoo visits, pantomimes, cinema screenings, barbecues and golf outings. Taking membership as a measure, the attractiveness of the Association to bank workers was considerable; by 2006, the number of members had climbed to 20,000.

Of necessity, this expansion was accompanied by an overhaul of the Association's channels of communication with members. The staid-looking *IBOA Newssheet* was replaced with the modern design of the *IBOA News* and later by *Spectrum*, but a more significant development was the establishment of an impressive web presence. The growth of the internet had transformed the business of banking in 1990s; now the IBOA, in keeping with best practice among progressive trade unions across the UK, Europe and the United States, looked to use the same technology to transform the way in which it interacted with its own members and the outside community.[58] The website, www.iboa.ie, was launched in 2003, enabling the Association to overcome the limitations of office hours and provide its members with a 24-hour service.[59] That it certainly did. Over the following months and years, the website won a big audience: in one month alone – January 2006 – it attracted 170,000 hits.[60] What drew people back to the site again and again was the breadth of material posted on the site which was regularly updated. The website became an online mirror to the wide spectrum of IBOA activity, carrying information on recruitment offers, members' services, union policies, sports and social events, a news archive and latest updates. A second website was added in 2009 – www.iboa.org.uk – with a password-protected members-only area incorporated into both sites.

The IBOA also expanded its focus on youth, given the increasing numerical strength of younger members within the Union. A combination of early retirements and voluntary severance schemes had resulted in the IBOA having the youngest profile of any trade union in Ireland. With over 60 per cent of its membership under the age of 40 by the mid-2000s, the question of how best to harness the potential of younger members was one that gave rise to considerable debate within the Association.[61] A youth committee was established in 2004 to address concerns about the apathy of young bank staff and while the work of this committee generated much publicity in internal publications, there remained a view that more radical action was required. One motion put to the 2005 biennial delegate conference asked that seats reserved for women on the Executive Committee be removed and replaced by seats for youth. Supporting the motion, Bernie O'Reilly, a Bank of Ireland Executive Committee member, argued that the reserving of seats for women had been intended to address a particular inequality and ensure better representation for women. Up to a point, this had been achieved – women by then constituted 49 per cent of Executive members. The progress of women within the IBOA reached a major landmark in 2001 when Susan Bustard, an employee of Ulster Bank in Belfast, was elected President. The Union's second female President, Margaret Browne, who had been employed by both AIB and Bank of Ireland, was elected for a two-year term in 2009. She was succeeded by Jessie Doherty, an AIB employee in 2011.

By 2005, it was being argued that what had been done for women in the past now needed to be done for youth. The benefits, Bernie O'Reilly believed, would be felt throughout the IBOA: 'Youth seats would help in the recruitment of new members, would help to encourage active participation by our young members and would ensure that our Executive Committee remains close and relevant to our membership.'[62] The proposition gave rise to much unease. Moya Cotton, who occupied one of the reserved seats for women on the Executive Committee, countered that she could not support any motion that would 'disenfranchise one group for another.'[63] The position of women within the Association – and within the wider banking sector – was not such as to justify the removal of support. It was true that women accounted for 49 per cent of the Executive Committee members, but it was equally the case that women comprised 72 per cent of all IBOA members. And a large proportion of that 72 per cent, it was suggested, were youth. For these reasons, Mary Sexton, an Ulster Bank Executive Committee member, stated that the removal of reserved seats for women to facilitate youth not only ran contrary to the principles of equality, it was also unnecessary. Indeed, Sexton said that she represented not just women, but all members 'regardless of age or sex.'[64]

The motion on reallocating Executive Committee seats was never put to a vote, but the debate around it was not in vain. If nothing else, it underlined the fact that the IBOA membership was predominantly female and predominantly under 40. These members were spread across four major banking groups and three different jurisdictions and, though they were by no means homogeneous, they shared many concerns. This much became apparent in 2007 when, in a unique attempt to capture opinions on a range of issues, the Association commissioned a massive survey of members. The survey was partly a response to the growing tendency among banks to commission their own employee surveys which were felt to be too limited in scope, taking little account of concerns around issues like pay and stress. The IBOA's survey was intended to be more rounded and would yield information that could be used in industrial relations negotiations with the various banks.[65] Carried out by Red C Research and Marketing Ltd and covering topics such as pay, pensions, health and safety, security, culture in banking and work environment, the survey involved a huge sample of 2,000 members who responded voluntarily to a fifteen-minute computer-aided telephone interview. The results of the survey, details of which were published in the *IBOA News*, were striking for the light they shone on Irish banking culture. The picture that emerged of Irish banking was one where bullying and harassment were widespread, where staff were overworked and stressed due to staff shortages and targets, and where many employees felt too afraid to report their concerns to management.[66] The vast majority of interview respondents – 87 per cent – were in agreement that the business of banking, as directed by senior management, had been reduced to the narrow pursuit of profit. Furthermore, more than half of respondents – 56 per cent – believed that in the drive towards increased profits, banks had forgotten not only about their staff, but their customers.[67]

III

IRISH BANKING: CULTURE AND COLLAPSE

To a large extent, there was nothing surprising about the IBOA's survey results. The exposure of a series of scandals in the late 1990s and early 2000s had already trained an unflattering spotlight on Irish banking culture. Indeed, a nadir appeared to have been reached in 2004 (wrongly as it turned out). That year saw a run of damaging reports and revelations about bank practices: the publication of a high court inspectors' report into overcharging and tax evasion at National Irish Bank, the disclosure of overcharging on certain foreign exchange transactions by AIB and the revelation that senior executives in that same bank had, over a number of years, operated a tax evasion scheme for their own benefit. The combined effect of all this was to lower further the reputation of an Irish banking system still stained by the disclosures of the DIRT scandal. Writing in *IBOA News*, Professor Ray Kinsella of UCD described the events of 2004 as 'seismic' and, echoing editorials in the same publication, he attributed the 'malaise' in banking to a wider corporate obsession with the maximisation of short-term shareholder value.[68]

The IBOA seized on the revelations to renew its call for a change in the culture of Irish banking. This became both a theme of its Bank Secretaries' Conference in November 2004 and a central plank in an earlier submission to an Oireachtas Joint Committee on Finance and the Public Service. In the course of that Oireachtas submission, the IBOA was explicit in its linking of the banks' short-term profit fixation with a decline in ethics. 'The rot set in the late 1980s or early 1990s. That was the turning point that has brought us to the current banking crisis,' Larry Broderick informed the committee in June 2004.[69] In charting the change in bank culture, the IBOA claimed that the obsession with profit had been manifest in the shift away from community banking and the growing prevalence across the banking sector of performance-related pay, downgraded jobs, low pay, outsourcing and the early retirement and severance packages offered to experienced staff.[70] This analysis of the underlying causes of ethical demise did not stand alone; it was accompanied by proposals for reform. The IBOA recommended a number of measures which it believed would address the existing problems within banking and ensure against their repetition. Included among them was the provision for representation on bank boards of staff and consumers, a review of human resource practices, a reduced emphasis on performance-related pay and the introduction of a whistleblowers' charter, enshrined in legislation, which would protect public-minded employees who felt compelled to bring to the attention of relevant authorities practices or activities that ran counter to the public good.[71]

This debate around the future of banking did not occur in a vacuum. The ethical issues highlighted by the IBOA were inextricably bound up with questions not only of culture, but of regulation. However, the process of overhauling the regulation of financial services in Ireland had already begun before the full scale of the scandals in NIB and AIB came to public light. In 2003, the Irish government had established the Irish Financial Services Regulatory Authority (IFSRA) as a single regulatory authority for the entire financial services industry. The new body assumed roles that were previously the preserve of the Central Bank (which regulated the banking and investment funds industry) and the Department of Enterprise, Trade and Employment (which regulated the insurance industry). The role of IFSRA was critical in shaping the regulatory environment in which the banks and their employees would function.

However, the new body adopted a 'principles-based' approach to regulation, which was heavily reliant on the observance of high standards by the senior management in financial service providers. This approach was in keeping with mainstream thinking at the time. And it was an approach with which the IBOA was in broad agreement. In a submission to the Department of Finance in December 2004, the IBOA declared its support for a 'self assessment' approach to compliance with regulation and expressed itself 'firmly of the view that the burden of compliance should not be excessive'.[72] However, the IBOA also insisted that safeguards were necessary to prevent the banks from neutralising IFSRA. In particular, the Association warned against 'the disproportionate influence of any one stakeholder over IFSRA' and 'the emergence of narrowly-defined pre-emptive voluntary codes reflecting bank interests rather than comprehensive statutory codes'. The IBOA also said the new arrangements must guard against 'the perception that the industry is engaged in self-regulation' and urged that the IFSRA should have sufficient powers to 'promulgate binding rules or codes'. Finally, it argued forcefully for the introduction of statutory protection for 'whistleblowers' to complement the new regulatory structures.

Although these concerns were not sufficient in themselves to lead the IBOA to oppose the establishment of IFSRA, the subsequent shortcomings of the new regulatory body, resulting from a combination of inadequate powers, insufficient resources and a lack of will, became a source of growing concern, leading the Union to declare in September 2009 that the 'principles-based approach' to banking regulation had 'not worked' – adding that the 'light touch' approach has been a significant contributory factor to the current crisis'.[73] The failure of regulation ultimately led to a situation where, according to Patrick Honohan, banking regulation was 'complacent and permissive'.[74] What did this mean in practice? It meant, for example, that Anglo-Irish Bank, the most irresponsible of Irish lenders, was able to grow unchecked its market share among Irish retail banks from 3 per cent to 18 per cent over the course of a decade. It meant too that banks met with little resistance when they relaxed their lending standards. Irish banks dangerously inflated the property bubble with decisions to lend massively to big property developers and homebuyers. The easing of loan conditions was such that by 2006, two-thirds of all loans to first-time buyers had a loan-to-value ratio of in excess of 90 per cent; the remaining one-third received 100 per cent loans.[75]

The simple truth is that Irish banking regulation was too 'business-friendly' to be effective. Its approach to industry was, as later acknowledged, 'unduly deferential'.[76] However, a lack of adequate regulation was only one of a complex of factors that contributed to the banking crisis of 2008. An investigation carried out in 2010 by Patrick Honohan, then Governor of the Central Bank, acknowledged the role of international factors (this was not a decisive role), but pointed more clearly to failings on the part of a cast of domestic Irish actors – bank managements, financial regulators, government and various professional bodies. The cost of these collective failings was great and was felt across the Irish economy and society. IBOA members were nevertheless left in a particularly vulnerable position. With the blame for the country's increasing economic tumult being laid at the door of their own industry, ordinary bank staff bore the brunt of public anger, meeting abuse not only in the workplace, but socially as well.[77] There was, of course, a perverse irony to their predicament: the IBOA, the voice of ordinary bank workers, had for many years warned of the corrosion of banking culture by the pursuit of short-term profit and high shareholder values; yet when this policy ended with the effective 'bailout' of the banks by the Irish state, the people who were left to confront an understandably angry public on a daily basis were those who bore the least responsibility within the banking system for the creation of the problem.

Public outrage was not all that bank workers had to contend with. The scale of the banking crisis was too great not to have more far-reaching consequences. This became increasingly obvious over time. Between September 2008 and November 2010, a series of government initiatives failed to bring closure to the problems of the Irish banking system. The state guarantee of all bank deposits, introduced on 30 September 2008 after late-night pressure by the chief executives and chairmen of the two major banks – Bank of Ireland and AIB – had been intended to bring about a resolution. It did not. Nor did the injection of significant state funds into AIB and Bank of Ireland as recapitalisation. And, again, nor did the establishment of the National Asset Management Agency (NAMA), which was intended to restore liquidity to the banks – freeing them to lend – by removing toxic loans from their books. Throughout this period, the IBOA adopted an approach that was pragmatic and principled. It offered guarded support for both the government's recapitalisation of the main banks and for the creation of NAMA.[78] It did so not because it believed them to be perfect solutions – there was none – but because it felt that these offered the best prospect of protecting the jobs, the pay and conditions of its members.[79]

The reality of the crisis, however, was that it brought nothing but bad news for Irish bank workers. In the eighteen months that followed the introduction of the guarantee, 6,000 job losses had either taken place or had been agreed across the financial services sector.[80] And this was not the end of it. Hopes that a line might be drawn under this number appeared to fade with the intervention of the IMF and the EU in November 2010 and their negotiation of a rescue package for Ireland. With plans to restructure and downsize the Irish banking system representing a core element of the agreement struck, further job losses became inevitable. Even so, the IBOA committed itself to a campaign of what might be described as constructive resistance. As well as reiterating calls for the reform of banking governance, the Union urged that the easy option of mass redundancies should be avoided. It argued instead that job losses not only needed to be kept to a minimum, they needed to be voluntary, negotiated and agreed with due consideration for their impact on customers and remaining staff. More than that, the IBOA railed against a policy of forced sell-offs, closures and mergers in the context of highly negative market conditions as the price of a restructuring plan that envisaged a slimmed down Irish banking system built around two pillar banks, each of them clearly focused on more core

Boom to bust: nothing symbolised the bursting of the Irish property bubble more than the sight of unfinished housing estates across the country. The Department of Environment reported that there were 2,800 'ghost estates' in 2010. The link of the fortunes of the banking and property industries would have devastating consequences for Irish society, resulting in, amongst other things, soaring unemployment. The new unemployed included thousands of bank officials. *(Mark Stedman/Photocall Ireland)*

operations.[81] Given the problems faced by Irish banks – even those deemed pivotal to Ireland's future economic requirements – the IBOA was playing with a seriously weakened hand, its arguments often drowned out in a public debate concentrated on the 'banking burden' being borne by the wider citizenry, a particularly unpalatable feature of an economic crisis characterised by spiralling unemployment, fiscal retrenchment and guillotined public services.

Although a restructured Central Bank began to develop a new regulatory regime as part of a wider effort to rebuild the reputation of the Irish banking sector, the IBOA continued to press the need for a broader strategic response – as opposed to simple expediency – in order to change the culture of Irish banking to minimise the risk of another banking collapse in the future. With the jobs of the rank and file being sacrificed all around them, the senior management of the Irish banks, like those in leading financial institutions in other countries, continued to reward themselves with lavish bonuses.[82] It was as if the crisis had never happened and the state guarantee never given. The culture of impunity was unshaken. In the case of the Bank of Ireland, assurances given to the Minister of Finance – subsequently read into the Dáil record – indicating that no performance-related bonuses had been paid out to staff were, on deeper scrutiny, exposed as erroneous, misleading, untrue.[83] A Department of Finance investigation revealed that in the two years that followed the introduction of the state's bank guarantee, more than €66m in performance-linked top-up payments were made, including €4.3m which the bank's senior executive team received as previously contracted bonuses.[84] Over the same period, more than 2,000 jobs in the same bank were lost through a combination of non-renewal of temporary contracts, non-replacement of retiring staff and the implementation of the first phase of the restructuring plan agreed with the EU Commission. Meanwhile those employees who remained were subject to pay freezes, a deferral of outstanding pay awards and a reduction in pension benefits.[85] The report highlighted how the disparities in treatment between ordinary staff and senior management which had been so pronounced during times of soaring bank profits were no less marked during times of crippling bank losses.

For the IBOA, the episode at the Bank of Ireland – then the only Irish bank not in majority state-ownership – poured acid on already gaping wounds. But it also pointed up the need, yet again, for boom-time reward practices to be finally jettisoned. The skewing of the balance between performance-related and basic pay had undoubtedly played its part in narrowing the vision of Irish banks on short-term gains, the unsustainability of which became appallingly evident with the onset of the Irish banking crisis in 2008. In the end, the wreckage caused by the recklessness of Irish banks was the logical conclusion of a culture against which the IBOA had been in opposition. The lesson for Irish banking is that it must, as the IBOA has made clear, 'return to the traditional banking values of prudence, integrity and the pursuit of long-term stability'.[86]

The Usual Suspects: IBOA members took part in a number of public demonstrations in protest at the wider economic consequences of the banking crisis. In one such protest organised by the ICTU in November 2010 on the eve of the visit of the IMF/EU/ECB Troika, the Union adapted the image of *The Usual Suspects* into a 'wanted' poster accusing leading financial figures of 'impersonating bankers'. *(Mark Stedman/ Photocall Ireland)*

References

Chapter 1: Foundations

1   J. F. Eager, *The inception and early history of the Irish Bank Officials' Association* (1930), pp. 10–11.

2   IBOA minutes, 18 March 1918.

3   *Ibid.*

4   For an excellent, accessible history of this period see Michael Laffan, *The Partition of Ireland* (1983).

5   Eager, *IBOA*, pp. 5–7.

6   Emmet O'Connor, *A Labour History of Ireland 1824–1960* (1992), p. 1.

7   Andrew Boyd, *The Rise of the Irish Trade Unions* (1985), p. 19.

8   *Ibid.*, p. 27.

9   O'Connor, *Labour History of Ireland*, pp. 10–12.

10   Stanley Palmer, *Police and Protest in England and Ireland 1780–1850* (1988), p. 406.

11   Boyd, *Irish Trade Unions*, p. 59.

12   John W. Boyle, *The Irish Labor Movement in the Nineteenth Century* (1988), p. 30.

13   O'Connor, *Labour History of Ireland*, pp. 24–5.

14   *Ibid.*, p. 28.

15 Boyd, *Irish Trade Unions*, p. 52.

16 Emmet O'Connor, *A Labour History of Ireland 1824–1960*, p. 32.

17 Boyd, *Irish Trade Unions*, p. 54.

18 Seán Redmond, *The Irish Municipal Employers Trade Union 1883–1983* (1983), p. 12.

19 Boyd, *Irish Trade Unions*, p. 66.

20 O'Connor, *Labour History of Ireland*, p. 35.

21 *Ibid.*, p. 47.

22 C. Desmond Greaves, *The Irish Transport and General Workers' Union. The Formative Years* (1982), p. 3. Dockers and coal porters had set up certain organisations, but these remained mostly temporary until the 1890s.

23 Redmond, *Irish Municipal Employers Trade Union*, p. 25.

24 *Ibid.*, p. 57.

25 Boyd, *Irish Trade Unions*, p. 67.

26 For more information about the Belfast strikes of 1907, see William McMullen, 'Early Days in Belfast', http://www.siptu.ie/AboutSIPTU/History/EarlyDaysinBelfast/ (accessed on 28 September 2010).

27 O'Connor, *Labour History of Ireland*, p. 69.

28 *Ibid.*, p. 82.

29 Boyd, *Irish Trade Unions*, p. 89.

30 *Ibid.*, p. 106.

31 O'Connor, *Labour History of Ireland*, pp. 95–99.

32 *Ibid.*, p. 98.

33 Report of the proceedings of the arbitration between the Irish banks and the Irish Bank Officials' Association (1920), p. 4.

34 *Ibid.*

35 Padraig McGowan, *Money and Banking in Ireland* (1990), p. 10.

36 *Ibid.*, p. 37.

37 Cormac Ó Gráda, *Ireland: A New Economic History, 1780–1939* (1994), p. 351.

38 Eager, *IBOA*, p. 22. These quotes are taken from a letter written by Eager on 15 February 1919.

39 IBOA minutes, 27 September 1917.

40 *Ibid.*

41 *Ibid.*

42 *Ibid.*

43 IBOA minutes, 30 November 1917.

44 Eager, *IBOA*, pp. 4–7. Eager dates the Dublin meeting as November 1917. It seems more likely, though still uncertain, that this meeting took place in early December 1917.

45 *Ibid.*

46 *Ibid.*

47 *Ibid.*

48 *Ibid.*

49 IBOA minutes, 18 March 1918.

50 *Ibid.*

51 Gordon McMullan, 'The Irish Bank "Strike", 1919', in *Saothar*, 5, pp. 39–49.

52 Eager, *IBOA*, p. 13.

53 McMullan, 'Strike', pp. 39–49.

54 *Ibid.*, p. 42.

55 J. M. Stott, 'The torch passes', in anon. (ed.), *IBOA: 70 years a-growing* (1998), pp. 7–16.

56 Eager, *IBOA*, p. 17.

57 *Ibid.*, p. 18.

58 McMullan, 'Strike', p. 43; Eager, *IBOA*, p. 21 and 26.

59 IBOA minutes, 17 March 1919.

60 *Ibid.*

61 Eager, *IBOA*, p. 26.

62 *Ibid.*, p. 25.

63 *The Irish Times*, 5 April 1919.

64 *Irish Banking Magazine (IBM)*, September 1919, p. 56.

65 Eager, *IBOA*, pp. 33–4.

66 *Ibid.*, p. 35.

67 *Anglo-Celt*, 22 November 1919.

68 *The Irish Times*, 24 November 1919.

69 Eager, *IBOA*, p. 47; *Irish Independent*, 22 November 1919.

70 Eager, *IBOA*, p. 47.

71 *Ibid.*, pp. 54–6.

72 *Ibid.*, pp. 54–6.

73 McMullan, 'Strike', p. 44.

Chapter 2: The 1920s

1 *Arbitration* (1920), p. 3.

2 Patrick Maume, 'Campbell, James Henry Mussen 1st Baron Glenavy,' in James McGuire and James Quinn (eds.), *Dictionary of Irish Biography*, (2009).

3 *Arbitration*, p. 1.

4 *The Freeman's Journal*, 28 February 1920.

5 McMullan, 'Strike', p. 39.

6 There is ample evidence of this in Smith and O'Brien, *Tales*, *passim*.

7 *Arbitration*, p. 20.

8 *Ibid.*, p. 20 and p. 68.

9 *Ibid.*, p. 91.

10 *Ibid.*, p. 6.

11 *Ibid.*, p. 7

12 *Ibid.*, p. 94.

13 IBOA Archives, letter dating from 1907. A copy of this letter was placed in the IBOA archives on the understanding of anonymity.

14 *Arbitration*, p. 10.

15 *Ibid.*, p. 23.

16 *Ibid.*, p. 15.

17 *Ibid.*, pp. 38–9.

18 *Ibid.*, p. 107.

19 *Ibid.*, p. 5 and 26.

20 *Ibid.*, p. 12.

21 *Ibid.*, p. 14.

22 *Ibid.*, pp. 47–8.

23 *Ibid.*, p. 26.

24 *Ibid.*, p. 52.

25 *Ibid.*, p. 8.

26 McMullan, 'Strike', p. 40 and *Arbitration, passim.*

27 *Arbitration*, p. 24.

28 *Ibid.*, p. 85.

29 *Ibid.*, pp. 29–30.

30 *Ibid.*, pp. 96–7.

31 *Ibid.*, pp. 96–7.

32 *IBM*, July 1920, p. 25.

33 Particulars of the agreement of 4 December 1919 between the Irish banks and the Irish Bank Officials' Association and of awards made thereunder and of agreements arrived at subsequently between the banks and the association (1920).

34 *IBM*, July 1920, p. 25.

35 Eager, *IBOA*, p. 58.

36 *Ibid.*, p. 58.

37 *IBM*, April 1920.

38 *IBM*, November 1920, p. 87.

39 *IBM*, December 1920, p. 105.

40 *IBM*, December 1920.

41 *IBM*, January 1921.

42 *IBM*, July–August 1922.

43 *IBM*, August 1921.

44 *IBM*, October 1922.

45 A copy of the circular, dated 13 February 1922 is reprinted in Smith and O'Brien, *Tales*, p. 45.

46 NAI FIN 1/3143, letter written by R. Buckley, Sec. Bank of Ireland, 11 November 1922.

47 NAI FIN 1/3144, letter written by R. Buckley, Sec. Bank of Ireland, 26 October 1923.

48 NAI FIN 1/3429, Report of F. A. King, Local Govt. Inspector, 2 May 1922.

49 NAI FIN 1/1051, file on bank raids of the Munster and Leinster Bank, 1921–22.

50 NAI FIN 1/3471, W. J. O'Reilly, solr., letter to Department of Finance, 20 July 1923.

51 *Ibid.*

52 *IBM*, August 1932.

53 See *IBM*, *passim*.

54 McMullan, 'Strike', p. 46.

55 Anon. (ed.), *Sixty Years in Residence*: booklet commemorating the restoration of 92 and 93 St Stephen's Green, Dublin, by the Irish Bank Officials' Association (1981), p. 15.

56 *IBM*, April 1920.

57 *IBM*, May 1919.

58 *IBM*, July 1919.

59 *IBM*, August 1919.

60 Desmond Ryan, 'A brief history of the Irish Bankers' Club, 1921–81', in Anon. (ed.), *Sixty Years in Residence*: booklet commemorating the restoration of 92 and 93 St Stephen's Green, Dublin, by the Irish Bank Officials' Association (1981), p. 21.

61 Ryan, 'Club', p. 21.

62 *IBM*, January 1923.

63 *IBM*, December 1929.

64 See, for example, *IBM*, May 1919.

65 *IBM*, June 1924.

66 *IBM*, April 1923.

67 See, for example, *IBM*, May 1923.

68 *IBM*, December 1919.

69 See, for example, *IBM*, April 1920 and July–August 1922.

70 *IBM*, May 1919.

71 *IBM*, April 1924.

72 See, for example, *IBM*, August 1925.

73 See, for example, *IBM*, August 1924.

74 *IBM*, December 1925.

75 *IBM*, April 1927.

76 *IBM*, November 1929.

77 *IBM*, October 1929.

78 *IBM*, September 1928.

79 *IBM*, January 1955.

80 *IBM*, August 1927.

Chapter 3: The 1930s

1   *IBM*, October 1936.

2   Quoted in Paul Daly, *Creating Ireland: the Words and Events that Shaped Us* (Hachette, 2008), p. 79.

3   Cormac Ó Gráda, *A Rocky Road: The Irish Economy Since the 1920s* (1997), p. 176.

4   Ó Gráda, *New Economic History*, p. 366.

5   *Ibid.*, p. 368.

6   *Ibid.*, p. 368.

7   *Irish Independent*, 14 April 1934; see, also, Agreements between the IBOA and the Banks' Staff Relations Committee, 1928–61.

8   Ó Gráda, *New Economic History*, p. 353.

9   *Ibid.*, p. 353.

10 Smith and O'Brien, *Tales*, p. 15.

11 *Ibid.*, p. 20.

12 R. F. Foster, *Modern Ireland 1600–1972* (1988), p. 554.

13 Smith and O'Brien, *Tales*, p. 22.

14 Diarmaid Ferriter, *The Transformation of Ireland 1900–2000*, p. 438.

15 *The Irish Times*, 17 October 1932.

16 IBOA minutes, 23 May 1932; *The Irish Times*, 5 May 1932.

17 *The Irish Times*, 23 June 1932.

18 *IBM*, July 1932.

19 *IBM*, July 1932.

20 *IBM*, December 1935.

21 *IBM*, January 1932.

22 *IBM*, March 1932.

23 *IBM*, November 1930.

24 *IBM*, January 1937.

25 *IBM*, January 1930.

26 *IBM*, February 1930.

27 *Ibid.*

28 *Ibid.*

29 *IBM*, April 1930.

30 *IBM*, May 1930.

31 *IBM*, June 1930.

32 *IBM*, October 1930.

33 IBOA minutes, 12 December 1932.

34 See, for example. *IBM*, January 1934.

35 IBOA minutes, 30 September 1935.

36 *IBM*, November 1937.

37 *IBM*, October 1938.

38 *IBM*, August 1939.

39 *IBM*, August 1938.

40 Margaret Browne, 'Equality for all', in anon. (ed.), *IBOA: 70 Years a-Growing* (1998), p. 17.

41 *IBM*, April 1939.

42 Smith and O'Brien, *Tales*, p.16.

43 Smith and O'Brien, *Tales*, p.17. Diarmaid Ferriter, 'Everett, James', in James McGuire and James Quinn (eds.) *Dictionary of Irish Biography* (2009).

44 *IBM*, September 1937.

45 *Ibid.*

46 *IBM*, December 1935; Patrick Long. 'Rooney, Philip', in James McGuire and James Quinn (eds.), *Dictionary of Irish Biography* (2009).

47 *IBM*, December 1935.

48 *IBM*, January 1939 and March 1939.

49 *IBM*, January 1939.

50 *IBM*, April 1930.

51 *IBM*, May 1930.

52 *IBM*, November 1935.

53 *IBM*, May 1938.

54 See, for example, *IBM*, December 1938.

55 *IBM*, August 1936, p. 34.

56 *IBM*, August 1935, p. 27

57 *Irish Independent*, 17 March 1933.

58 Ryan, 'Bankers' Club', p. 21.

59 *IBM*, August 1931.

60 IBOA minutes, 6 June 1932.

61 IBOA minutes, 28 November 1932.

62 *IBM*, April 1937.

63 IBOA minutes, 30 September 1935.

64 *IBM*, October 1938.

Chapter 4: The 1940s

1   *IBM*, October 1939.

2   *IBM*, June 1940.

3   *Ibid.*

4   *IBM*, July 1940.

5   *Ibid.*

6   *Ibid.*

7   *IBM*, May 1942.

8   *IBM*, September 1940.

9   *IBM*, February 1940.

10 *IBM*, October 1942.

11 *IBM*, May 1945.

12 Agreements between the IBOA and the Banks' Staff Relations Committee, 1928–61.

13 *IBM*, May 1942.

14 Agreements between the IBOA and the Banks' Staff Relations Committee, 1928–61.

15 Stott, 'Torch', p. 12.

16 *IBM*, May 1941.

17 *IBM*, June 1945.

18 *IBM*, August 1945.

19 *IBM*, July 1945.

20 McGowan, *Money*, p. 50.

21 *IBM*, September 1938.

22 McGowan, *Money*, p. 46.

23 *Ibid.*

24 *Ibid.*

25 *Ibid.*

26 *IBM*, April 1940.

27 Agreements between the IBOA and the Banks' Staff Relations Committee, 1928–61.

28 *IBM*, April 1941.

29 *IBM*, May 1942.

30 Sean Redmond, *The Irish Municipal Employees Trade Union 1883–1983*, p. 91.

31 Diarmaid Ferriter, *The Transformation of Ireland 1900–2000* (2004), p. 308.

32 Bill McCamley, *The Role of the Rank and File in the 1935 Dublin Tram and Bus Strike* (1981), p. 10. See also p. 30 of McCamley's pamphlet for a reference to the Communist Party of Ireland's newspaper, the *Workers' Voice*, from 25 May 1935, which stated that the 1935 transport strike was 'the longest of its kind in world history'.

33 McCamley, *Tram and Bus Strike*, pp. 9–11.

34 Statement by the IRA Army Council addressed 'To the Joint Strike Committee, Dublin Tram and Bus Workers', 22 March 1935. Quoted in full in Tim Pat Coogan, *The I.R.A.*, Glasgow (1980), pp. 113–4 and partially in McCamley, *Tram and Bus Strike*, p. 15.

35 *Ibid.*

36 'The Post Office Strike', *The Irish Times*, 12 September 1922 and the first episode of Diarmaid Ferriter's 'The Limits of Liberty', broadcast on 1 June 2010.

37 Joe Lee, 'Worker and Society since 1945', in Donal Nevin (ed.), *Trade Unions and Change in Irish Society* (1980), pp. 11–25, p. 14.

38 Niamh Puirséil, *The Irish Labour Party 1922–73* (2007), pp. 78–9.

39 Diarmaid Ferriter, *The Transformation of Ireland 1900–2000*, p. 373.

40 *Ibid.*, p. 453.

41 *Ibid.*, p. 493.

42 *Ibid.*, p. 493.

43 Eugene McCormick, *The INTO and the 1946 Teachers' Strike* (1996), p. 1.

44 *Ibid.*, p. 15.

45 Letter from McQuaid to the General Secretary of the INTO, 20 March 1946. Quoted in Eugene McCormick, *INTO*, p. 23.

46 Louie Bennett, letter to *The Irish Times*, 12 September 1946. Quoted in Eugene McCormick, *INTO*, p. 36.

47 McCormick, *INTO*, pp. 37–8.

48 Ferriter, *Transformation*, p. 531.

49 *IBM*, April 1946.

50 See IBOA minutes, 18 March 1947.

51 *IBM*, January 1946.

52 *IBM*, April 1946.

53 *Ibid.*

54 *IBM*, January 1946.

55 Agreements between the IBOA and the Banks' Staff Relations Committee, 1928–61.

56 *The Irish Times*, 12 July 1946.

57 *IBM*, January 1947.

58 *Ibid.*

59 William Knox, *Decades of the Ulster Bank 1836–1964* (1965), p. 230. See also Charles McCarthy, *The Decade of Upheaval*, p. 185.

60 *IBM*, August 1946.

61 *The Irish Times*, 19 July 1946.

62 *The Irish Times*, 17 July 1946.

63 *IBM*, September 1946. An article by one of the committee from which this quote is taken was entitled 'From the Inside'.

64 *The Irish Times*, 15 July 1946.

65 *IBM*, September 1946.

66 *The Irish Times*, 20 July 1946.

67 *IBM*, September 1946.

68 *Ibid.*

69 *IBM*, September 1946; *Irish Independent*, 19 August 1946.

70 *IBM*, September 1946.

71 *Ibid.*

72 *IBM*, June 1946.

73 *IBM*, January 1947; IBOA minutes, 18 March 1947.

74 *Ibid.*

75 *Ibid.*

76 *IBM*, February 1947.

77 IBOA minutes, 18 March 1947.

78 *IBM*, April 1947.

79 IBOA minutes, 29 March 1947.

80 *IBM*, June 1947.

81 *The Irish Times*, 3 July 1947.

82 IBOA minutes, 29 July 1947 and 14 August 1947.

83 *IBM*, September 1947.

84 Recommendation on a dispute between the Irish Bank Officials' Association and the Irish Bankers' Joint Committee concerning rates of pay and conditions on employment, 8 August 1947.

85 *IBM*, September 1947.

86 *Ibid.*

87 *Irish Independent*, 24 September 1947.

88 *The Irish Times*, 19 August 1947.

89 *Sunday Independent*, 5 October 1947.

90 *Irish Independent*, 8 October 1947.

91 *Sunday Independent*, 5 October 1947.

92 See Dáil Debates, 8 October 1947.

93 *Nenagh Guardian*, 11 October 1947.

94 *Times Pictorial*, 4 October 1947.

95 Charles McCarthy, *The Decade of Upheaval*, p. 185.

96 See Dáil Debates, 8 October 1947.

97 *The Irish Press*, 10 October 1947. See, also, NAI D/T S14143A, file on bank disputes.

98 *The Irish Times*, 22 October 1947.

99 *IBM*, December 1947; Agreements between the IBOA and the Banks' Staff Relations Committee, 1928–61.

100 *IBM*, April 1948; Agreements between the IBOA and the Banks' Staff Relations Committee, 1928–61.

101 *IBM*, December 1947.

Chapter 5: The 1950s

1 *IBM*, July 1953; see, also Ferriter, *The Transformation of Ireland 1900–2000, passim.*

2 *IBM*, September and October, 1958. A verse from Maura Fitzgibbon, an employee of the Bank of Ireland in Newcastle West read: 'Male clerks, if they wish, a moustache may exhibit; But the growth on the chin – known as a beard – we prohibit.'

3 *IBM*, April 1948.

4 Stott, 'Torch', p. 12.

5 *Ibid.*

6 *IBM*, January 1951.

7 *Ibid.*

8 *Ibid.*

9 IBOA minutes, 25 and 26 November 1950.

10 *IBM*, January 1951.

11 *Ibid.*

12 *Ibid.*

13 IBOA minutes, 25 and 26 November 1950.

14 See, for example, IBOA minutes, 12 December 1950.

15 IBOA minutes, 27 December 1950.

16 *IBM*, January 1951.

17 *Ibid.*

18 *Ibid.*

19 *The Irish Times*, 12 January 1951.

20 *Southern Star*, 20 January 1951.

21 *Munster Express*, 29 December 1950.

22 See, for example, *Irish Independent*, 13 January 1951.

23 *Irish Independent*, 1 February 1951.

24 *Southern Star*, 20 January 1951.

25 *Irish Independent*, 18 January 1951.

26 *Tuam Herald*, 30 December 1950.

27 NAI D/T S 14143 B, departmental note, 3 February 1951.

28 *IBM*, February–March 1951.

29 See, for example, IBOA minutes, 26 January 1951,

30 NAI D/T S 14143 B, departmental note, 3 February 1951.

31 *Irish Independent*, 2 and 3 February 1951.

32 *Irish Independent*, 9 February 1951.

33 *Sunday Independent*, 11 February 1951.

34 *Irish Independent*, 16 February 1951.

35 *IBM*, February–March 1951.

36 *IBM*, February–March 1951; IBOA minutes, 4 March 1951.

37 *IBM*, February–March 1951.

38 *IBM*, May–June 1951.

39 Report of Proceedings at the annual general meeting, May 1951.

40 *Ibid.*

41 *Ibid.*

42 NAI D/T, S 14143 B, letters between IBOA and Department of An Taoiseach, 27 and 31 July 1951.

43 *IBM*, September 1951.

44 *Anglo-Celt*, 26 March 1955.

45 *Sunday Independent*, 9 January 1955.

46 A full account of the proceedings of this conference is carried in NAI D/T S 14143 D, Mansion House Conference Proceedings, March 1955.

47 *The Irish Times*, 21 March 1921; *IBM*, April 1955.

48 *IBM*, April 1955.

49 IBOA Archives, IBOA internal memo, 29 January 1959.

50 *IBM*, April 1952.

51 *IBM*, March 1957.

52 *IBM*, April 1957.

53 *IBM*, July 1957.

54 Des Smyth and Éilis O'Brien (eds.), *Golden Guineas: Tales of Irish Bankers, 1920–1970* (1998), p. 7.

55 *Ibid.*

56 *Ibid.*, p. 49.

57 *IBM*, November 1958.

58 *IBM*, January 1958.

59 Smith and O'Brien, *Tales*, p. 57.

60 *IBM*, September 1955.

61 *IBM*, December 1955.

62 Smith and O'Brien, *Tales*, p. 56.

63 Ryan and Doyle, 'Bankers' Club', p. 21.

64 *IBM*, February 1957.

65 *IBM*, November 1955.

66 *IBM*, March 1957.

67 *IBM*, November 1958.

68 *IBM*, June 1958.

69 *IBM*, May 1952.

70 *IBM*, October 1952.

71 *IBM*, January 1953.

72 *IBM*, November 1958.

Chapter 6: The 1960s

1 McGowan, *Banking*, p. 55.

2 *Ibid.*, p. 55.

3 *IBM*, October 1966.

4 *IBM*, July 1962.

5 *IBM*, June 1967.

6 *Ibid.*

7 *IBM*, September 1968.

8 *IBM*, October 1968.

9 *IBM*, October 1961.

10 *IBM*, August 1963.

11 Smith and O'Brien, *Tales*, p. 71.

12 *IBOA Newssheet*, October 1993, p. 9.

13 Smith and O'Brien, *Tales*, p. 33 and p. 63.

14 *IBOA Newssheet*, October 1993, p. 9.

15 *IBM*, December 1958.

16 *IBM*, February 1961.

17 Ryan and Doyle, 'Bankers' Club', p. 21.

18 *IBM*, February 1968.

19 *IBM*, August 1969.

20 *IBM*, December 1962 and January 1963.

21 *IBM*, August 1961.

22 *IBM*, November 1965.

23 *IBM*, November 1965.

24 *IBM*, February 1966.

25 See, also, IBOA minutes, 6 November 1965.

26 *IBM*, December 1965.

27 See Agreements between the IBOA and the Banks' Staff Relations Committee, 1928–61.

28 *IBM*, November 1964.

29 *IBM*, May 1965.

30 IBOA minutes, 26 February 1966.

31 *IBM*, April 1966.

32 *Anglo-Celt*, 7 May 1966.

33 *The Irish Times*, 6 May 1966 and *Irish Independent*, 12 May 1966.

34 *The Irish Times*, 6 May 1966.

35 *The Irish Times*, 12 May 1966.

36 *The Irish Times*, 23 May 1966.

37 *Irish Independent*, 18 June 1966; IBOA minutes, 10 September 1966.

38 *The Irish Times*, 20 June 1966; IBOA minutes, 10 September 1966.

39 *Irish Independent*, 6 July 1966; IBOA minutes, 10 September 1966.

40 *The Irish Times*, 5 May 1966; IBOA minutes, 10 September 1966.

41 *IBM*, June 1966.

42 *The Irish Times*, 20 July 1966.

43 *IBM*, November 1966.

44 IBOA Archives, IBOA press statement, 8 July 1966.

45 IBOA Archive, John Titterington letter to members, 22 July 1966.

46 *Ibid.*

47 *Ibid.*

48 *Sunday Independent*, 30 July 1966.

49 *IBM*, September 1966; IBOA minutes, 10 September 1966.

50 *IBM*, July 1968.

51 *IBM*, July 1968.

Chapter 7: The 1970s

1 *The Irish Times*, 31 January 1970; *IBM*, February 1970; IBOA minutes, 10 September 1969.

2 *IBM*, February 1970.

3 'Their behaviour, symptomatic of a universal revolt of youth not always tempered with wisdom is best forgotten.': This is how the *Irish Banking Magazine* in February 1970 described the conduct of a minority of junior members at one of the meetings.

4 *IBM*, March 1970.

5 For a discussion on the causes of inflation in the late 1960s and early 1970s, see Patrick T. Geary's address to 'A Symposium on Inflation', delivered before a meeting of the Statistical and Social Inquiry Society of Ireland, 15 November 1974. It can accessed at http://www.tara.tcd.ie/bitstream/2262/8058/1/jssisiVolXXIIIPartII_0120.pdf

6 J. J. Lee, *Ireland 1912–1985: Politics & Society* (1989), p. 46.

7 The maintenance craftsmen's strike lasted from early January to early March 1969 and, at its peak, closed 142 firms, which employed 31,000 people. Those involved were building and engineering tradesmen – carpenters, plasterers, painters, plumbers, electricians and fitters – in manufacturing firms. In a report on the dispute, which was published shortly after its conclusion, Con Murphy described it as 'a clear demonstration of the irrational state of industrial relations in Ireland'. See *The Irish Times*, 17 September 1969.

8 Michael P. Fogarty, *Report of Banks Inquiry*, 1971.

9 See 'The Name of the Game is Money', *IBM*, February 1970.

10 Letter from J. Titterington, IBOA, to E. Grace, Banks' Staff Relations Committee 9 October 1969, in Michael P. Fogarty, *Report of Banks Inquiry, 1971*, p. 152.

11 *IBM*, March 1970.

12 *IBM*, January 1970.

13 IBOA Circular, 14 February 1970. Reprinted in Fogarty, *Report of Banks Inquiry, 1971*, pp. 158–161.

14 Labour Court Recommendation on the Bank Dispute of 1970, see Fogarty, *Report of Banks Inquiry, 1971*, pp. 165–173.

15 Fogarty, *Report of Banks Inquiry, 1971, passim.*

16 *Ibid.*, p. 29.

17 *The Irish Times*, 1 May 1970.

18 *Ibid.*

19 Address by John Titterington, *Report of Proceedings of Annual Delegate Meeting*, IBOA, 24 April 1971.

20 Address by John Titterington, *Report of Proceedings of Annual Delegate Meeting*, IBOA, 24 April 1971.

21 *IBM*, March 1970.

22 *Ibid.*

23 *IBM*, May 1970.

24 NAI Department of Taoiseach 2001/6/114, letter from Mary Mulcahy to Jack Lynch, 1 May 1970.

25 Some members of the Bank of Ireland Group had, it was claimed, taken it upon themselves to 'conduct a vile campaign' insinuating that the Executive Committee was more preferential in its treatment of the AIB over their own bank. This was dismissed by the Executive Committee which stated that at all times it acted 'nationally and impartially' for the good of all members. IBOA Circular 25 February 1970, in Fogarty, *Report of Banks Inquiry, 1971*, p. 161.

26 Report of Proceedings of Annual Delegate Meeting, IBOA, 24 April 1971.

27 *The Irish Times*, 2 May 1970, 17 November 1970; *Irish Independent*, 13 May 1970.

28 *Undated Report on IBOA Strikes, 1966–1976*, pp. 17–18, p. 26.

29 *IBM*, June/November 1970.

30 IBOA, *70 Years a-Growing*, p. 13.

31 Fogarty, *Report of Banks Inquiry*, 1971, p. 33.

32 Quoted in *Irish Independent*, 29 December 1999.

33 *Report of Proceedings of Annual Delegate Meeting*, IBOA, 24 April 1971.

34 *The Kerryman*, 17 July 1971.

35 *IBM*, March 1971.

36 *IBOA News*, January/February 2004.

37 *The Irish Times*, 2 February 2004.

38 Fogarty, *Report of Banks Inquiry*, *1971*, p. 24–5.

39 McGowan, *Money and Banking in Ireland*, pp. 55–9.

40 *The Irish Times*, 17 July 1971.

41 Fogarty, *Report of Banks Inquiry*, *1971*, pp. 114–115.

42 *Irish Independent*, 23 June 1971.

43 Rosemary Cullen Owens, *A Social History of Women in Ireland 1870–1970* (2005), p. 244.

44 *Ibid.*, p. 245.

45 *The Irish Times*, 2 November 1999, cited in Cullen Owens, *Women*, p. 245.

46 Fogarty, *Report of Banks Inquiry*, *1971*, p. 116; Browne, *Equality*, p. 17.

47 See Fogarty, *Report of Banks Inquiry*, *1971*, p. 60–1.

48 *Irish Independent*, 23 June 1971.

49 *IBM*, December 1975.

50 This was steadily reduced in subsequent years, see *IBM*, December 1975.

51 *Report of Proceedings of Annual Delegate Meeting*, IBOA, 24 April 1971.

52 *Irish Independent*, 23 June 1971.

53 *Ibid.*

54 *Ibid.*

55 See Linda Connolly, *The Irish Women's Movement: From Revolution to Devolution* (2002), Appendix 5, Chronology, Second Wave Feminism, p. 239–40.

56 *Irish Independent*, 23 June 1971; *IBM*, March 1974.

57 *IBM*, December 1975.

58 Browne, *Equality*, p. 17.

59 *Report of Proceedings of Annual Delegate Meeting*, IBOA, 22 April 1972.

60 Redmond, 'Bankers' Club', p. 24.

61 See, for example, *IBM*, August 1974 and April 1976; *Report of Proceedings of Annual Delegate Meeting*, IBOA, 27 April 1977.

62 *IBM*, February 1972, p. 180; *IBM*, April 1976.

63 *IBM*, March 1978.

64 *IBM*, December 1972 and April 1978.

65 *IBM*, November 1971.

66 *IBM*, December 1972.

67 *The Kerryman*, 31 July 1971.

68 *The Irish Times*, 29 December 1979; *Sunday Independent*, 4 July 1976.

69 *The Irish Times*, 6 March 1973.

70 *Sunday Independent*, 27 June 1927.

71 IBOA, *70 Years a-Growing*, p. 3–4.

72 *IBM*, July 1972.

73 *IBM*, October 1972.

74 *Report of Proceedings of Annual Delegate Meeting*, IBOA, 24 April 1971.

75 *IBOA Newssheet*, June 1979.

76 See http://group.ulsterbank.com/about-us/our-history/our-story.ashx, accessed on 12 October 2010; *Garda ar Lár*, RTÉ 1 Television.

77 *IBOA Newssheet*, February 1978.

78 *IBM*, 9 October 1975.

79 *IBOA Newssheet*, September 1979.

80 *IBOA Newssheet*, February 1978.

81 Joe Durkan, 'Social Consensus and Incomes Policy', *The Economic and Social Review*, Vol. 23, No. 3, pp. 347–63.

82 Durkan, 'Consensus', p. 354.

83 Lee, *Ireland*, p. 466.

84 Report of Proceedings of Annual Delegate Meeting, IBOA, 22 April 1972.

85 Regulation of Banks (Renumeration and Conditions of Employment) (Temporary Provisions) Act, 1973.

86 *IBM*, August 1973.

87 *IBOA Newssheet*, 12 December 1975; *Irish Independent*, 31 March 1976.

88 *Irish Independent*, 7 April 1976.

89 Report of Proceedings of Annual Delegate Meeting, IBOA, 24 April 1976.

90 Report on Bank Strike in Republic of Ireland 28 June to 31 August 1976.

91 *Irish Independent*, 18 June 1976.

92 *Undated Report on IBOA Strikes, 1966–1976*, pp. 19–20.

93 For government discussion on avoiding a strike, see NAI 2006/133/562.

94 *Undated Report on IBOA Strikes, 1966–1976*, p. 21; IBOA, *70 Years a-Growing*, p. 14.

95 *Irish Independent*, 1 July 1976.

96 *Undated Report on IBOA Strikes, 1966–1976*, pp. 22–4.

97 *IBOA Newssheet*, July 1979.

98 Report of Proceedings of Annual Delegate Meeting, IBOA, 22 April 1978.

99 Durkan, *Consensus*, pp. 354–5.

100 McGowan, *Banking in Ireland*, pp. 89–90.

101 *The Irish Times*, 5 April 1979.

102 *The Irish Times*, 22 November 1979.

Chapter 8: The 1980s

1 Richard Aldous, *Great Irish Speeches* (2007), pp.142–7.

2 In 1980–81, in the wake of Haughey's speech, exchequer borrowing was not reduced as planned. Instead, it rose by IR£208 million. See Roy Foster, *Luck & the Irish: A Brief History of Change 1970–2000* (2007), p. 81.

3 Diarmaid Ferriter, *The Transformation of Ireland 1900–2000* (2004), p. 669.

4 *The Irish Times*, 21 March 1979.

5 *Report of Proceedings of Annual Delegate Meeting*, IBOA, April1980.

6 *The Kerryman*, 13 August 1976.

7 *Ibid.*

8 See *Report of Proceedings of Annual Delegate Meeting*, IBOA, 27 April 1977 and *Report of Proceedings of Annual Delegate Meeting*, IBOA, 22 April 1978.

9 *Undated Report on IBOA Strikes, 1966–1976*, p. 27.

10 *The Irish Times*, 13 April 1978.

11 *The Irish Times*, 20 April 1978.

12 *IBM*, December 1984.

13 Derek Nally, 'Impact of the IBOA on the National Scene', Anon. (ed.), *IBOA: 70 Years a-Growing* (1988), pp. 18–9.

14 *IBM*, December 1984.

15 Anon., 'Symposium on Taxation: Some Implications of Tax Reform', *Journal of the Statistical and Social Inquiry of Ireland*, Vol. XXV, Part 1, p. 6.

16 *Report of Proceedings of Annual Delegate Meeting*, IBOA, 25 April 1981.

17 *Report of Proceedings of Annual Delegate Meeting*, IBOA, 25 April 1987.

18 *Report of Proceedings of Annual Delegate Meeting*, IBOA, 30 April 1983.

19 Anthony Leddin and Brendan Walsh, 'Economic Stabilisation, Growth and Recovery in Ireland, 1979–1996', *Irish Banking Review*, Summer 1997, p. 8.

20 Gary Murphy and John Hogan, 'Putting up the goodies and seeing who would vote for them . . .': *The Politics of Economic Performance, and the Trade Union Movement, 1970–1982 (2008)*, p. 24.

21 Niamh Hardiman, *Pay, Politics, and Economic Performance in Ireland 1970–1987* (1988) p. 221.

22 Joe Durkan, 'Social Consensus and Incomes Policy', *The Economic and Social Review*, Vol. 23, No. 3, p. 359

23 *Report of Proceedings of Annual Delegate Meeting*, IBOA, 30 April 1983.

24 This was a point Job Stott made in respect of a settlement reached for bank officials in the Republic of Ireland in 1984. From 1 June that year, they were given a 4.5 per cent increase and six months later, from 1 January 1985, a Labour Court award was set to deliver a additional 4 per cent. In 1986, Stott again drew favourable comparison between the fifteen-month salary increase of 7 per cent in the Republic for bank

officials and that which was achieved by workers in State and semi-state sectors. See *Report of Proceedings of Annual Delegate Meeting*, IBOA, 27 April 1985, and *IBM*, May 1986, p. 3.

25 The branch network of the two banks in Britain grew from 'a few branches in 1970 to thirty in 1975 and to some sixty in 1989'. See Padraig McGowan, *Money and Banking in Ireland: Origins, Development and Future* (1990), p. 71.

26 *IBOA Newssheet*, June 1986.

27 *Report of Proceedings of Annual Delegate Meeting*, IBOA, 27 April 1985

28 The dates of the disputes in the 1980s were: 11–15 February (Britain); 27 May 1987 (TSB, Northern Ireland); July–August 1987 (AIB Tralee, Newcastle West and Dromcollogher) 23 August 1989 (TSB, Northern Ireland).

29 See, for example, *IBM*, May 1981 and *IBM*, December 1981.

30 *Report of Proceedings of Annual Delegate Meeting*, IBOA, 30 April 1983

31 *IBOA Newssheet*, July 1980, p. 13.

32 Anon. (ed.), *IBOA: 70 Years a-Growing* (1988), p. 15.

33 *Report of Proceedings of Annual Delegate Meeting*, IBOA, 25 April 1981.

34 *Report of Proceedings of Annual Delegate Meeting*, IBOA, 22 April 1978.

35 *Ibid.*

36 *IBM*, March 1981.

37 *IBM*, July 1981.

38 *Report of Proceedings of Annual Delegate Meeting*, IBOA, 28 April 1984.

39 *Ibid.*

40 *IBOA Newssheet*, October 1986.

41 *Report of Proceedings of Annual Delegate Meeting*, IBOA, 27 April 1985 and *IBOA Newssheet*, October 1986.

42 *IBOA Newssheet*, December 1986.

43 See Northern Ireland Tribunal recommendations, February 1986, in *IBM*, March 1986.

44 *IBOA Newssheet*, June 1984.

45 *IBM*, October 1983.

46 *Report of Proceedings of Annual Delegate Meeting*, IBOA, 28 April 1984. FIET was the International Federation of Employees, Technicians and Managers.

47 *IBM*, March 1986.

48 *The Irish Times*, 24 April 1989.

49 *IBOA Newssheet*, May 1990.

50 *Ibid.*

51 *IBOA Newssheet*, September 1980.

52 *IBM*, June 1981.

53 *IBM*, June 1985.

54 See, for example, *IBM*, February 1982.

55 *IBM*, October 1980.

56 *IBM*, November 1980.

57 Republished in *IBM*, October 1980.

58 *IBM*, June 1981.

59 *IBM*, December 1981.

60 *IBM*, January 1980. See also, *IBM*, July 1981.

61 *IBOA Newssheet*, September 1980.

62 *IBM*, November 1982.

63 *IBOA Newssheet*, September 1987.

64 *IBM*, December 1980.

65 See *IBM*, February 1981 and *IBOA Newssheet*, September 1987.

66 *IBOA Newssheet*, September 1987.

67 *Ibid.*

68 *IBOA Newssheet*, November 1987.

69 *Report of Proceedings of Annual Delegate Meeting*, IBOA, 26 April 1986; *IBM*, November 1985.

70 *IBM*, July 1983.

71 From article in the magazine *Management*, reprinted in *IBM*, September 1985.

72 *IBM*, November 1986.

73 See, for example, *IBOA Newssheet*, September 1981 and October 1982.

74 *IBM*, February 1983.

75 *The Irish Times*, 29 April 1986.

76 *The Irish Times*, 7 May 1986.

77 *The Irish Times*, 15 July 1986.

78 *IBM*, November 1986.

79 *IBOA Newssheet*, May 1984.

80 *IBM*, September 1984.

81 *Report of Proceedings of Annual Delegate Meeting*, IBOA, 28 April 1984.

82 *IBOA Newssheet*, May 1984.

83 Report of Proceedings of Annual Delegate Meeting, IBOA, 28 April 1984.

84 *IBM*, September 1984.

85 Report of Proceedings of Annual Delegate Meeting, IBOA, 28 April 1984.

86 *IBOA Newssheet*, November 1988.

87 *IBM*, December 1986.

88 *IBM*, December 1986.

89 Peter Clarke, *Hope and Glory: Britain 1900–1990* (1996), p. 369.

90 *Report of Proceedings of Annual Delegate Meeting*, IBOA, 28 April 1984.

91 Steve Schifferes, 'Trade Unions' Long Decline', BBC News Online, 8 March 2004.

92 Rory O'Donnell and Colm O'Reardon, 'Ireland's Experiment in Social Partnership 1987–96', in Giuseppe Fajertag and Phillipe Pochet (eds.), *Social Pacts in Europe* (1997).

93 See Leddin and Walsh, p. 8.

94 *The Irish Times*, 12 May 1987. Job Stott summarised the developments sur-rounding the ending of the 1982 technology agreement in his General Secretary's address to the Annual Delegate Meeting in 1988. See *Report of Proceedings of Annual Delegate Meeting*, IBOA, 23 April 1988.

95 *The Irish Times*, 27 April 1987; 14 June 1988; 24 October 1988; 3 November 1988. The introduction of a new grade of lower-paid official in the Bank of Ireland won approval from the Labour Court, and

subsequently the members of the IBOA. In a ballot of members in November 1988 prior to plans to recruit the first group of school leavers, the Bank of Ireland's competitive-ness plan was endorsed by the IBOA. It was a result that ran contrary to the advice of the Association's leadership, who attributed the outcome to older bank officials who became eligible for voluntary redundancy or early retirement under the plan.

96 *The Irish Times*, 14 June 1988.

Chapter 9: The 1990s

1 *The Irish Times*, 30 December 1999.

2 Paul Sweeney, *The Celtic Tiger: Ireland's Economic Miracle Explained* (1998), p. 4.

3 R. F. Foster, *Luck & the Irish: A Brief History of Change 1970–2000* (2007), p. 35.

4 Ray McSharry and Padraig White, *The Making of the Celtic Tiger: the Inside Story of Ireland's Boom Economy* (2001), p. 318.

5 In 1995 the IFSC provided employment for 3,500 people and brought in £200 million in taxes, see Sweeney, *Celtic Tiger*, p. 47. In 2000, however, the IBOA and other trade unions complained that they had been 'precluded from recruiting' in what was a state sponsored initiative, see *Irish Independent*, 8 April 2000.

6 *IBOA Newssheet*, August 1989.

7 *IBOA Newssheet*, October 1990.

8 Report of Proceedings at Special Delegate Meeting, 17 November 1990.

9 Report of the Proceedings of Biennial Delegate Conference, 27 April 1991.

10 Report of the Proceedings of Biennial Delegate Conference, 27 April 1991.

11 IBOA, Industrial Action: Briefing Document, 1992.

12 IBOA, Industrial Action: Briefing Document, 1992.

13 *Industrial Relations News (IRN)*, 12 March 1992.

14 *IRN*, 12 March 1992.

15 Cited in Tom Hayes, 'The 1992 Bank Strike: An Analysis', in *Irish Industrial Review*, Vol.1, No. 3 June 1992, p. 25.

16 *Sunday Business Post*, 15 March 1992, cited in Hayes, 'Strike'.

17 Letter from C. Ryan, IBOA, to W. Brown, BSRC, 30 January 1992.

18 IBOA directive, 3 March 1992; IBOA, Industrial Action: Briefing Document 1992, Appendix 5.

19 *The Irish Times*, 21 March 1992. The intervention of the Labour Court came at the request of the Minister for Labour, Brian Cowen.

20 Dáil Éireann debates, Vol. 418, 2 April 1992; Labour Court Recommendation, No. LCR13601.

21 *The Irish Times*, 1 April 1992.

22 Hayes, 'Strike', p. 32.

23 Proinsias De Rossa, Dáil Éireann debates, Vol. 418, 2 April, 1992.

24 Hayes, 'Strike', p. 33.

25 *Ibid.*

26 *The Irish Times*, 25 April 1992.

27 Hayes, 'Strike', p. 34.

28 *Ibid.*

29 *Report of the Proceedings of Biennial Delegate Conference*, 24 April 1993.

30 *The Irish Times*, 27 April 1992.

31 *The Irish Times*, 29 October 1992.

32 *The Irish Times*, 27 April 1992.

33 *Report of the Proceedings of Biennial Delegate Conference*, 26 April 1997.

34 *The Irish Times*, 11 December 1992; *IBOA Newssheet*, December 1992.

35 *Report of the Proceedings of Biennial Delegate Conference*, 27 April 1991.

36 *IBOA Newssheet*, July 1992.

37 *Ibid.*

38 *IBOA Newssheet*, August 1992.

39 *Report of the Proceedings of Biennial Delegate Conference*, 24 April 1993, p. 2.

40 *IBOA Newssheet*, July 1992.

41 *IBOA Newssheet*, March 1994.

42 See, for example, *IBOA Newssheet*, July 1993; *IBOA Newssheet*, February 1998.

43 The spike in general robbery rates in the early 1990s is shown in a graph in John Brewer, Bill Lockhart & Paula Rodgers, 'Crime in Ireland since the Second World War', in *Journal of the Statistical and Social Inquiry Society of Ireland*, Vol. XXVII, Part III, p. 148.

44 *Irish Independent*, 16 March 2009; *IBOA Newssheet*, January 1990.

45 *IBOA Newssheet*, November 1992.

46 See, for examples, the *IBOA Newssheet*, November 1993 and October 1996.

47 Department of Environment, Heritage and Local Government, *Referendum Results 1937–2009*, p. 51.

48 *IBOA Newssheet*, March 1996.

49 *IBOA Newssheet*, June 1994.

50 *IBOA Newssheet*, January 1994.

51 *Report of the Proceedings of Biennial Delegate Conference*, 22 April 1995.

52 *IBOA Newssheet*, May 1990.

53 *IBOA Newssheet*, June 1990.

54 Northern Bank Dispute 1994, unidentified document held in the IBOA archive.

55 *IBOA Newssheet*, October 1994.

56 *IBOA Newssheet*, January 1995.

57 *Report of the Proceedings of Biennial Delegate Conference*, 22 April 1995.

58 *Ibid.*

59 *Newry Reporter*, 27 April 1995. Dr Paisley had also met with the chief executive of the Northern Bank, see *Portadown Times*, 14 April 1995.

60 *Report of the Proceedings of Biennial Delegate Conference*, 22 April 1995.

61 *Ibid.*

62 For example, Ulster Bank's salary restructuring policy was launched in 1996, containing many similarities with that introduced by the Northern Bank. According to the IBOA, the plan was to reduce the salary at the top of the pay scale from IR£24,000 to IR£16,000. In addition, existing staff would be 'red-circled', with their salary frozen until such time as the new scales caught up with them through national or sectoral pay rises, see *The Irish Times*, 13 April 1996.

63 *Report of the Proceedings of Biennial Delegate Conference*, 26 April 1997.

64 *Belfast Telegraph*, 12 April 1995.

65 *Report of the Proceedings of Biennial Delegate Conference*, 22 April 1995.

66 *The Irish Times*, 28 April 1997.

67 See, for example, Ciaran Ryan's article 'Profits and Jobs', in *IBOA Newssheet*, March 1995.

68 *Report of the Proceedings of Biennial Delegate Conference*, 24 April 1999.

69 *Ibid.*

70 *Report of the Proceedings of Biennial Delegate Conference*, 26 April 1997.

71 The *IBOA Newssheet* regularly published an industrial relations update providing progress reports on developments within each of the banks. See, for example, *IBOA Newssheet*, February 1995.

72 *Report of the Proceedings of Biennial Delegate Conference*, 24 April 1999.

73 *Ibid.*

74 *IBOA Newssheet*, July 1993.

75 *Report of the Proceedings of Biennial Delegate Conference*, 26 April 1997.

76 *IBOA Newssheet*, January 1999.

77 *IBOA Newssheet*, January 1999 and August 1999.

78 Simon Carswell, *Something Rotten: Irish Banking Scandals* (2006), pp. 132–135.

79 *Ibid.*, p. 137.

80 *Ibid.*, pp. 145–6.

81 *IBOA Newssheet*, April 1998.

82 *Report on Investigations into the Affairs of National Irish Bank Limited and National Irish Bank Financial Services Limited, by High Court Inspectors Mr Justice Blayney and Tom Grace FCA*, 30 July 2004, p. 167.

83 *Ibid.*, p. ii.

84 Fintan O'Toole, *Ship of Fools: How Stupidity and Corruption Sank the Celtic Tiger* (2009), p. 48.

85 *Parliamentary Inquiry into D.I.R.T.: First Report*, Part 1, Chapter 1, Introduction.

86 *Ibid.*

87 *Report on Special Delegate Conference*, 13/14 October 2005, p. 14.

88 *IBOA Newssheet*, September 1999.

89 *IBOA Newssheet*, January 1999.

90 *IBOA Newssheet*, November/December 1999; *Report of the Proceedings of Biennial Delegate Conference*, 24 April 1999, p. 9. In 2001, the Irish Banking Federation and its affiliate the Irish Mortgage Council did publish a Code of Ethics, but it was not of the type envisaged by the IBOA. While the Association welcomed it as a positive development, it stressed the need for it to be placed on a statutory basis and for penalties to be applied to those who contravened it. See IBOA, Submission to the Department of Finance: Consultation on Consolidation and Simplification Bill, 10 December 2004, p. 8.

91 *The Irish Times*, 19 June 2009.

92 *Report of the Proceedings of Biennial Delegate Conference*, 27 April 1991, p. 20.

Chapter 10: The 2000s

1 Patrick Honohan, 'Policy Paper: Resolving Ireland's Banking Crisis', in *Economic and Social Review* , Vol. 40, No. 2, Summer 2009.

2 By November 2010 the Irish government had injected €7 billion into the two largest banks, AIB and Bank of Ireland. Estimates of the amount of money which would be put into Anglo Irish Bank ran to an astonishing €35 billion.

3 The results of the 2011 general election can be accessed on the RTÉ website at http://www.rte.ie/news/election2011/results

4 *The Irish Times*, 31 March 2011; *Sunday Business Post*, 3 April 2011.

5 *Irish Independent*, 10 February 2010; *Irish Examiner* 5 August 2011; *Irish Independent*, 20 August 2010.

6 National Economic and Social Council, *The Irish Economy in the Early 21st Century* (June 2008), p. xiii.

7 *Ibid.*, p. 1.

8 Morgan Kelly, *The Irish Property Bubble: Causes & Consequences*, 15 January 2009. Accessed on 22 November 2010 at http://www.irisheconomy.ie/ Crisis/KellyCrisis.pdf

9   http://www.globalpropertyguide.com/Europe/Ireland/Price-History. Accessed on 22 November 2010; See also Karl Whelan, 'Policy Lessons from Ireland's Latest Depression', a paper delivered to the McGill Summer School, 20 July 2009, p. 7.

10 *Irish Independent*, 29 August 2000.

11 *IBOA News*, September/October 2005. The original building at 93 St Stephen's Green was acquired by the Association in 1921 and 92 was subsequently purchased in 1967.

12 *Report of the Proceedings of Biennial Delegate Conference*, 20–21 April 2007.

13 *Report of the Proceedings of Biennial Delegate Conference*, 19 and 20 October 2001.

14 Larry Broderick was speaking as General Secretary Designate at the biennial delegates conference in 2001.

15 *Report of the Proceedings of Biennial Delegate Conference*, 19 and 20 October 2001.

16 *IBOA News*, January/February 2002; *Report of the Proceedings of Biennial Delegate Conference*, 25 and 26 April 2003, p. 4.

17 For an example of what a simple euro changeover transaction might involve, see *Report of the Proceedings of Biennial Delegate Conference*, 19 and 20 October 2001, p. 43.

18 *IBOA News*, January/February 2002.

19 *Ibid.*

20 European Foundation for the Improvement of Living and Working Conditions, *Developments in the Financial Services Sector: an analysis of EIRO articles* (2001), p. 12

21 *Ibid.*, p. 2.

22 *IBOA News*, September/October 2004.

23 *Report on Special Delegate Conference*, 13–14 October 2005.

24 *IBOA News*, Autumn 2006. The IBOA argued that inflation had 'rocketed' since it had made its 10 per cent pay claim and that it was, by late 2006, running at a rate of 4.2 per cent.

25 Feelings on this issue were already running high following Bank of Ireland's plans to downgrade the pensions of their staff while enhancing the entitlements of their senior executives. See *IBOA News*, Autumn 2006.

26 *IBOA News*, Autumn 2006.

27 William K. Roche, 'The Trend in Unionisation in Ireland since the mid-1990s', in Tim Hastings ed., *The State of the Unions: Challenges Facing Organised Labour in Ireland* (2008), pp. 18–20.

28 *Ibid.* p. 24.

29 *Report on Special Delegate Conference*, 13–14 October 2005.

30 *Ibid.*

31 Eilis Kelly, Séamus McGuinness and Philip O'Connell, *Benchmarking, Social Partnership and Higher Renumeration: Wage Settling Institutions and the Public-Private Sector Wage Gap in Ireland*, ESRI, Working Paper, No. 270, December 2008, p. 11.

32 *Report of Special Delegate Conference*, 13–14 October 2005, p. 11.

33 *Report of the Proceedings of Biennial Delegate Conference*, 20–21 April, 2007, p. 31.

34 *IBOA News*, Spring 2006, p. 19.

35 RTÉ News, 9 December 2005.

36 *IBOA News*, Spring 2006.

37 *IBOA News*, March/April 2003.

38 *IBOA News*, March 2000.

39 *Report of the Proceedings of Biennial Delegate Conference*, 25 and 26 April 2003.

40 *Ibid.*

41 *Irish Examiner*, 21 July 2003.

42 *Ibid.*, 9 July 2003.

43 Kieran Mulvey, *Recommendations in the Dispute between the IBOA and the Bank of Ireland on The Transfer/Outsourcing of the Bank's I.T. Infrastructure (ITSIS) to Hewlett Packard*, 20 August 2003, p. 2.

44 *Sunday Business Post*, 6 July 2003.

45 Kieran Mulvey, *Recommendations*, p. 3.

46 *Report of the Proceedings of Biennial Delegate Conference*, 25 and 26 April 2003, p. 42.

47 *Irish Examiner*, 1 August 2003.

48 *The Irish Times*, 2 August 2003.

49 *Irish Examiner*, 2 August 2003.

50 Kieran Mulvey, *Recommendations*, p. 15. The biggest points of

difference between the parties were on issues of job security and the right to redeployment.

51 *The Irish Times*, 9 September 2003

52 *Report of the Proceedings of Biennial Delegate Conference*, 22 and 23 April 2005, p. 50.

53 The figure of 12,500 is the sum of figures produced in *IBOA News*, November/ December 2004, p. 3 and *IBOA News*, Spring 2006, p. 14. Between 1999 and 2004 it was stated that over 10,000 new members joined the Association; in 2005 alone, a further 2,500 members joined.

54 *IBOA News*, Spring 2006.

55 *IBOA News*, August/September 2001.

56 *Report of the Proceedings of Biennial Delegate Conference*, 19 and 20 October 2001, p. 33–4.

57 For examples of the savings available to members in Northern Ireland and Britain, see *IBOA News*, Autumn 2006 and 2007. For savings available to Republic of Ireland members, see *IBOA News*, Spring 2006.

58 Tim Hastings (ed.), *The State of the Unions: Challenges Facing Organised Labour in Ireland* (2008), p. 8.

59 *IBOA News*, August 2003.

60 *IBOA News*, Spring 2006.

61 *IBOA News*, September/October 2003.

62 *Report of the Proceedings of Biennial Delegate Conference*, 22 and 23 April 2005.

63 *Ibid.*

64 *Ibid.*

65 *Report Special Delegate Conference*, 3 February 2007.

66 *IBOA News*, Spring 2007.

67 *IBOA News*, Spring 2007.

68 *IBOA News*, Sept/Oct 2004.

69 *Irish Examiner*, 18 June 2004.

70 *IBOA News*, July/August 2004.

71 *IBOA News*, July/August 2004.

72 IBOA, Submission to the Department of Finance: Consultation on Consolidation and Simplification Bill, 10 December 2004, pp. 4 and 9.

73 See *Spectrum*, September 2009.

74 Patrick Honohan, *What Went Wrong in Ireland, A Report for the World Bank*, May 2009, p. 5.

75 *Ibid.*, p. 5.

76 Patrick Honohan, *The Irish Banking Crisis: Regulatory and Stability Policy 2003–2008, A Report to the Minister for Finance by the Governor of the Central Bank*, 31 May 2010, p. 9.

77 *Irish Independent*, 22 February 2009.

78 See IBOA Press Releases, 21 January 2009 and 9 September 2009.

79 IBOA Press Release, 9 September 2009.

80 IBOA Press Release, 29 March 2010.

81 For instance, the IBOA resisted the sell-off of profitable international arms of both the Bank of Ireland and AIB, see IBOA Press release; 4 November 2010; 1 November 2010. On the broader restructuring plans for Irish banks, see *The Irish Times*, 31 March 2011; IBOA Press Release, 31 March 2010.

82 In 2010, by way of example, the Royal Bank of Scotland paid over 100 senior executives more than £1m each. Despite the bailed-out bank reporting losses of £1.1bn for that year, total bonus payouts reached nearly £1bn. See *The Guardian*, 24 February 2011.

83 *The Irish Times*, 4 March 2011.

84 Department of Finance, *Report on payment of bank bonuses in Bank of Ireland*, 3 March 2011. Accessible at: http://www.finance.gov.ie/ documents/ publications/reports/ 2011/boibonus.pdf

85 *Sunday Business Post*, 3 April 2011.

86 IBOA Press Release, 9 October 2008.

Select Bibliography

Primary Sources

MANUSCRIPT:

Irish Bank Officials' Association Archives

IBOA Minute Books.

Miscellaneous letters and documents.

Report of Proceedings at the Annual General Meetings, 1919–2010.

Particulars of the agreement of 4th December 1919 between the Irish banks and The Irish Bank Officials' Association and of awards made thereunder and of agreements arrived at subsequently between the banks and the association (1920).

Report of the proceedings of the arbitration between the Irish banks and the Irish Bank Officials' Association (1920).

Report on Investigations into the Affairs of National Irish Bank Limited and National Irish Bank Financial Services Limited (2004).

National Archives of Ireland

Department of An Taoiseach Files

Department of Finance Files

Department of Justice, Equality and Law Reform Files

PRINTED SOURCES:

Parliamentary Papers

Dail Éireann Debates

Labour Court Recommendations

Parliamentary Inquiry into D.I.R.T.: First Report.

Regulation of Banks (Remuneration and Conditions of Employment) (Temporary Provisions) Act, 1973.

The Irish Banking Crisis: Regulatory and Stability Policy 2003–2008, A Report to the Minister for Finance by the Governor of the Central Bank.

Newspapers and Magazines

Anglo-Celt

Belfast Telegraph

Cork Examiner

IBOA News

IBOA Newssheet

Irish Banking Magazine

Irish Independent

Kerryman

Munster Express

Nenagh Guardian

Newry Reporter

Portadown Times

Southern Star

Spectrum

Sunday Independent

The Freeman's Journal

The Irish Times

The Sunday Business Post

Times Pictorial

Secondary Sources

Aldous, Richard (ed.), *Great Irish Speeches* (2007).

Anon. (ed.), *IBOA: 70 Years a-Growing* (1998).

Anon. (ed.), *Sixty Years in Residence: booklet commemorating the restoration of 92 and 93 St. Stephen's Green, Dublin, by the Irish Bank Officials' Association* (1981).

Anon., 'Symposium on Taxation: Some Implications of Tax Reform', *Journal of the Statistical and Social Inquiry of Ireland*, Vol. XXV, Part 1.

Boyd, Andrew, *The Rise of the Irish Trade Unions* (1985).

Boyle, John W., *The Irish Labor Movement in the Nineteenth Century* (1988).

Carswell, Simon, *Something Rotten: Irish Banking Scandals* (2006).

Clarke, Peter, *Hope and Glory: Britain 1900–1990* (1996).

Connolly, Linda, *The Irish Women's Movement: From Revolution to Devolution* (2002).

Coogan, Tim Pat, *The I.R.A.*, Glasgow (1980).

Cullen Owens, Rosemary, *A Social History of Women in Ireland 1870–1970* (2005).

Daly, Paul, *Creating Ireland: the Words and Events That Shaped Us* (2008).

Durkan, Joe, 'Social Consensus and Incomes Policy', in *The Economic and Social Review*, Vol. 23, No. 3.

Eager, J. F., *The Inception and Early History of the Irish Bank Officials' Association* (1930).

European Foundation for the Improvement of Living and Working Conditions, *Developments in the Financial Services Sector: an analysis of EIRO articles* (2001).

Ferriter, Diarmaid, *The Transformation of Ireland 1900–2000* (2004).

Foster, R. F., *Modern Ireland: 1600–1972* (1988).

Foster, R. F., *Luck & the Irish: A Brief History of Change 1970–2000* (2007).

Greaves, C. Desmond, *The Irish Transport and General Workers' Union. The Formative Years* (1982).

Hardiman, Niamh, *Pay, Politics, and Economic Performance in Ireland 1970–1987* (1988).

Hastings, Tim (ed.), *The State of the Unions: Challenges Facing Organised Labour in Ireland* (2008).

Hayes, Tom, 'The 1992 Bank Strike: An Analysis', in *Irish Industrial Review*, Vol.1, No. 3 June 1992.

Honohan, Patrick, 'Policy Paper: Resolving Ireland's Banking Crisis', in *Economic and Social Review*, Vol. 40, No. 2, Summer 2009.

Kelly, Eilis, McGuinness, Seamus and O'Connell, Philip, *Benchmarking, Social Partnership and Higher Remuneration: Wage Settling Institutions and the*

Public-Private Sector Wage Gap in Ireland, ESRI, Working Paper, No. 270, December 2008.

Knox, William, *Decades of the Ulster Bank 1836–1964* (1965).

Laffan, Michael, *The Partition of Ireland* (1983).

Leddin, Anthony and Walsh, Brendan, 'Economic Stabilisation, Growth and Recovery in Ireland, 1979–1996', in *Irish Banking Review*, Summer 1997.

Lee, J. J., *Ireland 1912–1985: Politics & Society* (1989).

Lockhart, Bill and Rodgers, Paula, 'Crime in Ireland since the Second World War', in *Journal of the Statistical and Social Inquiry Society of Ireland*, Vol. XXVII, Part III.

Lyons, F. S. L., *Bank of Ireland, 1783–1983: Bicentenary Essays* (1983).

McCamley, Bill, *The Role of the Rank and File in the 1935 Dublin Tram and Bus Strike* (1981).

McCarthy, Charles, *The Decade of Upheaval* (1973).

McCormick, Eugene, *The INTO and the 1946 Teachers' Strike* (1996).

McGowan, Padraig, *Money and Banking in Ireland* (1990).

McGuire, James and Quinn, James (eds.), *Dictionary of Irish Biography*, (2009).

McMullan, Gordon, 'The Irish Bank "Strike", 1919', in *Saothar*, 5, pp. 39–49.

McSharry, Ray and White, Padraig, *The Making of the Celtic Tiger: the Inside Story of Ireland's Boom Economy* (2001).

Murphy, Gary and Hogan, John, *'Putting up the goodies and seeing who would vote for them': The Politics of Economic Performance, and the Trade Union Movement, 1970–1982* (2008).

National Economic and Social Council, *The Irish Economy in the Early 21st Century* (2008).

Nevin, Donal (ed.), *Trade Unions and Change in Irish Society* (1980).

O'Connor, Emmet, *A Labour History of Ireland 1824–1960* (1992).

O'Donnell, Rory and O'Reardon, Colm, 'Ireland's Experiment in Social Partnership 1987–96', in Giuseppe Fajertag and Phillipe Pochet (eds.), *Social Pacts in Europe* (1997).

Ó Gráda, Cormac, *Ireland: A New Economic History, 1780–1939* (1994).

Ó Gráda, Cormac, *A Rocky Road: The Irish Economy since the 1920s* (1997).

O'Toole, Fintan, *Ship of Fools: How Stupidity and Corruption Sank the Celtic Tiger* (2009).

Palmer, Stanley, *Police and Protest in England and Ireland 1780–1850* (1988).

Puirséil, Niamh, *The Irish Labour Party 1922–73* (2007).

Redmond, Seán, *The Irish Municipal Employers Trade Union 1883–1983* (1983).

Roche, William K., 'The Trend in Unionisation in Ireland since the mid-1990s', in Tim Hastings ed., *The State of the Unions: Challenges Facing Organised Labour in Ireland* (2008).

Smyth, Des and O'Brien, Éilis (eds.), *Golden Guineas: Tales of Irish Bankers, 19201970* (1998).

Sweeney, Paul, *The Celtic Tiger: Ireland's Economic Miracle Explained* (1998).

Index

Page numbers in italics refer to illustrations.

INDEX

293